D0479997

THE MIDDLE EAST
The Fertile Crescent
BLACK SEA
MEDITERRANEAN SEA
ITALY
Rome
Naples
SARDINIA
SICILY
Tunis
MALTA
YUGOSLAVIA
BULGARIA
GREECE
Athens
CRETE
Istanbul (Constantinople)
SEA OF MARMARA
BOSPORUS
DARDANELLES
Ankara
TURKEY
Izmir (Smyrna)
Konya (Iconium)
Tarsus
CYPRUS
SYRIA
Tripoli
Beirut
LEBANON
Damascus
Tel Aviv
JORDAN
Amman
ISRAEL
Jerusalem
Gaza
DEAD SEA
Port Said
Alexandria
El Alamein
Ismailiya
SUEZ CANAL
Suez
Cairo
Eilat
Aqaba
SINAI PEN.
Sharm el Sheikh
Tripoli
Benghazi
Tobruk
LIBYA
SAHARA DESERT
EGYPT
Asyut
NILE RIVER
Luxor
Aswan
ASWAN DAM
SUDAN
Merowe
Atbara
Khartoum
0 MILES 500
0 KM 500
palacios

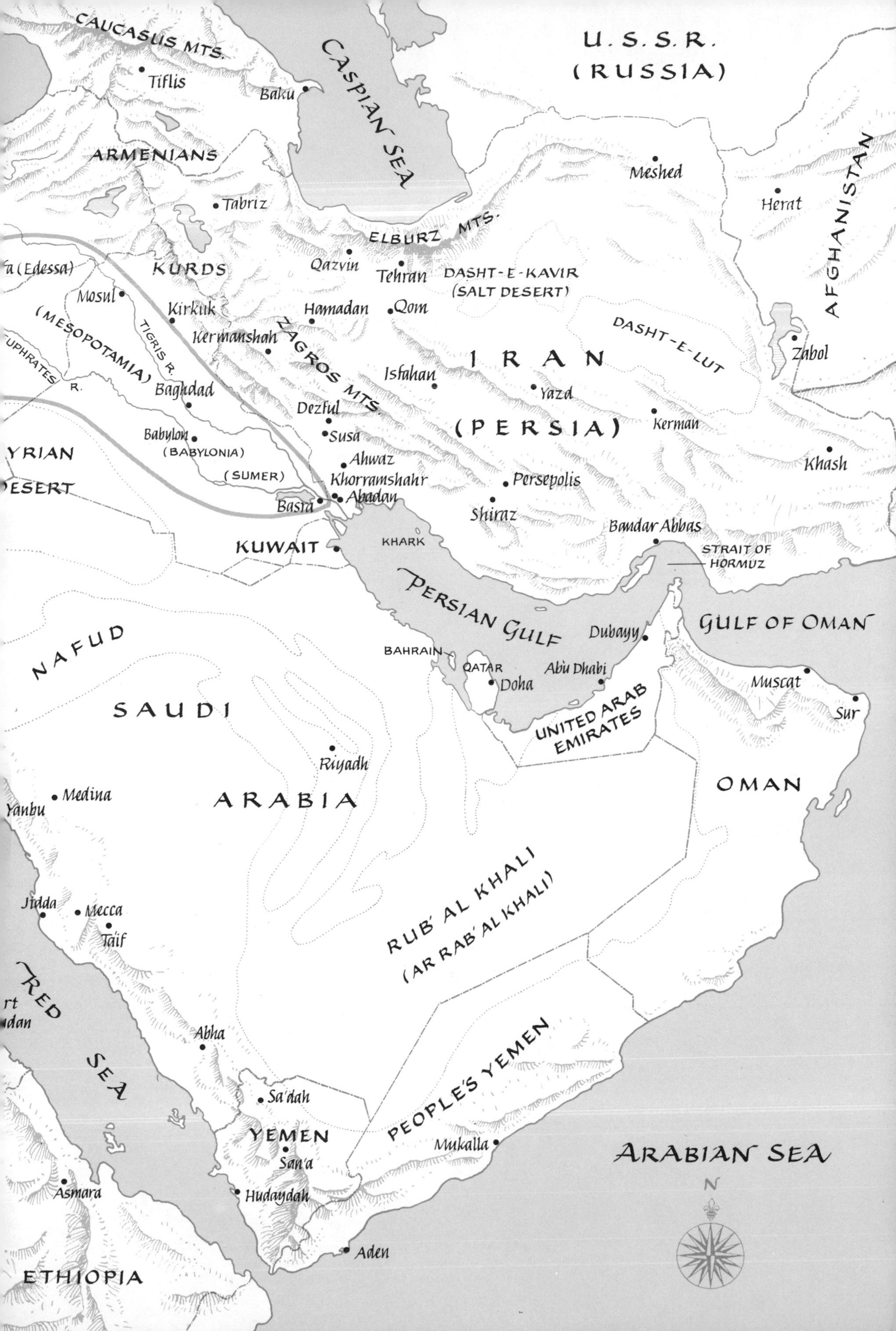

CAUCASUS MTS.
Tiflis
Baku
CASPIAN SEA
U.S.S.R.
(RUSSIA)
ARMENIANS
Meshed
Herat
AFGHANISTAN
Tabriz
ELBURZ MTS.
KURDS
(Edessa)
Qazvin
Tehran
DASHT-E-KAVIR
(SALT DESERT)
Mosul
Kirkuk
Hamadan
Qom
(MESOPOTAMIA)
TIGRIS R.
Kermanshah
ZAGROS MTS.
DASHT-E-LUT
Zabol
EUPHRATES R.
Baghdad
Isfahan
IRAN
Yazd
Dezful
(PERSIA)
Kerman
Babylon
(BABYLONIA)
Susa
Ahwaz
Khash
(SUMER)
Khorramshahr
Persepolis
Abadan
Basra
Shiraz
Bandar Abbas
KUWAIT
KHARK
STRAIT OF HORMUZ
PERSIAN GULF
GULF OF OMAN
NAFUD
Dubayy
BAHRAIN
QATAR
Abu Dhabi
Doha
Muscat
Sur
SAUDI
UNITED ARAB EMIRATES
Riyadh
OMAN
Medina
Yanbu
ARABIA
RUB' AL KHALI
(AR RAB' AL KHALI)
Jidda
Mecca
Taif
RED SEA
Abha
PEOPLE'S YEMEN
Sa'dah
YEMEN
San'a
Mukalla
ARABIAN SEA
Asmara
Hudaydah
N
Aden
ETHIOPIA

A PICTORIAL HISTORY OF

THE MIDDLE EAST

A PICTORIAL HISTORY OF THE MIDDLE EAST

War and Peace from Antiquity to the Present

EDWARD JABLONSKI

Maps by Rafael Palacios

DOUBLEDAY & COMPANY, INC.
Garden City, New York

For Joseph F. Oravec

Once Eighth Air Force
Now Clarks Summit, Pennsylvania

Library of Congress Catalog Card Number 81-43565
Library of Congress Cataloging in Publication Data
Jablonski, Edward.
A pictorial history of the Middle East.
Bibliography: p.
Includes index.
1. Near East—History, Military—Pictorial works.
I. Title.
DS62.5.J3 1984 956
ISBN 0-385-18504-9
Printed in the United States of America
9 8 7 6 5 4 3 2 1

Contents

Author's Note

A deep bow of gratitude to editor Mary Sherwin, patient, meticulous, and forbearing over a long stretch of time. Her thoughtful editing of our manuscript is much appreciated. Thanks too to another editor, Harold Kuebler, who helped to shape the manuscript from inception and was, as usual, there when I needed him.

Emily, Carla, and David Jablonski have also been most helpful from the beginning. They have been wise guides through the several shadings of Middle East history. Carla, who presented me with a volume of collected issues of the Jerusalem *Post,* also did some on-the-spot research in the Middle East in the summer of 1981. The insights of all three have been as humanistic as they have been scholarly, with emphasis on the first quality.

Mary and I are grateful to others who have assisted in the making of this volume: American Museum of Natural History, Library Services Department, New York; Shulamit, Leon, and Rhona Bitner, New York; Major Lars Hedstrom, Jr., U.S. Army Office of Public Affairs, New York; Mehrdad Izady, Middle East Institute, Columbia University, New York; Joe Luppino, United Press International, New York; Metropolitan Museum of Art, Photo Library, New York; Rachel Palmer, United Nations Photo Library, New York; Jamil Shammout, United Nations Relief and Works Agency (UNRWA), Vienna; Betty Sprig, Department of Defense, Washington, D.C.; Valerie A. Walker, UNRWA, New York; Paul White, National Archives, Washington, D.C.; C. Zabel, French Embassy Press and Information Division, New York; and Mrs. Sylvia Landress and Mrs. Rebecca Sherman, the Zionist Archives, New York.

E. J.
December 1982

Foreword

SINCE THE end of the Second World War, that little-known and even less-understood part of our world called the Middle East has been impinging upon the consciousness of the rest of the world, and, not the least, in recent history, upon a perplexed and frustrated United States.

Before the fall of Iran's Shah in January 1979, and the seizure of the American Embassy by "students" in Tehran and the subsequent captivity of its personnel in November, Americans gave little thought to "exotic" Iran. When that nation's religious leader, the Ayatollah Ruhollah Khomeini, returned after fifteen years of exile to scourge the United States and to equate its President with Satan, Americans were appalled by the fury of his malevolence. As time went by, they were even more distressed by the prolonged confinement and psychologically callous treatment of the American hostages.

Additional realities became apparent when the price of oil continued to spiral upward, when the Soviets moved into Afghanistan (which shares a border with Iran), and when Iraq (on Iran's western boundary) went to war with Iran in September 1980. Two Muslim nations, both predominantly of the Shi'ite sect, taking up arms against one another implied civil war; the strategic importance of the Persian Gulf and the Gulf of Oman, to the southeast, to the world's oil-consuming nations, became obvious with startling clarity.

The war in the Persian Gulf distracted attention from other conflicts in the Middle East: Israel versus the Arab states, and the explosive question of the fate of displaced Palestinians. The political position of Egypt, an Arab state, and the enmity of other Arab states, Iraq among them, because of President Anwar el-Sadat's attempts at peace between Egypt and Israel, emphasizes inter-Arab instability and hostility.

North of Israel, on the Mediterranean, lies the small nation of Lebanon (smaller by some four thousand square miles than the state of Connecticut); its capital, Beirut, is a shambles after years of tangled civil war. Christians battle Muslims—and Christians—for control of a government in chaos. Muslims, in turn, fight Christians and Muslims. The Shi'ites of Lebanon have been tendered financial support by Shi'ite Iran. The Palestinians of Lebanon, allied with the leftist Lebanese militia (which receives aid from Libya and Iraq), contribute to the uneasiness of the Shi'ites. In addition, Palestinian guerrilla incursions into Israel from Lebanese bases bring retribution from Israel.

Israel is the most Westernized—politically, technologically, and militarily—of the nations in the Middle East. It is also the most democratic; the voice of its people is heard and often heeded. The most recent of the Arab-Israeli wars, the incursion into Lebanon to shatter the Palestine Liberation Organization, and the tragic aftermath, the slaughter of Palestinians in Beirut by Lebanese Christian Phalangists, have revealed Israeli instabilities. The public outrage and the subsequent investigation into the murders in the Palestinian camps threw light on an Israeli Government in disarray. While Israelis, civilian and military, searched their consciences, their leaders at that time—Prime Minister Menachem Begin and Defense Minister Ariel Sharon—appeared to be intent on establishing a Greater Israel, the former basing his incentive on the Old Testament and the latter on Clausewitz. This fusion of biblical ideology and military strategy promises no true solution to what is known as the "Palestinian question," especially as posed on the West Bank of the Jordan River.

As a historical crossroads since antiquity—a bridge between Asia, Africa, and Europe—the Middle East is as much a state of mind as a geographic area. The term was originally of European—Western—derivation. The nineteenth-century "Near East" and "Far East" were useful in the French and English rivalry for trade and political-military dominance from the Mediterranean Sea to the Indian Ocean. The American military writer Alfred T. Mahan is credited with devising "Middle East" early in the twentieth century; his thinking was centered on the strategic importance of the Persian Gulf to the navies of the world, still a dozen years before World War I. Mahan's conception of what today is called the Middle East remains the popular, if not totally precise, term. It remains a relic of Western colonialism and military adventurism.

The roots of today's confrontations between the Middle East and the West can be traced to Napoleon's invasion of Egypt, in 1798. In the next two centuries, exploitation by the major, often contending, European powers came to fruition as the French colonized portions of North Africa—e.g., Egypt and Algeria—and the British moved into Africa and appropriated Egypt and its vital Suez Canal, built by the French, to ensure a sea route to Afghanistan and India, in the Far East. On the northern areas of this vast region (in the Caucasus and Turkestan), the Russians, from the eighteenth to the nineteenth centuries, occupied Muslim lands and waited.

The subject peoples of these colonies or protectorates did not welcome the invasions with joy, but they were no match for the armies and guns of European military forces. They bided their time, a depressed, slighted people whose wishes and history were overlooked or distorted.

Not that European scholars did not study the "Mysterious East"; a vast literature grew out of Europe's contact with the East in the years since Napoleon. Much of this has been rejected and deprecated as "Orientalism" by contemporary scholars, most eloquently by the Palestinian-American professor of literature (Columbia, Stanford, Princeton, Harvard) and member of the Palestine National Council, Edward W. Said. In his book *Orientalism* (1978), Said finds that most of the studies by Europeans since the Napoleonic invasion are little more than compilations of stereotyped exotica, with minimal understanding of the peoples of the Middle East, their cultures, and their religions. The emphasis, Said believes, is on the "ineradicable distinction between Western superiority and Oriental inferiority." By his definition, "Orientalism" . . . is "a Western style for dominating, restructuring and having authority over the Orient." In short, the scholars who perhaps in all sincerity and to the best of their capabilities studied the Middle East, merely provided the intellectual ammunition and rationalization for colonialism.

Such thinking, Said asserts, has determined the Western view of the Middle East from the eighteenth century to this day. To a tragic extent this may be true, but it is not an absolute. Not all the students, even travelers, brought back tales of the irrational wild Arab horseman, illiteracy, harems, pitiless codes of justice, and technological backwardness.

The "Orientalists," prejudiced as they were (and are), may have based their stereotypes on facts, exaggerated by repetition into sweeping generalizations. Many students subsequently sought out the stereotypes, because they were fascinating and colorful. Still, the plight of women throughout most of the Middle East is no stereotype (in parts of Egypt, circumcision of girls of six or eight is still practiced); nor is the fact of public whipping for (in Western eyes) minor crimes. Amputation for theft is common in Islam, and, in Iran, death by stoning is often the fate of the prostitute, female adulterer, or sexual deviant. Public hangings for assorted crimes ranging from drug dealing to alleged treason may not occur every day, but they occur; the "fair" trial of the West is held in contempt in some Islamic nations.

Although these barbaric forms of retribution may not delineate cultural inferiority, they do confront the Western student with a difficult-to-grasp—"mysterious," if you will—attitude toward human life and suffering, not to mention justice.

Aside from certain shocking indisputable realities (which might be classified as Orientalism because they are shocking and therefore more interesting), stereotypes do abound and distort our perceptions of a complexity of peoples and their histories. Before 1945, when the United States began its inroads into this volatile, factious part of the world, few Americans realized its implications.

Where and what was the Middle East? Who are these Arabs, Muslims, Kurds, and Iranians?

Visions of swarthy, wild-eyed warriors in flowing robes on charging camels or compact Arabian horses were conjured: Veiled women in harems! *The Arabian Nights.* How about "The Lustful Turk"? Or "A jug of Wine, a loaf of Bread and Thou"? Lawrence of Arabia. Bustling bazaars, wretched poverty, and ineffable wealth. Cadillacs and oil. Such were—and are—the popular images evoked by the words *Middle East.*

Between World Wars I and II, business as usual was carried on in the Middle East and, despite the Arabic contribution to the Allies' defeat of Germany in World War I, the Allies' promises made to the Arab nations were not kept after 1918. But there were stirrings; one of the most significant occurred in the early 1920s, when a nationalist movement led by Kemal Atatürk broke centuries of imperialist rule, introducing an end to colonialization, and advocated modernization. From various nations in the Middle East, the sons of the wealthy were sent to the West to be educated in finance, technology, industrialization, and other arts of "modern civilization." Often these Westernized Muslims and Arabs were regarded with suspicion by the more orthodox, but their skills proved most useful in a changing Middle East. Few in the West noticed this, for it was supposed to be a backward, stagnant region.

Then, virtually the moment World War II ended in Europe, the Algerian revolt (beyond the scope of this volume) erupted, demonstrating to the West that the indigenous Algerian neither loved his French overseers nor was as compliant, docile, and pacific as had been assumed. The outcome was one of the most savage wars in history (1954–62). The image of the prayerful, patient Muslim required drastic revision after the Algerian revolt.

In October 1973, the United States suffered an unexpected and unsettling jolt when, in reprisal for its aid to Israel in what has come to be called the Yom Kippur War, a few small Arab states demonstrated their power by cutting off their shipments of petroleum to the West. Then came the Iranian revolution, in 1979, which magnified the situation with its emphasis on Islam: the religious dimension. Ayatollah Khomeini intimated its implications in a broadcast: "I hope that all Islamic nations, which have been set against one another by the evil foreign propaganda against them, will wake up and join hands to form a great Islamic government under the banner of 'There is no God but Allah' and prove victorious the whole world over."

If this theocracy were to evolve and unite, it would encompass much of the globe, stretching across North Africa from Morocco to Egypt, across the Sinai Peninsula into Jordan, Syria, Lebanon, Turkey, Iraq, Iran, the nations of the Arabian peninsula, Afghanistan, and on into Asia (northwestern China, Indonesia), Southeast Asia, and part of the Philippines. In addition, much of Africa south of the nations on the south shore of the Mediterranean has embraced the Muslim religion. (An exception is Ethiopia, which is predominantly Christian.) In Europe there are substantial Islamic pockets in Bulgaria and Yugoslavia; likewise in the Soviet Union. In the Americas, only the Caribbean area and South America have small groupings of Muslims: in Trinidad and Tobago, Guyana, and Surinam. In short, there are some 700 million Muslims in forty countries throughout the world.

The entity called the Arab world is superimposed over the Muslim world, with important exceptions. What is popularly called the Middle East is nearly congruent with the Arab world, which, for the purposes of this volume, includes Libya, Egypt, Jordan, Syria, Iraq, Saudi Arabia, and the rest of the Arabian peninsula (Oman, North Yemen, South Yemen, the United Arab Emirates, Qatar, Behrain, and Kuwait).

The important omissions are Turkey, which although it may properly be placed in the Middle East, is not an Arab state—its official language is Turkish, though its principal religion is Islam; and Iran, which is not an Arab state either—its language is Persian, although it, too, is an Islamic country.

Another obvious omission is what Middle East authority Herbert Mason has termed "neo-Western Israel," which is a Jewish state, of which the primary language is Hebrew (which, it might be noted, belongs to the Semitic family of languages—as does Arabic but not Turkish or Persian).

These generalities oversimplify the complexity of peoples in the Middle East, which also include Armenians, Kurds, and other tribal peoples, as well as Europeans. So it would seem that to state categorically that the inhabitant of the Middle East (even in its rather limited usage in this book) has a defined national personality determined by his Arabic or Semitic culture or Islam is misleading because of this wide range of peoples, cultures, languages, and denominational variants.

It is also a grave error to attempt to separate government from religion in Islam, one of the three major religions of the world, along with Judaism and Christianity. The Muslims view their faith differently (although Islam has borrowed from these earlier religions as well as from its Greek and Roman experiences). There is no Islamic priesthood, for example, as in the Roman Catholic Church. Islam is not a "Sunday religion," either, but is practiced daily; it permeates every facet of the devout Muslim's life. "Islam is not a religion in the common, distorted meaning of the word, confining itself to the private life of man," Islamic scholar Khurshid Ahmad has written. "It is a complete way of life, catering for all the fields of human existence. Islam provides guidance for all walks of life—individual and social, economic and political, legal and cultural, national and international."

The stirrings, the unrest, the revolutions and wars that have flared in the Middle East, whether to end European-American dominance or to settle disputes between the Islamic and Arabic peoples themselves, are triply sanctioned: by economic reality; by a surge of militant nationalism of individual states (there is no such thing as a Middle Eastern nationalism); and by the Deity.

The last is the most difficult to understand, to rationalize in Western terms and, in turn, to handle. It is virtually impossible to discuss with an individual who holds you in contempt as a child of Satan, who believes in a god-given invincibility, and who, should he die in battle, is assured of eternal paradise.

This Middle East, this mercurial creation of an imperialist West, suppressed for so long, is even more of a "melting pot" than the United States. It is boiling over. How it became that way and what has occurred since World War II are the subject of this volume.

Emphasis will be on those nations whose futures have an immediate meaning to the United States. Due to modern transportation, communication, and military technology, the Middle East is no longer some place east of London and Paris and far from Washington; it is right next door—and angry.

Introduction: The Setting

SAND IS the Middle East's most abundant substance; its near-hypnotic undulations define the landscape. Its lifeless but shifting dunes encroach on cities, towns, settlements, farms, and oases. Arid, with extremes in temperature ranging from blistering during the day to freezing at night, the desert is a constant, inexorable, often deadly presence.

A great swath of desert sweeps across the nations of the Middle East: the Sahara in Libya and Egypt, across the Sinai Peninsula into the Arabian Desert of the Arabian Peninsula, with the Red Sea along its western, mountainous edge and the Persian Gulf, the Gulf of Oman, and the Arabian Sea on the east and the southeast.

Four fifths of the Arabian Peninsula is desert: the Syrian in the north, the Nafud below that, and the vast "Empty Quarter" (Ar Rub' al Khali), in southern Saudi Arabia. In Iran, across the Persian Gulf and to the east of the Zagros Mountains, are the Salt Desert, or more precisely, salt plain (*Dasht-e-Kavir*) in central Iran, and, roughly, sand plain (*Dasht-e-Lut*) in eastern Iran.

Thus, the landscape of the Middle East varies from flat and rolling to jagged, from very dry to wet—all of which combine to determine its characteristic way of life. The major mountainous regions of the Middle East lie in the north, extending through Turkey and Iran into southern Asia, with its spectacular

American Museum of Natural History; photo by Walter Fairservis

Himalayas. Parts of Turkey and some parts of Iran get some of the meager rainfall of the area, permitting a moderate amount of agriculture. In the foothills of the mountains and on the edges of sparsely flowering desert, tribesmen and farmers tend their herds of sheep, goats, and camels. Such nomadic grazing (especially by goats) consumes the scattered vegetation to the roots, contributing to the further spread of the desert wasteland, rendering that way of life more precarious than ever.

Mountains and their foothills, nurtured by the rainfall they collect, contribute to the growth of forests in Turkey, particularly. These mountains harbor the Kurds, a non-Arabic-speaking Muslim people who, like so many of the Middle Eastern peoples, are seeking self-determination: a homeland (once Kurdistan) of their own. They have been fighting the government of Iraq intermittently since the 1960s.

Although every nation of the Middle East has access to shipping ports—on the Mediterranean, Black, Red, Caspian, and Arabian seas—its arid climate

Lifeline in Egypt: an irrigation ditch in the agricultural belt, Nile Valley.

Photos courtesy of American Museum of Natural History

The lateen-rigged dhow, *traditionally used for travel and fishing on the Nile River.*

Wide World Photos

The Holy City, Jerusalem, in a view looking east toward the Mount of Olives. The Garden of Gethsemene, the scene of Christ's betrayal by Judas, is in the foreground. A Russian church rises out of the trees in the center.

The Church of the Holy Sepulcher, in the Christian quarter of Jerusalem, is the site of Christ's burial and Resurrection.

Consulate General of Israel

The Dome of the Rock, in eastern Jerusalem, was built on the site of Herod's Temple. According to Islamic tradition, Mohammed ascended to heaven from the spot over which the Dome of the Rock is standing. Completed in A.D. 691, it is the oldest Muslim monument.

Photos courtesy of Consulate General of Israel

Nativity Square, Bethlehem, site of the birthplace of Christ.

and deserts make its fresh-water streams, rivers, and lakes crucial to life and agriculture. The greatest population concentrations are in the agriculturally rich river valleys such as the Nile, in Egypt, or in areas that have ample rainfall—the northern sections of Turkey and Iran, for example.

Another important area in dispute, known as the "Fertile Crescent," extends northeastward roughly from the Nile to the Euphrates and Tigris rivers. This well-watered arc swings through portions of today's Israel, Lebanon, Jordan, Syria, and Iraq.

The Euphrates and Tigris rivers are important to Iraq's agriculture, rather than to shipping. Ranging from sluggish to rushing flood, they are only navigable—when navigable—by raft or small boat. The rivers merge in southern Iraq north of Basra, the nation's major port on the Persian Gulf. This body of water is essential to the water transport of Iraq as well as to the major oil-producing states of the Arabian Peninsula (Saudi Arabia, Kuwait, Bahrain, Qatar, the United Arab Emirates) and Iran.

Crude oil from inland oil fields is carried to the Gulf ports through a network of pipelines constructed during the European-American domination of the Middle East oil industry. One of the longest lines traverses the Arabian Peninsula east to west, through Jordan and Syria to ports in Lebanon, on the Mediterranean; Iraqi oil is pumped from its fields near Kirkuk through Turkey to the Mediterranean. Some of these pipelines were constructed aboveground, making them vulnerable to vandalism, sabotage, and military strikes.

The Great Mosque of Medina, the city in which the Prophet Mohammed died.

Wide World Photos

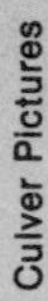

Nineteenth-century etching of Mecca, the Holy City of Islam. In the foreground: the Great Mosque; the Kaaba is the square structure at left center. Pilgrims fill the courtyard.

Contemporary pilgrims in Mecca, with spires of the Great Mosque in the background. All pilgrims wear a white gown, whatever their station in life, symbolizing the equality of all in the eyes of Allah.

Wide World Photos

Culver Pictures

The goal of every devout Muslim: the Kaaba, containing the sacred Black Stone of Islam.

Wide World Photos

Interior view of the Great Mosque, Mecca.

Culver Pictures

The call to prayer in Islam. The pious Muslim fulfills salat *(the ritual prayer) five times a day, upon hearing the* muezzin *in the mosque's minaret calling the faithful.*

Photos courtesy of Culver Pictures

A Syrian Muslim prays to Allah.

Desert Arabs at prayer.

Another critical Middle Eastern waterway is the Jordan River, which forms a two-hundred-mile boundary between what were called Palestine and Transjordan from 1922 until 1948. Partitioned in 1947 by the United Nations into Jewish and Arab sections to establish a long-promised homeland for the Jews, this land of the Bible, this Holy Land, became an instant trouble spot.

When Israel was declared a state, the following year, and the United Nations peacemaking forces—and the British—withdrew, the first of a series of Arab-Israeli wars erupted. To the surprise of many, particularly the more numerous Arabs, Israeli military prowess proved to be most effective. The result was that Israel held, when the conflict was over, even more of Palestine than had been granted by the partition. Jordan, however, continued to hold onto a bulge of

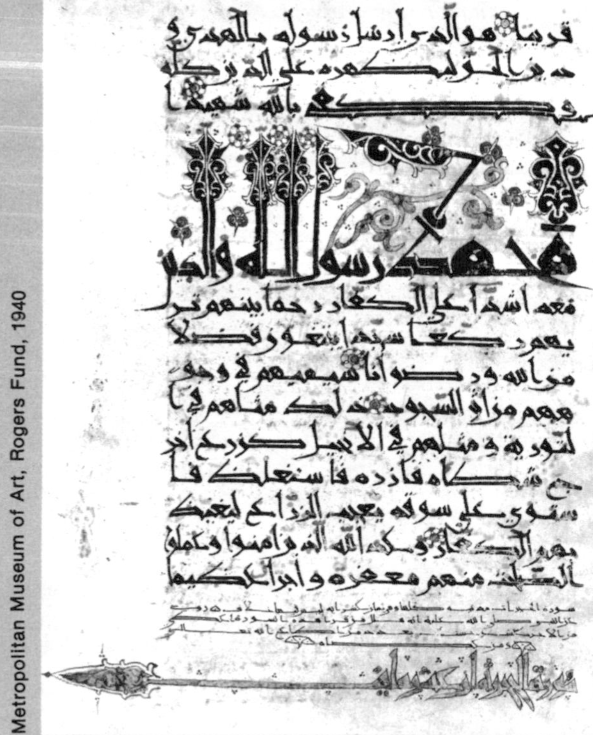

Metropolitan Museum of Art, Rogers Fund, 1940

A page from the Koran, the sacred book of Islam; the text is in Iranian (Persian) Kufic calligraphy, circa A.D. *1050.*

Despite the major changes that have occurred in the Middle East since World War II, the strength of Islam has not waned. Misjudging the powerful hold of this religion on the Middle Eastern peoples has led to serious problems for Americans and Europeans in the Middle East.

Culver Pictures

American Museum of Natural History

Arab mother and child in traditional costume. The man on the left carries a scimitar, the centuries-old sword of the Mideast.

Bedouin desert camp; these nomadic "desert dwellers" (i.e., Bedouin*), fiercely independent and proud, have greatly shaped Middle Eastern society.* ▼

Consulate General of Israel

Arab family group from the village of Dabbuniah, near Mount Tabor, in the Jezreel Valley, east of Nazareth. Christian tradition places the Transfiguration of Christ on or near Mount Tabor. ▼

Consulate General of Israel

territory on the Jordan's west bank and north and west of the Dead Sea. Inside this constricted area were gathered hundreds of thousands of Arab refugees—Palestinians who had fled from Israeli-occupied territories.

The even more stunning "Six Day War," of 1967, another serious and electrifying jolt for the Arabs, concluded with the Israeli occupation of Egypt's Sinai Peninsula as well as all of the West Bank, including the city venerated by three worldwide religions: Jerusalem. This conquest also exacerbated the grievous problem of the Palestinian refugees and hardened Arab hostility toward Israel (and allies) even more.

The Arabs may have lost control over the Jordan River, but they do command the other critical fluid of the Middle East: oil. Its significance in this ancient region is of recent origin. The Middle East for centuries had been regarded as predominantly an agricultural area, with its grain, fruit, and olives and Egypt's long-staple cotton. Petroleum did not figure into the Middle East's economic picture until the beginning of the twentieth century, when a young British entrepreneur-prospector, William Knox D'Arcy, negotiated an agreement with the government of Persia (now Iran) enabling him to explore, produce, and refine any oil within an area of 480,000 square miles. After several years of discouraging drilling, D'Arcy finally struck oil, in 1908, at Masjed-Soleyman, northeast of Ahwaz, in southwestern Persia. By 1914, the Anglo-Persian Oil Company was producing enough fuel oil to supply the Royal Navy, only recently converted from coal to oil by the wily First Lord of the Admiralty, Winston Churchill.

After World War I, Britain expanded its oil interests in the Middle East, followed by investors from the United States, France, and other Western nations. Until the surge of Arab nationalism and the subsequent nationalization of the petroleum industry since World War II, few of the peoples in the area shared much of this wealth. Since D'Arcy's time, the Middle East has emerged as the major oil depository of the world, with some two thirds of the oil reserves under its sands, mostly inside the borders of Saudi Arabia, Iran, Kuwait, and Iraq.

This reserve, as well as smaller deposits in other Arab states, draws the attention and concern of the highly industrialized nations, among them Japan and the United States (the two most oil-dependent nations), West Germany, France, and the United Kingdom.

Since reclaiming the oil fields, the Arabs have found themselves in possession not only of a valuable natural resource, but also of a potent international bargaining weapon. The income has raised living standards in many of the Arab states (Kuwait has had especially spectacular growth), and it has made possible Arab investments in Western business, from real estate to banking. It also pays for sophisticated weaponry: jet fighter bombers and modern tanks. The oil itself, either by being withheld from the West or by having its price raised, is even more forceful than money.

It also makes the Middle East very alluring indeed to such competitors as

An American oil refinery at Ras Tanura, near the Persian Gulf, Saudi Arabia. This area is one of the world's major oil reservoirs.

An American oil derrick drilling throughout the night. This photo was taken in 1947 in Saudi Arabia; the United States was in the Middle East to stay.

An oil exploration party sets out prepared for several weeks of searching. Besides the usual equipment, the caravan consists of air-conditioned living and working quarters (the trailers, center). Two Bedouin observe the strange caravan which contributes to a drastic change in their way of life.

Photos courtesy of Wide World Photos

National Council of Tourism in Lebanon

*The famed Cedars of Lebanon (*Arz el-Rab = *"Cedars of God"), which grow in the mountains near the town of Becharre, southeast of Tripoli, in northern Lebanon. The wood of these hardy trees was used by the ancient Egyptians in fashioning their barges. Only about 300 carefully guarded cedars exist today; some are 1,000 years old. In this scene, snow covers the mountains on which the trees grow, which shows that the Middle East is not all sand.*

the United States and the Soviet Union. The Soviet invasion of Afghanistan in late 1979 places it on the rim of the strategically situated, oil-rich Middle East.

What once appeared to be a relatively simple "Middle East" problem, in the halcyon empire years, when France and Britain dominated the region, has become, in recent years, especially since 1945, a tangle of overlapping, intersecting, and divergent culture currents and objectives: the rise of a "Militant Islam" to drive Western influence out of their nations—and the divisions among the Islamic sects themselves; the inter-Arab rivalries that seem to ebb and flow with the winds; the presence of the new state of Israel, a tiny island in an Arab sea; the "Palestinian question," which grows more complex following the convulsions in that sea. Another factor is the Westernization (i.e., modernization) that has led to a population growth in an area incapable of sustaining a high density of population. Great areas of the Middle East are uninhabitable, and only about 10 percent of the land is arable. There is also a wide gap between the wealthy and the poor, the urban dweller and the farmer.

And there is oil. About two thirds of the world's known oil reserves are buried under the sand of the Middle East.

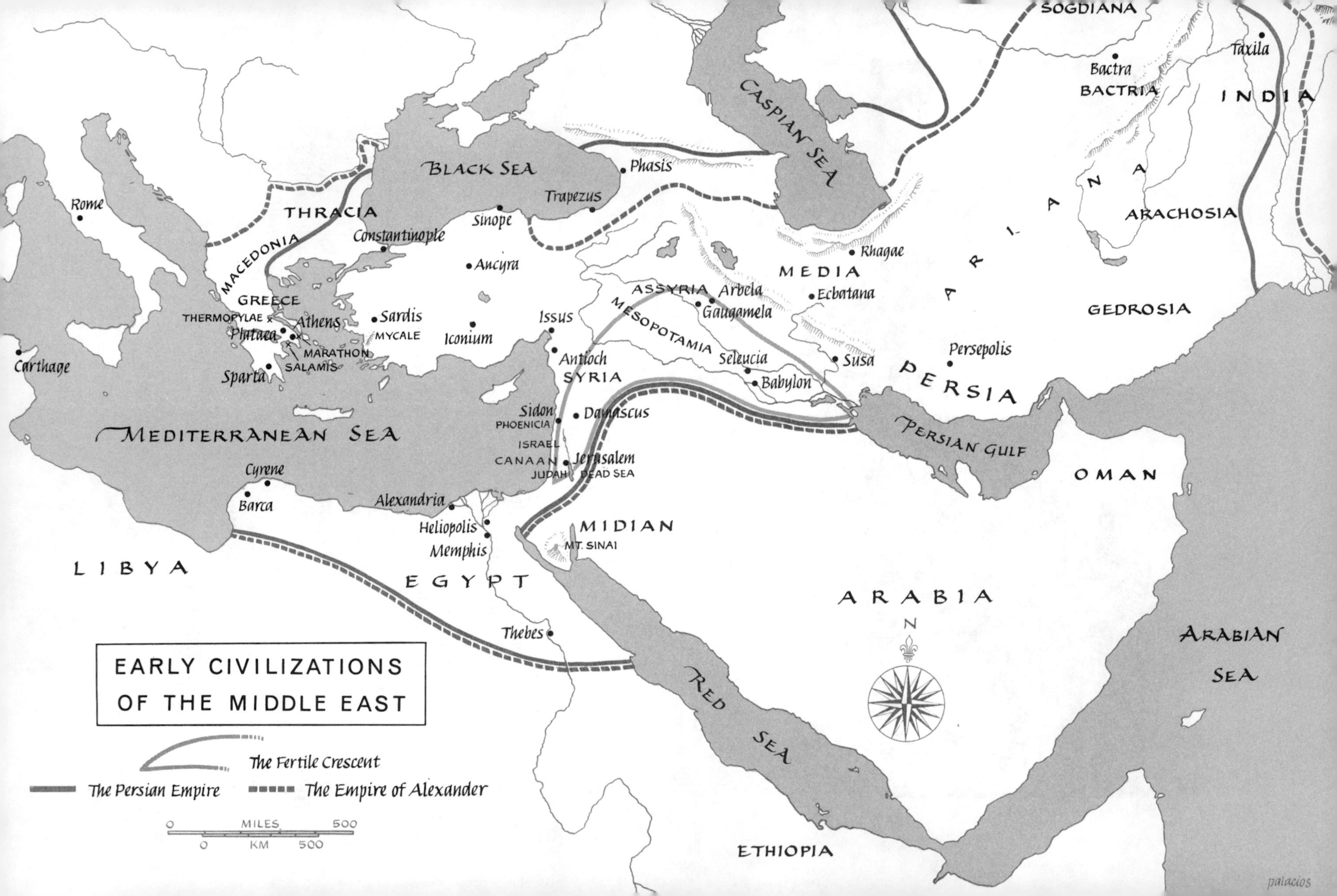

EARLY CIVILIZATIONS OF THE MIDDLE EAST
The Fertile Crescent
The Persian Empire
The Empire of Alexander
0 MILES 500
0 KM 500
SOGDIANA
Taxila
Bactra
BACTRIA
INDIA
CASPIAN SEA
BLACK SEA
Phasis
Trapezus
Sinope
Rome
THRACIA
MACEDONIA
Constantinople
Ancyra
ARIANA
ARACHOSIA
Rhagae
MEDIA
Ecbatana
GEDROSIA
ASSYRIA
Arbela
Gaugamela
MESOPOTAMIA
GREECE
THERMOPYLAE
Athens
Plataea
Sardis
MYCALE
Iconium
Issus
MARATHON
SALAMIS
Carthage
Sparta
Antioch
SYRIA
Seleucia
Babylon
Susa
Persepolis
PERSIA
Sidon
PHOENICIA
Damascus
MEDITERRANEAN SEA
ISRAEL
CANAAN
Jerusalem
JUDAH
DEAD SEA
PERSIAN GULF
OMAN
Cyrene
Barca
Alexandria
Heliopolis
Memphis
MIDIAN
MT. SINAI
LIBYA
EGYPT
ARABIA
N
Thebes
ARABIAN SEA
RED SEA
ETHIOPIA
palacios

1

"Cradle of Civilization"

THE ANCESTORS of all humans who have ever lived on this earth were born in Africa in what are now Kenya, Uganda, and Ethiopia. Six or so million years ago, these manlike creatures began migrating northward down the Nile Valley and, at its delta, over long periods of time, disseminating westward along the southern shore of the Mediterranean Sea in North Africa and eventually into Europe.

Other migrants fanned northeastward into the Fertile Crescent and continued eastward. From there these peoples, adapting to climates and environments widely different from their ancestral African homeland, filtered into the Americas and Australia during the most recent ice age, some 20 million years ago, when sea levels had lowered throughout the planet.

Conditions favorable to agricultural and pastoral life (as opposed to nomadic life, which did not encourage communities) were found in the Nile Valley and the Fertile Crescent. In the latter region were born the first recorded civilizations. In the "Land Between the Rivers" (the Euphrates and the Tigris, in contemporary Iraq), Mesopotamia, Sumerian cities united in agricultural, commercial, and other enterprises, including metallurgy, that required human cooperation. This occurred in southern Mesopotamia circa 3000 B.C.

With the establishment of cities, farms, and trade, "civilization" began. From the fertile land between the rivers came not only the yield of their irrigated fields, but also the alphabet and writing (cuneiform = "wedge-shaped") of the Sumerians, and a Babylonian system of laws, codified by King Hammurabi. The idea that laws should be administered more or less equally by the state, instead of by individuals or by cities, was almost as revolutionary as putting things in writing to record business transactions. The "eye for an eye and tooth for a tooth" edict, one of the less humane features of Hammurabi's Code, was later absorbed into the Old Testament and other Oriental systems of law.

Almost simultaneously with the rise of Mesopotamian city-states, the unification of farming villages in the Nile Valley produced another flowering of civilization, in Egypt. This was the Egypt of the great pyramids, superbly engineered canals, an elaborate polytheistic religion ministered by a powerful priesthood, and a system of writing (hieroglyphics = "priestly carving") applied to rolls of papyrus, rather than more cumbersome stone tablets. Like the

Babylonians, the Egyptians excelled in the arts, especially sculpture, mathematics, and literature.

Between Babylonia and Egypt, at the southwestern end of the Fertile Crescent's arc, in Canaan (later known as the Levant), Natufians, whose traces date back to the Middle Stone Age, circa 10,000 B.C., had practiced farming even before these two great civilizations, perhaps by as much as five thousand years. In this narrow strip of land, around the period of Babylonian and Egyptian flowering, the Phoenicians and the Hebrews had moved into the Levant and flourished independently, but not without hostility. The Phoenicians settled predominantly in the north (contemporary Lebanon) and evolved from farmers into the great seamen of the ancient world; the most important cargo they transmitted to the world was undoubtedly the alphabet, in which each symbol (or letter) represented a single sound, rather than a picture of something or an entire word.

To the south, the Israelites, who had migrated into Canaan from the Arabian Desert, were primarily agriculturists and herdsmen. They, too, eventually united into a national state under King David (circa 1012–972 B.C.). During his reign, the religious-literary heritage of the Israelites was collected and preserved on papyrus scrolls, which the Greeks called *biblia*. This was, of course, the Old Testament of the Bible, a collection of writings containing poetry, genealogies, histories, stories, and the belief in a single God. The Israelites contributed those beliefs that eventuated in three of the world's major religions: Judaism (named for the fourth son of Jacob, one of the early Jewish patriarchs), Christianity, and Islam.

The civilization of the Israelites reached a peak during the reign of King Solomon (circa 972–932 B.C.), in which a great temple was constructed in Jerusalem, trading cities flourished, and the Jews enjoyed a period of peace with their neighbors, Egypt and Phoenicia. After Solomon's death, the kingdom split in two: Judah in the south and Israel in the north. This division led to internecine quarrels, which left the divided kingdom open to conquest by Assyrians and Babylonians from the north. The Babylonians destroyed Solomon's Temple in Jerusalem (586 B.C.) and sent many of their captives to Babylon (the biblical exile). The Assyrians were a formidable military people whose weaponry included war chariots and iron swords and spears.

Warring, too, emerged as a questionable "contribution" of burgeoning civilizations. "Spring, the season of war, " brought not only plantings but invasion and plundering. The Assyrians, who so concentrated on making war that they neglected agriculture, eventually fell to the Babylonians—whose empire, in turn, fell to an Indo-European people from the east, the Persians.

Persians came from that area known today as Iran. Under the leadership of their legendary king, Cyrus the Great, the Persians conquered an empire that spread from Asia Minor to the Fertile Crescent. Cyrus' successors took Egypt and, moving eastward from the Iranian Plateau, dominated portions of India to the Indus River. By 500 B.C., the Persian Empire was the most expansive of its time. Persian rule, which lasted for around two hundred years,

American Museum of Natural History; photo by Edward L. Bailey

The dawn of urbanization: a reconstruction of the city of Ur, in Sumer (now southeastern Iraq), about 2000 B.C. The city was a major commercial center because of its location on the Euphrates River.

American Museum of Natural History; photo by Julius Kirschner

Babylonian tablets: the symbols, representing sounds, were based originally on pictures of objects and impressed on the tablets of soft clay with a wedge-shaped stylus. The tablets were used for keeping records and accounts by both merchants and priests.

The Roman Temple of Bacchus, built circa A.D. *150 in Baalbek, Lebanon, serves as the setting for the Baalbek International Festival's ballets and concerts.*

National Council of Tourism in Lebanon

Culver Pictures

The Temple of Jupiter, Baalbek, Lebanon. The foundations of the structure are thought to be pre-Roman; the building was probably completed around A.D. *60.*

American Museum of Natural History; photo by L. Boltin.

The pyramid of Khafre and a portion of the Great Sphinx, Egypt. The sphinx generally represented the Pharaoh as a reincarnation of the sun god, Ra. Pyramids were used as royal tombs, and construction was begun years before the death of the monarch.

American Museum of Natural History; photo by Rota

Assyrian warriors invaded the Middle Eastern states of Mesopotamia, Egypt, Syria, and Israel. With their well-trained armies, war chariots, and iron weapons, the Assyrians plundered and pillaged. Their cruelty in the conquered lands led to many revolts and to their eventual downfall.

was reasonably enlightened, and the subject peoples retained their own customs, culture, religions, and even their own self-government, provided they paid their taxes (and proper obeisance to the emperor). There was the usual cultural exchange, with the Persian contribution notably represented by an extensive system of roads for communication, trade, and military movement. The Persians were among the first to use the horse as an efficient, fast means of delivering messages and for transportation.

Where the Persians failed, militarily, was in their attempts to push westward out of Asia Minor into Macedonia and Greece. The reaction to these Persian wars (500–449 B.C.) eventually led to the first fateful collision between East and West.

Under the reign of Darius I of Persia, Greek colonists who had settled on the coastal edges of Asia Minor revolted against Persian rule, in 500 B.C. In this the colonists were given military aid by Athens, the great Greek city-state. Darius succeeded in crushing the revolt and wanted more: the punishment of the Greeks and the annexation of all of Greece. He failed in this when he was defeated at Marathon (490 B.C.).

A student of Aristotle, Alexander (356–323 B.C.) was a great admirer of Greek culture, like his father, Philip II, and also like him, he planned to avenge the Persian assault on Athens one hundred fifty years before. Assembling an army of Macedonians and Greeks, Alexander, at the age of twenty, set out in 334 B.C. to crush the Persians. In a military campaign that lasted ten years, Alexander the Great, as history would come to know him, "Hellenized" the Persian Empire and beyond.

Alexander's dream was to unite east and west into one vast empire, in which the vanquished and the enlightened conquerer would live in harmony. By 334 B.C., Alexander's empire stretched from the Aegean Sea in the west to the Himalayas in the east, and from the Black and Caspian seas in the north to

Reconstruction of a Roman theatre in Byblos, Lebanon. Byblos (modern Jubayl) is believed to be the oldest continuously inhabited city in the world (a distinction also claimed by Damascus); its ancient city walls date back to 2800 B.C. During the third millennium B.C., Byblos (or Gebal, in the Bible) was the most important shipping center on the eastern Mediterranean. Its prime products were cedar timber and oil.

the Persian Gulf and the Arabian Sea in the south. Roughly, his empire covered an area that would have reached from the California coast of the United States, crossing the continent and continuing about five hundred miles into the Atlantic. It was the greatest empire in the known world.

Alexander's empire began to crumble even during his short lifetime, from corruption and favoritism, and it was soon divided after his death, with three of his generals assuming control of Macedonia in the west, Syria in the east, and Egypt in the south. Thus divided, they were open to another invasion from the west, from the Romans, who carried Alexander's dream of the unification of east and west to greater fruition than he himself had done. Hellenization, with a Roman accent, was continued under the Roman conquerers, who admired the higher civilization of the Greeks and borrowed from its literature, art, and science—which, in turn, had been borrowed partly from conquered peoples of the Middle East. Roman roads, reservoirs, and other public works exploited the goods—papyrus, spices, incense, silk, and jewels of the Mediterranean world—for centuries.

Under the Pax Romana (Roman Peace), administered roughly from 27 B.C. to A.D. 180, governments were locally run under the often indifferent eye of a Roman procurator. This did not always make for peace. For example, the venal house of Herod ruled over Palestine and, between the reign of Herod the Great (circa 73–4 B.C.) and Herod Antipas (circa 4 B.C.–A.D. 40), a revolutionary religious movement grew among the Jews of Palestine. Led by a preacher, Joshua ("Jesus" in Latin), a small band defied both the Roman Emperor Augustus and the established Jewish religious hierarchy.

By the time the Romans executed Joshua, by crucifixion (circa A.D. 30), Christianity (from the Greek *Christos*, "the anointed one, the Messiah") had taken root in the Middle East and had spread, despite persecution, throughout the Roman world. This was the second of the three great world religions that originated in the Middle East.

The persecution was officially ended by the emperor Constantine (288–337 A.D.), who converted to Christianity and, in the twilight of the Roman Empire, moved the center of government from Rome eastward to Byzantium, in A.D. 324, renaming it Constantinople (today's Istanbul, Turkey).

Germanic tribes from central and eastern Europe had gnawed at the northern edges of the Roman Empire for centuries, most disastrously under the leadership of Attila the Hun (the "Scourge of God"). In the fifth century, the Huns ravaged the Roman Empire and, although they were eventually defeated, at the Battle of Châlons (451), they had so weakened the Roman armies that the Empire was prone to future invasions. Rome fell to a Germanic chieftain, Odoacer, in 476, which left only the Eastern, or Byzantine, portion of the great empire as a reminder of the glory that had once been Rome.

The Byzantine Empire flourished (circa 527–65) under the Emperor Justinian, who governed from Constantinople. Here the cultures of Greece and the Middle East melded, and trade and industry made it one of the richest empires in the world. It also functioned for centuries as a buffer between the Eastern invaders (predominantly Arabs and Turks) and Western Europe. The end finally came when the Ottoman Turks captured Constantinople, in 1453.

Before that, however, an even more significant—if not very successful militarily—intrusion occurred. Constant warring between Byzantium and the Sassanian dynasty in neighboring Persia weakened both empires, which made them susceptible to a vigorous challenge from an unexpected quarter, the vast, stark Arabian Desert.

The Western intruders into the Middle East had found little to profit them in the forbidding wastes of the Arabian Peninsula. The northern portion, touching on the Fertile Crescent, and the settlements on the western shore of the Red Sea, were fine for trading, and caravans carried frankincense, myrrh, gold, and other precious goods to North African and European markets.

Having domesticated the foul-tempered camel, the Arabs did commerce with their neighbors and the West. However, because of their virtual isolation in desert settlements, and the nomadism of the Bedouin, they experienced little of the impact of Alexander and the Roman Empire. Arab culture, to a large degree, retained its own language, customs, and beliefs.

One of the major centers of trade near the Red Sea coast was Mecca, situated about halfway down the peninsula. It was also an important religious center, because of the Kaaba, a sanctuary housing the Black Stone (a meteorite) and some three hundred fifty idols. Because of its commercial importance, Mecca came under Jewish as well as Christian influence, although the Arabs clung to their own religions. Even so, tradition assigns the building of the Kaaba to the biblical patriarch Abraham, the founder of Judaism. His son Ishmael is believed by the Muslims to be the father of the Arabs, as opposed to Isaac and his son Israel, who were Jews.

East meets West: Alexander the Great and Darius III clash in the battle of Issus, 333 B.C. Outmaneuvered by the youthful conqueror, Darius fled in panic, abandoning his troops, weapons, family, and possessions.

Metropolitan Museum of Art, Gift of Alexander Smith Cochran, 1913

Mecca was also the birthplace of Mohammed (circa 570–632), the great prophet of Islam. He was about forty years old, a successful Mecca merchant, when he underwent a profound religious experience. An angel appeared in a dream and revealed to him that he had been chosen to lead the idol-worshiping Arabs in a new religion. Acquainted with the teachings of Judaism and Christianity, Mohammed denounced Arab idolatry and proclaimed the existence of one God (Allah). Such blasphemy stirred up the Meccans to the degree that Mohammed was forced to flee, in 622 (year 1 in the Muslim calendar) to Yathrib (later Medina, the City of the Prophet), about two hundred miles north of Mecca. This was also an important caravan stop, and one of the few centers of population that accepted Mohammed's teachings.

Mohammed claimed no special divinity (he accepted Jesus merely as another prophet), only that he was the intermediary between Allah and his followers. His messages from Allah are preserved in the great book of Islam, the Koran ("recitation"), believed to be the word of Allah as transmitted to Mohammed by the angel Gabriel.

The Arabic word *Islam* translates roughly into "submission to Allah" (or God), and a Muslim is "one who submits." The words *Islamic* and *Muslim* are synonymous. However, to refer to a Muslim as a "Mohammedan" (as has been the practice for centuries) is to insult him. This is regarded as blasphemy, since it implies that the founder of the religion should be the object of worship (as is the case with Buddhism and Christianity).

The presence of Mohammed in Medina, and his teachings there, which began to diffuse through the Arabian Peninsula, led to clashes between Medina and Mecca. The people frequently raided one another's caravans; in 624, Mohammed himself led one of the raiding parties and seized the goods of the caravan as spoils of war. The Meccans raised an army to avenge the plundering, but were defeated by Mohammed with a much smaller force. This was believed to be a certain sign that Mohammed had been truly chosen by Allah to be the last of the prophets.

By 629, Mohammed's renown as Prophet and warrior—no "Prince of Peace" he—was so pervasive throughout Arabia that he made a pilgrimage to Mecca without fear and began the conversion of his former enemies. The next year, he entered in triumph at the head of a small army and occupied the city without a battle. His single stipulation after the victory was to call for the destruction of the idols in the Kaaba; the Black Stone remained (and is there today, the object toward which all devout Muslims face five times a day in prayer).

The Arabs, united at the time of Mohammed's death by a common language and religion (which assured them a paradisiacal afterlife if they died in battle), were ready for conquest. After the death of Mohammed, in 632, leadership of the Muslim community passed to his successor, Abu-Bakr, who was designated caliph (which means "successor" in Arabic). Since Mohammed was considered the last of the prophets, no other Muslim could take the title or engage in prophecy. The caliph combined religious as well as civil authority over Islam. Abu-Bakr had been one of Mohammed's most zealous followers; he was also the father of one of Mohammed's favorite wives. He lived only two years after Mohammed and was in turn succeeded by his trusted adviser, 'Umar (also Omar). During the decade of 'Umar's caliphate, Islam made its great expansion and created a vast Muslim Empire.

By 732, the Arabs had conquered an empire that extended from Spain to

India. Although this brought about the spread of Islam, the Arabs did not attempt to convert the Jews of Palestine, or the Copts of Egypt or the various other Christians in their empire. Only pagans were forced to become Muslims or die. The Arabs, accustomed to tribal ways generally, adapted Persian and Byzantine forms of government and laws. The nonpagans who chose not to convert to Islam were taxed. The promise of eternal life (often referred to as Eden in the Koran), the Muslim code of ethics, and avoidance of the tax all contributed to the spread of Islam among the conquered peoples.

These conquered peoples found their new masters more tolerant and kind than the Byzantine governors. In time, with trade, intermarriage, and conversion to Islam, the division between conqueror and conquered faded and, as other nations became Muslim, Islam was recognized as one of the great international religions, as it is today.

Internecine power struggles, political and religious, contributed to the disintegration of the great Arabian Muslim Empire, a breakdown that coursed with blood. Following the murder of 'Umar by a Christian slave, the new caliph, selected by conclave, was Othman, husband of Mohammed's daughter Ruqayya. This rankled Ali, the Prophet's cousin and husband of Fatima, the Prophet's daughter. Although both belonged to the Quraish tribe, Ali was a member of the Hashim branch, and Othman, the Omayyad branch; this division would have a grave effect on the future of Islam.

National Council of Tourism in Lebanon

Fortress/castle north of Batrun, Lebanon. This type of citadel stood in the path of the crusaders on their march to Jerusalem.

Certain tribal chieftains, who had led the Arabian conquests into Byzantine territories, grew to resent the rule of the caliph, safe in Medina, and his favoritism toward his fellow Omayyads. Not the least was a bitterness, voiced by their preachers, over Othman's establishment of a single official form of the Koran and his order to destroy all other versions. A party of dissidents, led by the son of Abu-Bakr, the first caliph, marched from Egypt to Medina, besieged the home of Othman, broke in, and slaughtered him as he sat reading the Koran. This set off the struggle between Arab and Arab, Muslim and Muslim—a struggle that continues in the twentieth century.

The murder of Othman left the caliphate open to Ali, who was held responsible for the assassination by both the Prophet's young widow, Aisha (who led an early, unsuccessful uprising against Ali) and Mu'Awiyah, the Omayyad governor of Syria. In putting down the Aisha rebellion, Ali moved the capital of Islam from Medina to al-Kufa (to the north, in what is now Iraq). This slighting of the city where Mohammed gave birth to Islam led to open rebellion among the more zealous Muslims, which, in turn, generated further breaks and the formation of dissident sects.

A member of the first of these sects, the Kharijites ("the outgoers," who deserted al-Kufa in open rebellion), murdered Ali near al-Kufa's mosque in 661. Mu'Awiyah proclaimed himself caliph of Jerusalem. He led his forces into Iraq and convinced Ali's son Hasan that he should relinquish whatever claim he had to the caliphate. Hasan agreed, and Mu'Awiyah proclaimed himself caliph over all of Islam. Although not accepted by every Arab tribe (the Kharijites, especially), Mu'Awiyah governed reasonably, formed an efficient Islamic army, and abandoned the old, divisive method of election to the caliphate. He introduced the concept of hereditary descent, with his son next in line. In effect, he founded an Omayyad dynasty.

This was offensive to some Muslims, which incited further unrest. Factionalism divided the Arabs and resulted in rebellion and slaughter. Those who had favored Ali broke away from the main body of Islam to form the Shi'ah Ali ("the party of Ali"), believing that the caliphate could be filled only by descendents of Ali. The more orthodox faction, deeply opposed to the Shi'ites, believed in the *sunna* ("the way," as revealed by Mohammed in his lifetime) and have since been called Sunni; the Omayyads belonged to this sect.

These factions are the two major opposing forces in contemporary Islam. Both are Muslim; both consider the Koran to be the Holy Book of Islam; but they have deep-rooted, irreconcilable differences as to the origins of their faith. The dissension, interweaving political and religious elements, weakened the empire and eventually caused the fall of the Omayyad dynasty. In a revolt led by Abu-al-Abbas, who could trace his descent to an uncle of Mohammed, the new holy city, Damascus, was attacked and fell in 750. The Abbasids assured the end of the Omayyad dynasty by slaughtering about eighty members of the family during a banquet (Abu-al-Abbas called himself al-Saffah, "The

Bloodshedder") and later killed most surviving members of the family. One Omayyad managed to flee and set up a new dynasty at Córdoba, Spain.

The Abbasids then transferred the caliphate from Damascus to Baghdad, Iraq, farther east. The name Baghdad (meaning "God-given") is Persian, not Arab; Islam was no longer purely Arabian, but borrowed ideas and practices from the Persians and other eastern cultures. Once a small market town, Baghdad grew into one of the great culture centers of the eighth century, and although Arab feudalism and political and religious factionalism would lead to the disintegration of the Muslim Empire by the tenth century, Arab Islam enjoyed a golden age.

As a center of learning, Baghdad's House of Knowledge integrated varied cultural mansions—Arabic, Persian, Greek, Roman, Jewish, Christian, and Indian—translating, preserving, and adding to the sciences and the arts. This was the period that produced *The Thousand and One Nights* (*The Arabian Nights*) during the caliphate of Harun al-Rashid (786–809). This compilation of tales from various sources not only reflected Islamic values and beliefs, but also the lush life in the courts and other major commercial centers. Poetry flourished (always in the language of the Koran, Arabic), as did geography, medicine, chemistry, architecture, and the law.

Some two hundred years after the death of Mohammed and the diffusion of Islam over vast distances and among various peoples, it was obvious that there was a need for a codification of beliefs, rules, and practices—all, of course, within the Koranic view of life. The result was an inseparable binding of religion and politics. These laws were based to a great degree on the Hadith ("Traditions"), believed to be a collection of Mohammed's sayings, views, and aphorisms recalled by his wife, disciples, and others, eventually numbering in the hundreds of thousands. These commentaries, guidelines for living, and rules were, and are today, administered by religious courts. Rival sects disagreed on some points, but the ultimate source was the Koran. Still the body of Islamic theological law remains rather complex to the Westerner, whose laws, generally, are not bound up with religion. The separation of church and state is inconceivable in Islam.

Although the Abbasid Empire prospered, and nurtured the arts and sciences, the grand scale of living of the caliph and the upper classes provoked civic unrest. By the tenth century, the empire had broken up into several independent Muslim provinces and the caliph had dwindled to a symbol whose rule depended upon an army comprising hired warriors, the most impressive of whom were Turks. This would prove to be a fateful miscalculation.

The most important revolt from within the empire came out of Egypt, with the formation of the Isma'ili movement within the Shi'ite sect. Calling themselves the Fatimids (claiming descent from Mohammed's daughter and her husband, Ali, and the only rightful caliphs), they established a splinter caliphate at Cairo. The Fatimids won the allegiance of disgruntled peasants and townsmen, although their rule was confined to Egypt primarily and to other sections of North Africa, Arabia, Palestine, and Syria.

In the east, Persian nobles began asserting themselves and broke away from Baghdad, leaving only Iraq under the caliph's rule—and even that fell eventually (in 945).

The dissolution of the Islamic Empire left it open to invasion from the West. As the power of the caliphate waned, more Turks were hired for its army. The Turks embraced Islam, and so when the Seljuk Turks (named for their chieftan) invaded the empire and took Baghdad, the caliph remained as a figurehead, and the Turks became masters of the Muslim Empire, ending the dominance of the Arabs and Persians.

The Turkish rulers assumed the title of sultan ("ruler"); one of the greatest and most enlightened was Malik Shah (d. 1092). He established his capital in Isfahan and beautified it with magnificent mosques. However, he may be best known as the sultan who was associated with the poet-astronomer Omar Khayyám, author of the celebrated Rubáiyát and deviser of a new, more accurate calender than was in use at the time. Before Malik Shah's death, his rule, too, began to disintegrate.

After the Seljuk Turks' power waned and the army weakened, the final destruction was administered in 1258 by the Mongols, who overran Persia and Mesopotamia and, when the caliph refused to remove the defenses of Baghdad, destroyed the city. The last caliph of the Abbasids was then kicked to death. The pagan Mongols, under Hulagu Khan, a grandson of Genghis Khan, were welcomed by some factions of the conquered—the Shi'ites believed them to be their allies against the Sunnis, and the Christians saw them as a deliverance from the caliphs, who had become less tolerant of non-Islamics.

Behind them, however, the fierce warriors left thousands slaughtered (fifty thousand in Baghdad alone) and destroyed libraries, art, and religious buildings. The great Muslim golden age was over.

The compressed empire's flame was kept flickering in Cairo by the Mamluks ("slaves," who had been brought in to man and officer the Egyptian Army); one of their number, an officer, had had the perspicacity to marry a sultan's widow, and thus initiated a new dynasty. The Mamluks ruled Egypt and even placed one of the surviving Abbasids in the caliphate in Cairo, to serve as a front for the Mamluk regime.

The Mongol invaders were checked by a hardy breed of warrior who have gone down in history as the Ottoman Turks. Like the Seljuks, they had moved down from Central Asia; converting to Islam, they often served as mercenaries in the Seljuk armies, taking as their reward the spoils of war and grants of land.

The Turkish tribesmen—not yet called Ottoman Turks, but *ghazis* ("warriors of the faith")—fought primarily against the Byzantines and established themselves, land grant by land grant, in Anatolia (today's western Asiatic Turkey), with Byzantium to the west and the Mongols in Mesopotamia in the east. Raiding of Christian Byzantines by Muslim Turks was in keeping with the Islamic concept of *jihad* ("striving" for one's faith, but more popularly translated as "holy war").

In Anatolia, the Ottoman Turks began reforming. In 1453, under Mehmed

II (the name is a variant of Mohammed), the Ottoman Turks achieved their centuries-old objective, the capital of Byzantium, Constantinople. Attacked from the land and from the sea, under siege for more than fifty days, the great city fell to the Ottoman invaders, who pillaged and massacred for three days. The fall of Constantinople had a tremendous effect throughout the Muslim world, for it had symbolized the Roman-Christian domination of the eastern Mediterranean. Mehmed delineated the symbolism by establishing his new capital in the vanquished city and authorized the continued use of a more recent name, the Turkish variant of a Greek phrase, *eis tēn polin* ("in the city"), Istanbul (the official change, however, did not occur until 1930).

Having defeated the Byzantines, the Ottoman sultans set out to consolidate and expand their empire in the Middle East, to Syria, Egypt, and North Africa. In accomplishing this, they introduced an innovative form of warfare to Islam: field artillery. A grandson of Mehmed, Selim the Grim, after succeeding to the sultanship (acceding to his grandfather's Law of Fratricide by murdering his two brothers), moved southward and defeated the Mamluks at Aleppo by blasting them with artillery. This relatively new weaponry had been made possible by the discovery of gunpowder in China (circa the ninth century). The Mamluks, who depended on classical cavalry, were readily shattered by what they regarded as a disreputable form of warfare.

Under Selim's successor, Suleiman the Magnificent, the Ottoman Empire expanded into the Balkans, Austria, Hungary, southern Russia, and by 1529, to the gates of Vienna, although Suleiman's troops never did take the city. This was the last flowering of the Ottoman Muslim Empire, rich in architecture, literature, and the law. For the Arabs, eclipsed as leaders of Islam, it was a dark age—even as Europe was in the midst of its Renaissance, many elements of which had been preserved by Islamic scholars who had settled in Sicily and Spain.

Religious antipathies between Christians and Muslims did not interfere greatly with trade and, as Europe reawakened and grew stronger, traders began making inroads into the Ottoman Empire. The French moved into Syria and Egypt; the English and the Dutch followed. But the Empire was in decline; some Arabs eluded Ottoman rule. In Persia, the heretical Shi'ite sect established a dynasty and made Shi'ism the state religion (which, in Iran, it continues to be). By the middle of the eighteenth century a young reformist, Mohammed ibn-Abd-al-Wahhab, began preaching a return to pure Islam, to the Koran, and rejection of modernist, infidel ways. This movement was centered in Arabia (generally termed the Wahhabi Movement, after the latter-day prophet).

By the early-nineteenth century, virtually all of Arabia had embraced Wahhabi doctrines and further disturbed the already disintegrating Ottoman rule. Retaliation for caravan raids and the capture of Medina by Wahhabi forces led to the crushing of the rebellion in 1818 by the Ottomans, but the spirit remained smoldering among the Bedouins.

These proud desert warriors had resented their treatment by Turkish caliphs and sultans; the Turks generally regarded them as second-rate Muslims. The Arabs, isolated as they were in their vast, sandy landscapes, regarded themselves as the true carriers of Islamic truths and, unlike their rulers, spoke the language of Mohammed, Arabic. In their desert they preserved their ways and waited.

Although the Ottoman Empire tottered through history until its dissolution after World War I, it went into decline after the death of Suleiman, in 1566. Divided into difficult-to-govern provinces, weakened by corruption, it was an easy mark for European exploitation, commercial and military. The rejuvenated, vigorous, ambitious Europeans found the Middle East a perfect setting for profitable colonialism—an exploitation that planted the seeds in which contemporary Islamic militancy is rooted.

The cradle of civilization had been transmuted into a hotbed of war.

House of War

The first major impact of the Western world on Islam, a collision of religious conflict that remains unforgotten and unforgiven to the present, occurred between the eleventh and the fourteenth centuries. These invasions of portions of the Middle East, ostensibly to wrest the Holy City of Jerusalem from the hands of the Muslim "infidels," were collectively known as the Crusades (from old French, "to bear the cross").

As the Muslim journeys to Mecca, so did the medieval Christian make a pilgrimage to the Holy City of the Saviour. Traditional Muslim tolerance toward other nonpagan religions precluded interference with these pilgrimages for some time, until the installation of the Fatimid caliph Hakim (985–1021), who persecuted Christians under his rule, destroyed Christian shrines, and went so far as to desecrate the Church of the Holy Sepulcher, in Jerusalem, in 1010. His death, eleven years later, eased the persecutions, but after the Seljuk Turks took Jerusalem, in 1071, their practice of intolerance caused a severe strain between Muslim and Christian. Farther to the north, the Turks proved to be a threat to Byzantium, the Christian bastion between Europe and the Middle East. The Emperor in Constantinople, Alexius I (1081–1118), appealed to the West for aid in stopping the invasions by the Turks (who, in turn, believed themselves to be on a *jihad*—"holy war"—against the unbelieving Christians). The direct inspiration for launching the Crusades was a speech, by Pope Urban II, calling for vengeance for what Hakim had done to the Holy Sepulcher and promising full penance for their sins to all participants and protection for their families. With the battle cry "God wills it!" the First Crusade was underway.

From 1095 until the Ninth Crusade, which began in 1271, Christian armies set out from Europe to wrest the Holy City from "infidel" hands. Western histories have tended to romanticize these military-religious expeditions. (The spiritual impetus was frequently overshadowed by disputes among the leaders,

RISE OF ISLAM
MONGOL DOMINIONS
N
ATLANTIC OCEAN
SCOTLAND
IRELAND
ENGLAND
London
HOLY ROMAN EMPIRE
Frankfurt
Paris
FRANCE
BURGUNDY
LEÓN
CASTILE
Toledo
Córdoba
ALMORAVIDS
Fez
Oran
Algiers
Tunis
ZIRIDS
Tripoli
Marseilles
LOMBARDY
PAPAL STATES
Rome
POLAND
Vienna
HUNGARY
RUSSIA
Novgorod
Moscow
Kiev
PETCHENEGS
BYZANTINE EMPIRE
Constantinople (Istanbul)
Nicaea
Nicomedia
Dorylaeum
Angora
Athens
BLACK SEA
Trebizond
MEDITERRANEAN SEA
Alexandria
Cairo
FATIMITES
PALESTINE
Jaffa
Jerusalem
Damascus
Krak des Chevaliers
Tripoli
Antioch
Aleppo
Edessa
Arbela
Baghdad
Kufah
ABBASID
SELJUK TURKS
CASPIAN SEA
Raghae
Isfahan
PERSIA
Herat
Samarkand
Lahore
INDIA
ARABIA
Medina
Mecca
RED SEA
INDIAN OCEAN
Muslim area
at the time of the First Crusade
Christian area at the time of the First Crusade
The Ottoman Empire in the 17th Century
0 MILES 1000
0 KM 1000
palacios

by looting, and by wholesale butchery.) It was a period in which the myth of knighthood and chivalry blossomed. (England's Richard the Lion-Hearted was one of the leaders of the Third Crusade, 1189–92.)

The First Crusade, one of the most successful, established the tenor of these pietistic adventures, which readily underscored Mohammed's division of the world into two inimical factions: *dar al-Islam* ("the house of Islam") and *dar al-harb* ("the house of war").

Christian armies—Norman, Frankish, German, Lombardian, Burgundian, among others—converged on Constantinople after long marches through France, Italy, and the Balkans. Looking out upon the not-always-disciplined forces that almost engulfed his city, Byzantine Emperor Alexius suffered second thoughts about his appeal to Rome for aid against the Turks. His daughter Anna reflected his apprehension when she wrote that the "whole of the West, and all the barbarian tribes which dwell between the further side of the Adriatic and the Pillars of Hercules, had all migrated in a body and were marching into Asia . . . with all their household." It may have seemed so to Alexius and his daughter, who feared, and not without reason, that the military leaders of the Crusade may have had their eyes on Constantinople as much as Jerusalem. To the fearful leaders of Byzantium, the sixty thousand or so crusaders who clustered around the capital may have appeared to be the "whole of the West," especially after they began looting to replenish their supply of food and other necessities.

Culver Pictures

Knights of the Crusades; the kneeling knight is dressed in the uniform of the First Crusade (1095). The other uniform dates from the thirteenth century, around the time of the Ninth, and final, Crusade. Mail and other armor protected the crusaders from arrows and swords, but not from the scorching weather of the Holy Land.

Alexius, exhibiting a hasty diplomacy, was generous in his welcome gifts and in providing guides and transportation across the Bosporus to speed his untrustworthy guests on their way. Although the Crusade had begun from its various starting points in the spring of 1096, it was 1097 before Alexius breathed easier in Byzantium.

Without a unified military leadership, the motley armies set out for the Holy Land. A rabble, led by a French preacher, Peter the Hermit, encountered a disciplined Turkish army near the Bosporus in October 1096, and was destroyed. Peter survived, because he had returned to Constantinople for help, but was too late. This easy victory over a most unmilitary band of pilgrims established a Muslim contempt for the ineffectual Christian fighting man—a misplaced self-confidence that would bring disasters to the Turks.

So in May 1097, when the Christians began surging into Anatolia, the Seljuk sultan was little concerned. The crusaders, on their way to Nicaea, passed by the remains of Peter the Hermit's "army." One of them, Fulcher of Chartres, wrote in sorrow: "Oh, how many severed heads and bones of the dead lying on the plains did we then find beyond Nicomedia near that sea! In the preceding year the Turks destroyed those [i.e. crusaders] who were ignorant of and new to the use of the arrow. Moved by compassion . . . we shed many tears there."

In the Seljuk capital, Nicaea (today's Iznik), the sultan waited. The Christian armies, in early June, encircled the walls of the city and laid siege. By the time the sultan realized his miscalculation and sent for reinforcements, Nicaea was doomed. A French account relates the annihilation of a Turkish relief unit: "The Count [Raymond of Toulouse] . . . found Turks coming against us here. Armed on all sides with the sign of the Cross, he rushed upon them violently and overcame them. They turned in flight, and most of them were killed. They came back again, reinforced by others, joyful and bearing along with them the ropes with which to lead us bound . . . As many as descended remained there with their heads cut off at the hands of our men; moreover, our men hurled the heads into the city."

The siege went on for six weeks, with heavy and merciless casualties on both sides. When it appeared that Nicaea's fall was imminent, the apprehensive Alexius surreptitiously slipped his own envoys into the capital to negotiate a sur-

Culver Pictures

Peter the Hermit exhorting crusaders. In 1096, he led a disorganized army across Europe; the Turks wiped it out in an ambush near the Bosporus. Peter survived and eventually reached Jerusalem with the crusaders in 1099.

Crusaders prepare a mangonel for firing into a Muslim walled city. Such siege machines were shipped from Europe in parts and assembled near the battlefield.

render and keep the city for himself. When the crusader knights prepared to storm the walls, they were astonished to find the standards of Byzantium fluttering over their heads and Nicaea occupied by Byzantine troops. This did not endear Alexius to the crusaders, whom he bought off with gifts of food, gold, and jewels. Raymond of Toulouse, though he accepted the gifts, said of Alexius, "The people will curse him and proclaim him a traitor."

Still it had been a great victory, and the emboldened crusaders marched through Asia Minor. Divided into two groups, marching a day apart, the spearhead met the Turkish Army on a plain near Dorylaeum. The Turks, not realizing they were meeting only half of the crusader army, were certain they had ambushed them. The hapless Normans, virtually surrounded, would have agreed. "We were all huddled together . . . like sheep," Fulcher of Chartres later wrote, "trembling and frightened, surrounded on all sides by enemies . . . It was clear to us that this befell us as a punishment for our sins."

The crusaders held off the Turkish forces who were mounted on horses and showered them with arrows for several hours, when, to the surprise of the at-

More deadly than the Muslim warriors was the scarcity of water in the deserts through which the crusaders marched into the Holy Land. Many died of thirst or starved in the barren country.

Culver Pictures

tackers, the second crusader unit appeared. The tide turned and, after bitter fighting, the Turks retreated from the plain; organized Turkish resistance was broken in Anatolia. This fact did not make the progress of the crusaders easy; they had to contend with desert—"We suffered such extreme thirst," wrote Fulcher, "that many men and women died from its torments"—and with a ravaged countryside, despoiled by the retreating Turks, so that food became impossible to find. Pack animals were eaten; there were mass desertions; and heavy armor was discarded along the way to their next major objective, Antioch (Antakya, Syria).

This was accomplished with great suffering over desert and mountain, under blistering sun and engulfing rains, but, with the Holy City closer than ever, the survivors persisted. "The mountains took more lives than ever the Turks had done," observed Crusades historian Sir Steven Runciman.

When the depleted, nearly exhausted European army approached Antioch, in October 1097, they were confronted by a great and forbidding fortified city astride the road to Jerusalem. Expecting the crusaders, the Turkish commander, Yaghi-Siyan, sent for reinforcements throughout the Muslim world: Damascus, Baghdad, and distant Persia. For months the knights laid siege to Antioch, consuming their provisions until, by January 1098, desertions depleted their number. Even zealous Peter the Hermit set out for home, until he was caught and returned to the fray.

One leader, Stephen of Blois, decided that Antioch was impregnable and led his northern French unit away from the battle. On the road to Constantinople he met a Byzantine relief army and informed Emperor Alexius, who led it, that the situation was hopeless, so Alexius returned to Constantinople himself.

The next day, June 3, 1098, however, the crusaders were inside the walls of Antioch. The Turks were betrayed by one of their captains, who permitted the knights to scale a wall and to open the city gates. Even Yaghi-Siyan took

Culver Pictures

Crusaders in the mountains of Judaea. The valley afforded little protection from the sun and was often a fatal setting for ambush by Muslim warriors.

to his horse, but he was apprehended and beheaded. Inside the fortress city, the Greek and Armenian citizens of Antioch joined in the carnage.

By nightfall of June 3, Runciman noted in his *History of the Crusades*, "there was no Turk left alive in Antioch . . . You could not walk on the streets without treading on corpses . . ."

The Turks, however, continued to hold on to certain portions of the wall, and a relief force that arrived after the investment of Antioch entrapped the crusaders inside their own prize. "Those profane enemies of God held us so enclosed," one historian wrote, "that many died of hunger . . . Horse and donkey flesh was sold and eaten."

The encirclement and blockade continued for nearly a month, until a servant, Peter Bartholomew, approached the leaders with the claim that he had seen St. Andrew in a vision and that the saint had told him that the very lance that had pierced Christ's side was buried beneath the Church of St. Peter. After what seemed to be a fruitless search, Peter Bartholomew himself found the Holy Lance.

On the morning of June 28, with Raymond of Aguilers carrying the Lance affixed to a spear staff in the vanguard, the crusaders attacked the Muslim armies. They fought with impassioned savagery, breaking up the Turkish formations, which fled the battleground in terror. The Turks abandoned their families, treasures, and tents, with the knights in pursuit; so zealous were they that they did not stop, as was the practice, to plunder the Turkish encampments. They trailed the panicky Turks, killing them in great numbers and then returned to claim their loot.

There they found not only the treasure, but also the wives and concubines of the Turks. They acted with what was then a characteristic Christian attitude toward "the enemies of God."

"When the women were found in the tents," wrote Fulcher of Chartres, "the Franks did nothing evil to them except pierce their bellies with their lances."

And so were the Muslims introduced to the nature of Christian charity in the eleventh century.

It took another year before the European armies pushed southward deeper into Syria, Lebanon, and Palestine, finally arriving at the walls of the Holy City, Jerusalem. Behind them they had left their starved, dehydrated, and battle dead; their leaders revealed their petty jealousies, suspicions, and envy in bickering over spoils, over command. Baldwin of Lorraine left the Crusade with his forces to establish his own Christian stronghold at Edessa (Urfa, Turkey). It was a battle-weary, depleted army of some twelve thousand that arrived in Jerusalem after three blistering years, on June 7, 1099.

Inside the Holy City's awesome walls, under the command of the governor, Iftikhar ad-Daula, were some sixty thousand Muslim troops. The governor was prepared for the invaders; the herds that had grazed around Jerusalem and that might have been a source of food were brought inside the walls of the city; all Christians were ejected from Jerusalem; wells had been poisoned and all springs dammed, save one: the Pool of Siloam, six miles away. Men and beasts competed for this meager water supply. Those men and animals that died in the Pool contaminated it for the survivors.

The thirsty, starving crusaders remained outside the gates of Jerusalem for days, unable to breach or scale the walls, from which they were jeered and taunted by the "unbelievers." Then unexpectedly, on June 17, six Genoese and English ships arrived at Joppa (in the vicinity of today's Tel Aviv) with sorely needed supplies. (After the Muslims captured the ships, the surviving crews were drafted by the crusaders as reinforcements.)

Nearly a month was devoted to building ladders, scaling towers, and various forms of catapult and battering rams. Wood for these implements of war was acquired by raids in Samaria's forests, some forty miles distant.

In early July the crusaders got word that a large Egyptian army was moving north to reinforce the Muslims inside Jerusalem. There was despair in Christian tents, and then, another vision. Peter Desiderius came forward and told of a visitation from their former religious leaders the Bishop of Le Puy, who had died at Antioch. The bishop had advised the knights to purge themselves of their sins, to fast, and to march barefoot around Jerusalem. This was done, and the barefoot army, led by clergy bearing crosses, were jeered by Muslims who "placed many crosses on the walls," a crusader recalled, "and mocked them with blows and insulting deeds."

Thus inspired and incited, the crusaders began their siege on the night of July 13, but were held off by a rain of arrows, stones, and liquid fire (Greek fire, the napalm of antiquity). By nightfall of July 14, the crusaders had placed a scaling tower against the south wall, but without success; the next morning, it was wheeled and placed against the north wall (in the vicinity of what is now Herod's Gate).

The Muslims fought ferociously, shooting flaming arrows into the towers and holding off the Christian warriors. Then, as an anonymous French account in the *Gesta Francorum* records, "when the hour approached on which our Lord Jesus Christ deigned to suffer on the Cross for us, our knights began to fight bravely in one of the towers—namely, the party with Duke Godfrey and his brother Count Eustace. One of our knights, named Lethold, clambered up the wall of the city, and no sooner had he ascended than the defenders fled from the walls and through the city."

Soon more crusaders swarmed over the walls, opened a gate (today's Damascus Gate), and swept through the city. Jerusalem's governor, Iftikhar, bargained with the invaders, and he and his bodyguard were permitted to leave after paying a staggering ransom. But the surviving inhabitants—men, women, and children—were killed without mercy, by sword or by fire. The Jews who took refuge in their main synagogue were burned alive in it; not a single Jew is known to have survived the crusaders' occupation of Jerusalem.

The new religious leader, Daimbert of Pisa, proudly informed the Pope:

"If you desire to know what was done with the enemy who were found there, know that in Solomon's Porch and in his temple our men rode in the blood of Saracens [a blanket term then for Arabs and therefore Muslims] up to the knees of their horses." Subsequently they spread through the city and "took possession of the gold and silver, the horses and mules, and the houses filled with goods of all kinds."

Finally, in the evening of July 15, 1099, the crusaders filed barefoot into the damaged Church of the Holy Sepulcher, where they "rejoiced and exulted and sang a new song to the Lord!" Drenched in blood, the Holy City was once again in Christian hands.

The crusaders established a Christian kingdom of Jerusalem, as well as other such Latin kingdoms, or counties, as Edessa (in Turkey), Antioch, and Tripoli.

Culver Pictures

Using scaling ladders, the crusaders attempt to invade a fortified city. On July 15, 1099, the walls of Jerusalem were breached, and the Crusaders took the Holy City.

Knights of the Second Crusade (1147–49), led by Roman Emperor Conrad III and King Louis VII of France, come upon the remains of the dead of the First Crusade. The crusaders failed in their attempt to take Damascus, and the pilgrimage was marred by treachery, envy, and pillaging of Christian settlements along their route. The Second Crusade was a failure.

These were developed by merchants into great commercial centers, for the Crusades were not totally dedicated to the Cross. Along the route through the Levant, the knights constructed fortresses to protect the pilgrims en route to the Holy City. One of the most famous, built by Knights Hospitalers, Krak des Chevaliers ("Castle of the Knights"), still stands, in Syria.

The Christians occupied Jerusalem for eighty-eight years before the Muslims, led by one of the great commanders and thinkers of Islam, Salah al-Din ("Honor of the Faith," best known in Western histories as Saladin), launched a *jihad* and occupied the city in October 1187. Unlike the crusaders, Saladin did not massacre Christian inhabitants (infidels, to him). His victory led to the Third Crusade (1189), in which German, French, and English knights were not successful in retaking Jerusalem. The mutual respect that grew between Saladin and Richard the Lion-Hearted has become a classic tale of chivalry.

Although Saladin retained Jerusalem for Islam, he granted in the Peace of Ramla (1192) a narrow strip along the coast near the city which could be used by pilgrims for safe passage into Jerusalem. The five subsequent Crusades failed to take back the Holy City; the infamous Fourth Crusade resulted in the sacking of the Christian capital of the East, Constantinople, by Christians, and the tragic Children's Crusade (1212) ended at Marseilles for some, when they were sold into slavery, and for others, a German group, when they perished in Italy of hunger and disease.

And so, as cogently phrased by the editors of the Encyclopaedia Britannica, "the bloody and useless fury of the Crusades" dwindled into vain strivings and failures (Jerusalem remained in Muslim jurisdiction [i.e., Turkish] until December 1917, when it was taken by the British during World War I).

Historians agree that among the positive effects of the "bloody and useless fury" was that it brought on the close of the European Middle Ages. The magnificent cities the crusaders found (and sometimes plundered), the evidence of arts and sciences, architecture and industries little known or unknown in Europe, made a deep impression on them (one small example: the technique of producing Syrian glass, which would result in the beautiful cathedral windows of the Renaissance).

The stimulation of trade encouraged the growth of towns, the rise of a merchant (middle) class, and the importation of the products of the East. Italian cities traversed by the crusaders prospered, setting the scene for the prosperity and influence that would nourish the Renaissance. European feudalism was weakened, along with its major beneficiary, the nobility. Not only did the knights sell their lands to finance their expeditions to the Holy Land, many never returned, further debilitating the nobility and initiating the end of serfdom.

Arabic learning made a significant impression upon the crusaders. Their preservation of Greco-Roman learning and literature, their universities, and their arts and sciences inspired the more enlightened crusaders and stimulated learning—all but ignored in medieval Europe. Beginning in Italy and Spain, where Muslim scholars enjoyed positions of importance, the roots of the Renaissance were planted; it marked the beginning of a modern Europe.

But there was a negative side, too. The crusaders not only perpetrated atrocities of plunder and massacre, but their savagery served to deepen the Muslim hatred for the infidel; the tolerance once so readily practiced by Muslims toward Christians and Jews was severely abraded. Islam withdrew into itself, nurtured

The beginning of the Westernization of the Middle East: Napoleon's invasion of Egypt in an attempt to strike at the British in the Sudan. The invasion force, after eluding Lord Nelson at sea, landed in Egypt in July 1798.

Napoleon introduced weapons of modern warfare into the Middle East in battling with Mamluk cavalry.

Napoleon's decisive victory in the Battle of the Pyramids, near Cairo, with musket and cannon against scimitar and horse, placed Egypt under French domination.

Photos courtesy of Culver Pictures

its own religion, ignored the infidel as much as possible, and a once magnificent culture withered. As Europe flowered, Islam found bitter solace in a resplendent past and rejected the modern world coming into existence.

Having shattered a culture (which, in truth, also contributed to its own dissolution through internal conflicts), a vigorous Europe, in time, added another thorn: colonialism. The incursion by a modern Alexander, Napoleon Bonaparte, in 1798 initiated palpitations in Islam and particularly among the Arabs, who had—under the rule of the Turks—slipped into the background of history. As expressed by historian Philip K. Hitti, "The people of the Arab world were generally leading a self-contained, traditional, conventional life, achieving no progress and unmindful of the progress of the world outside. Change did not interest them. This abrupt contact [through Napoleon] with the West gave them the first knock that helped to awaken them from their medieval slumber. It kindled the intellectual spark that was to set a corner of the Moslem world on fire." This fire, it might be noted, is now ablaze.

Napoleon was not concerned with revitalizing the Muslim world. Having established himself as a military master of France by 1797 (when he was not yet thirty) in his successful Italian campaign, he was determined to counter France's major mercantile competitor, Great Britain. His strategic eye was on India, a British colony and a treasury of resources. His first step was to invade Egypt; by July 1, 1798, he and his disciplined army easily captured Alexandria, and the Nile Valley soon followed. The Mamluk defenders of Egypt were overwhelmed in the face of Napoleon's "cowardly" cannon and rifles.

Napoleon's public objective was to contribute to the preservation of Islam and to end the tyrannical Mamluk rule in Egypt by restoring the Ottoman sultanship. Besides his guns and troops, Napoleon brought nearly two hundred artists, writers, and scientists of various disciplines to study, and to instruct, Muslim cultures. In Cairo, printing presses were established to produce books, pamphlets, and papers in Arabic and French. An Institut d'Égypte was founded; engineers began to survey a projected canal through the Isthmus of Suez. Educated, French-speaking Egyptians were invited to participate in the "reawakening." Napoleon offered the Egyptians the opportunity to rule themselves (under French supervision, of course) after centuries of Turkish domination.

The Egyptians, in fact, were more impressed with Napoleon's army, which, in the Battle of the Pyramids (July 21, 1798), defeated the Mamluk army decisively and took Cairo. European organization and technology proved more than a match for Muslim cavalry, sword, and arrow. Napoleon's conquest, in turn, was frustrated by the technology of the British as he attempted to invade Palestine and Syria to secure his Egyptian holdings from Turkish retaliation. The nominal leader of the Muslims, Selim III, a great admirer of French culture, decided that French occupation was more than he wanted and allied himself with Britain and Russia against Napoleon.

His progress north was stopped by the British and Ottoman forces at Acre (today's 'Akko, Israel, where some eighty thousand crusaders had died in

1189–90). An outbreak of the plague weakened the French, and a British blockade virtually sealed Napoleon off from outside aid. He and his army were stranded in Egypt when the British admiral Horatio Nelson found the French fleet, after tracking it for some time, at Aboukir Bay (today's Abu Qir), on August 1, 1799. In what has come to be called the Battle of the Nile, the British fleet destroyed the French fleet. Although he made one more attempt at the British- Turkish forces, and demonstrated the superiority of his army, Napoleon realized he had no future in Egypt. On August 23, he slipped out of Egypt to attend to matters at home, where, in time, he would declare himself Emperor Napoleon I.

Two years later, the Ottomans, with British aid, defeated the French and drove them out of Egypt. Not only did this establish the British in the Middle East, it introduced another Muslim leader, whose ideas and reforms would

Napoleon's Egyptian expedition was not purely military; besides troops, he also brought scholars, engineers, and artists to study the culture of Egypt, as caricatured in this drawing.

The "Little Corporal" contemplates the Great Sphinx.

Photos courtesy of Culver Pictures

Napoleon's engineers began planning a canal through the Isthmus of Suez, but their plan was thwarted in August 1798, when the British wiped out the fleet that had brought Napoleon to Egypt. Despite their military defeat, the French won a political victory over the British by building the canal (1859–69).

have a deep impact on Islam. He was Mehemet Ali (Mehemet is a variant of Mohammed), a Turkish junior officer who had fought the French with the Ottoman Army. With the supposed sultan of all of the Muslim world, Selim III, ineffectually ruling from far-off Istanbul, Mehemet Ali exploited the Ottoman-Mamluk rift and the turmoil following the French defeat, and moved himself into power as the pasha of Egypt, in 1805. To ensure his position, he invited three hundred Mamluk chieftains to a conference in Cairo, where they were tendered a magnificent banquet—and massacred.

Although Napoleon's impact on the Middle East was magnified by many historians, his militarily fruitless Middle East adventure was not without its consequences. European intellectual and commercial interests were stimulated by the tales and goods brought back from Egypt. Napoleon's ethnologists practically initiated the entire field of Egyptology and, eventually, the fascinating, exotic, and (by some despised) field of "Orientalism."

Mehemet Ali's remarkable dynasty lasted from 1805 until 1902. Although he fought to drive the French out of Egypt, he was an unabashed admirer of French technology as applied to military devices. Having ousted the French, he then proceeded to invite them to return as technicians, teachers, engineers, and craftsmen to contribute to the modernization of Egypt—and perhaps to Mehemet Ali's ambition to expand his empire. Under French direction, a large Egyptian Army was created; the French established and managed the factories that equipped that army. French agriculturists contributed to the evolution of long-staple cotton, one of Egypt's most important exports. Under Mehemet Ali's son, Said, French construction of the Suez Canal was begun.

This was all part of the pasha's plan to modernize Egypt and to free it of dependence on European industry. But in accomplishing this he was heavily dependent on European advisers and investors (conservative, wealthy Egyptians were wary of innovative industry). Mehemet Ali had begun to sow the seeds of European colonialism in Islam.

Although he was nominally the Sultan's Egyptian governor, Mehemet Ali devised his own aggressive power plays. If the Sultan, in Istanbul, followed these with apprehension and suspicion, so did concerned eyes in Paris and London. With his French-trained troops, Mehemet Ali began making incursions into the Sudan, to the south, and once Egypt controlled the Upper Nile, he profited from the ivory and African slave trades. In 1833, he began to drive through Syria, with Istanbul his objective, before British and French intervention stopped him. Under Anglo-French pressure, the Sultan granted the pasha hereditary governorship of Egypt and appointed him governor of Palestine and Syria. Five years later, when Mehemet Ali challenged the Sultan again, European powers convened in London and advised the pasha to put "the desert between his troops and the . . . sultan." The Egyptians withdrew from Syria and relinquished the lands east of Suez taken from the Ottoman troops.

Just how insidious was this European attention to Islam—and specifically Egypt—was demonstrated by the establishment, by the English, of a railway

Culver Pictures

The Khedive of Egypt, Ismail, officially opened the Suez Canal on November 17, 1869. The hundred-mile-long waterway connected the Mediterranean and Red seas.

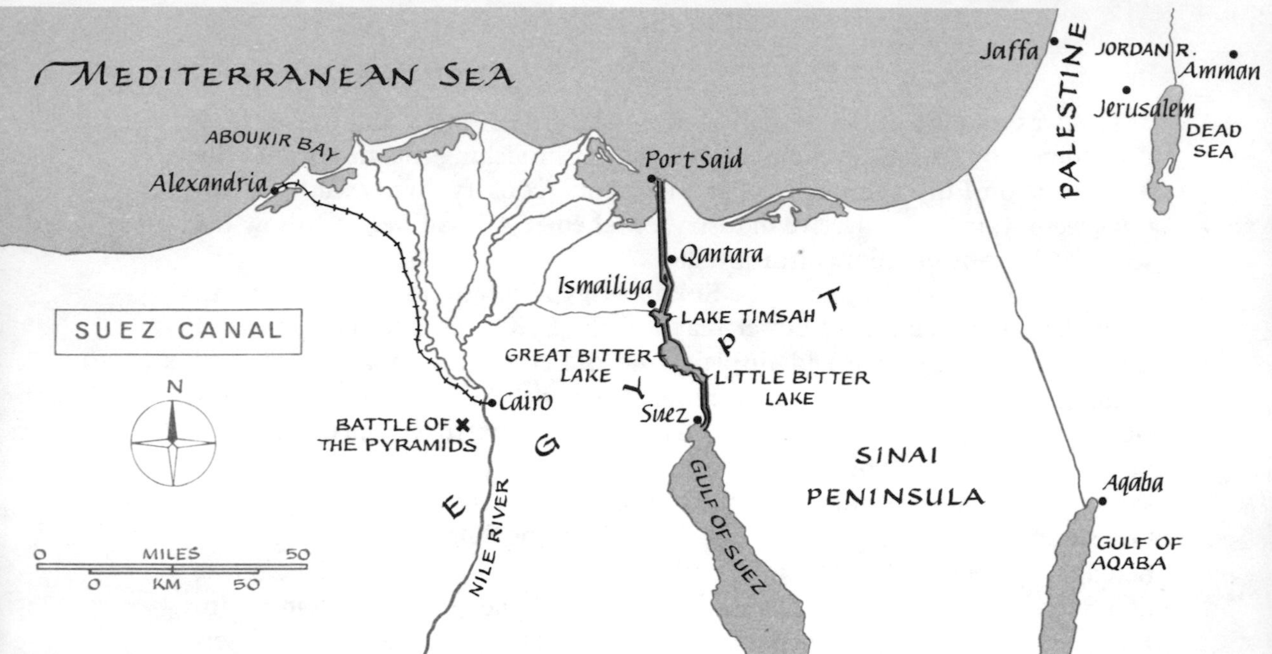

joining Cairo and Alexandria. The British opposed the building of a canal at Suez, the right to which the new pasha, Ismail (a grandson of Mehemet Ali) granted to the French. The British feared that such a strategically situated waterway would be a challenge to their interests in the Far East, India, and the Persian Gulf. What such innovations meant to the Egyptians was immaterial. French engineer Ferdinand de Lesseps, who had acquired the right to build the canal from the pasha, arranged for Egypt to provide much of the financial backing (a prelude to later bankruptcy) and for Egyptian laborers to dig the canal. In turn, Egypt would receive 15 percent of the net profits of the canal. De Lesseps was granted the concession in 1854; he formed the Suez Canal Company in 1858; and construction continued from April 1859 until the canal's completion, in November 1869.

Ismail celebrated this 101-mile wonder with a lavish opening at which thousands of European guests observed the first ships passing from the Mediterranean to the Red Sea, and onward into the Indian Ocean, without having to sail around the southern tip of Africa. In his enthusiasm, the Egyptian governor commissioned Italian composer Giuseppe Verdi to compose an opera to celebrate the inauguration of the canal. The result was *Aida*, but Verdi didn't make the deadline, and the opera was premiered in Cairo two years later.

By this time Ismail, through his profligacies and awards of privileges to European businessmen, was in serious financial trouble. His European creditors convened, found Egypt bankrupt, and in 1879 deposed Ismail in favor of his son, Tewfik. Hoping to extricate himself from his debts, Ismail sold the Egyptian share in the canal to the British, who recognized its importance to a maritime Britain. This fruitless attempt did not save Ismail, but it brought about a virtual British occupation of Egypt by 1882.

Port Said, at the northern entrance to the Suez Canal. Although the Egyptians funded its construction and the French built it, the British benefited most from the Suez Canal, which they bought in 1875. In 1882, after putting down an uprising over foreign interference in Egypt, Britain occupied Egypt; the era of colonialism in the Middle East had begun.

Culver Pictures

Foreign domination of Egyptian affairs aroused nationalist emotions among the exploited "natives." Attempts to dislodge the colonial powers were quashed by British sea power as well as other French and British pressures. So it continued until World War I; in theory, Egypt was part of the Ottoman Muslim Empire, but in fact it was virtually a British colony (although never officially so designated). British control brought its advantages and improvements—modern medical advances, financial stability, an expanded irrigation system—but it did not bring about an Egypt for Egyptians. Like the Arabians, who were temporarily out of the international limelight in their great desert, the Egyptians waited, bitterly smoldering.

The two had much in common despite their differences: a rich past they had all but forgotten; resentment of their Ottoman rulers and patronizing European protectors; and the unifying, invisible, but powerful bond of Islam.

2

Wars and Duplicity: 1914-45

THE MAJOR factor in the uneasy unification of Arabs was their treatment at the hands of the major European powers during and after the two world wars of the twentieth century. Exploited and betrayed, the Arabs, particularly of the middle class—the intellectuals and professionals (most of whom had learned about nationalism in European schools or European-managed schools in their homelands)—pondered their own nationalism. They dreamed of self-government—free of the Turks, the French, and the British.

Preoccupied with Egypt (primarily a Muslim, Arabic-speaking country), the British and the French tended to overlook the turbulent but no doubt parochial events in the Arabian Peninsula. However, the British did exhibit concern over Russian interest, farther east, in Persia. The British were worried, too, by the autocratic Kaiser Wilhelm II, whose imperialism was expressed in a powerful army and, to their dismay, an imposing navy. Besides, even before 1900, German businessmen had obtained permission from the Turks to construct a railroad connecting Berlin and Baghdad.

The history of today's Arabia began early in the twentieth century, when a twenty-one-year-old warrior, Abdul-Aziz ibn-Saud, in command of a small force of about two hundred, led fifteen of his band over the walls of Riyadh, the capital, and overthrew its governor.

Abdul-Aziz had returned to reclaim his birthright, which had been denied his tribe since it had been subdued and scattered, in 1890, by a rival tribe, the Rashidis. The Sauds were members of the Wahhabi Muslims, while the overthrown governor, a member of the Rashid family, belonged to the less puritanical sect. The son of an exiled tribal leader, Abdul-Aziz began the reconquest of ancestral lands.

For the next thirty years, beginning in 1902, when he captured Riyadh, Abdul-Aziz led his Wahhabi warriors in a struggle against the Turks and toward a unification of Arabia. He formed cooperative farming communities, which

The Metropolitan Museum of Art

The great ruins of ancient civilizations of the Middle East attracted scholars and scientists from the West. Here, members of a British Museum archaeological expedition to Mesopotamia (contemporary Iraq), 1911, display their finds at a dig at Carchemish. In the center is T. E. Lawrence, who chose to remain in the Mideast until 1914, learning Arabic and surveying the sites of ruins. With the outbreak of World War I, he returned to Britain and, in turn, came back to the area as a member of British Army Intelligence. By 1916, he had transferred to the Arab cause and became the legendary Lawrence of Arabia.

Culver Pictures

Symbol of British influence in the Middle East: T. E. Lawrence, a writer/archaeologist prominent in the Arab revolt against the Turks during World War I. Like the Arabs, he believed that he and his small army were fighting for an Arab homeland by aiding the British.

stabilized the nomadic Bedouin in central Arabia, and assured him a following of fierce fighting men. By 1913 he succeeded in driving the Turks out of the Eastern Province, along the Persian Gulf; in 1921 he annexed Asir, in the South, then moved northward to take Mecca and Al-Hijaz, on the western coast. In 1932 he proclaimed a dynasty, officially named his country Saudi Arabia, and declared himself king. When he died, in 1953, Abdul-Aziz left thirty-four sons and the proviso that the succession to the throne be by the oldest capable surviving son. The throne cannot pass to the son of the current king, only to one of Abdul-Aziz's sons; what will happen when the last of his surviving sons dies has yet to be determined.

During King Saud's reign, American explorations brought tremendous changes to his kingdom and affected other Arab countries in the Middle East—

Children of early settlers in Palestine; beginning in 1882, most had fled from Russia or Romania. Although they were predominantly city-bred, agriculture was critical to their survival.

and the world as well. American engineers discovered oil deposits in Saudi Arabia in the mid-1930s, and Saud was convinced by an American adviser that he should grant a sixty-year concession to American investors. Commercial production began in 1938 under the direction of the Arabian-American Oil Company (Aramco). Undreamed-of riches were showered upon Saud and his dynasty.

During the period before World War I, in which Abdul-Aziz embarked on his conquests in the Arabian Peninsula, Russian and British imperialism began to encroach on Persia (Iran). This was a time of "spheres of influence," in which the smaller countries were powerless against technologically advanced nations. Russian annexation of several northern Persian provinces, in turn, animated Persian claims on territories in Afghanistan, to the east. Because Afghanistan bordered on British India, the powers in London looked aghast at any foreign power taking over and controlling the mountain passes on India's western frontier. So, with impeccable colonial logic, the British occupied portions of Afghanistan and forced the Persians out. This move also served to restrict Russian trespass into Persia.

Then another burgeoning European power entered the picture. Because of the growing military strength of Kaiser Wilhelm's Germany, in 1907 the British and the Russians agreed to settle their Persian differences: northern Persia would fall into the Russian sphere of influence for economic development, and the southern portion would be under British supervision. The Persians got to keep a neutral zone in the middle. A year later, the Anglo-Persian Oil Company was formed. (English adventurer-entrepreneur William Knox D'Arcy had discovered oil the previous May, after several years of fruitless searching.)

Although the strategic significance of the oil strike in Persia and the later one in Saudi Arabia were not fully understood until after World War I, there were unavoidable facts confronting the world: the Persian Gulf area was rich in oil—and both the Saudis and the Persians were Muslim.

Islam, for so long indifferent to modern Western technology, controlled the lifeblood of its machinery.

The international rivalries that subdivided the homelands of subject peoples into "spheres of influence" burst into unexpected flame in June 1914, with the assassination of Austrian Archduke Franz Ferdinand, by a young Serbian terrorist, in the Yugoslavian city of Sarajevo. The Alliances, the Ententes, and national jealousies, mixed with the state of militarism they had accumulated, radiated what might have been an insignificant flame into the conflagration that we now call World War I.

Islam was drawn into what at first seemed to be a quick little war when Turkey, in hopes of defeating its traditional enemy Russia, joined the Central Powers (Germany and Austria-Hungary). In Baghdad, the sultan called for a *jihad* ("holy war") against the enemies of Turkey; this call for unity did not work. The British declared Egypt (i.e., the Suez Canal) a protectorate, and Egyptians chose to remain under the protection of the Crown. The Muslims of India wore British uniforms, and the French Army had good numbers of Arabs in its forces. Field Marshal Horatio Herbert, Lord Kitchener, in Egypt during the early weeks of World War I, had befriended the sharif of Mecca, Husayn (whom the British recognized as the king of the Arabs, not Saud). Kitchener, who had been virtual sovereign of Egypt from 1911 to 1914, no doubt was partially responsible that no call for a *jiḥad* emanated from Mecca, the Holy City of Islam. The sharif's son, Faisal, had already met with Kitchener in Cairo, initiating the promise of an Arab uprising against the Ottoman Turks in exchange for Arab independence.

The next year, 1915, Sharif Husayn exchanged a series of letters with the

Zionist Archives and Library

Birth of a suburb, Talpiot, which is now absorbed into the city of Jerusalem.

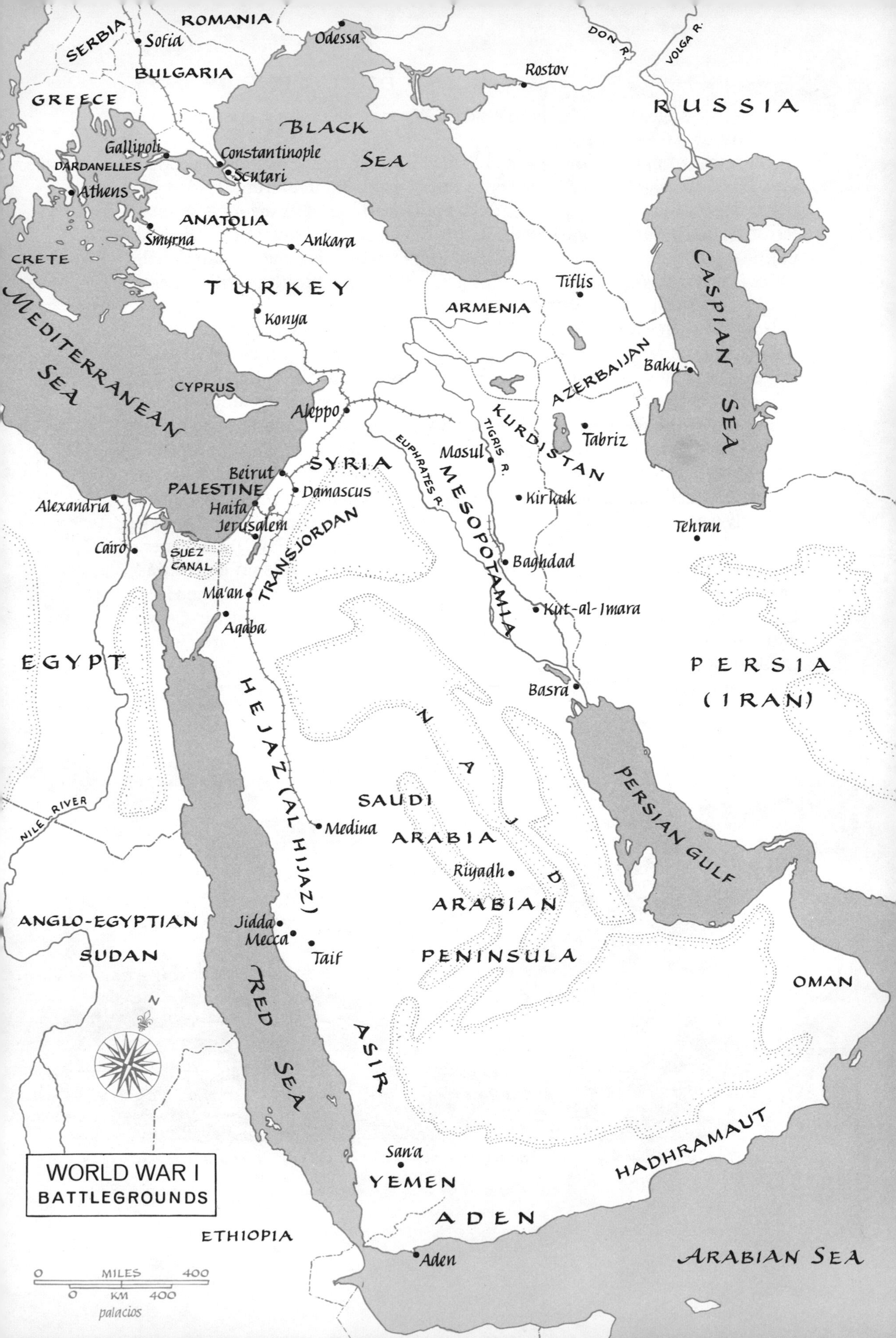
WORLD WAR I
BATTLEGROUNDS
ROMANIA
SERBIA
Sofia
Odessa
DON R.
VOLGA R.
BULGARIA
Rostov
GREECE
RUSSIA
BLACK
SEA
Gallipoli
DARDANELLES
Constantinople
Scutari
Athens
ANATOLIA
Smyrna
Ankara
CRETE
TURKEY
Konya
Tiflis
ARMENIA
MEDITERRANEAN
SEA
CYPRUS
AZERBAIJAN
Baku
CASPIAN SEA
Aleppo
KURDISTAN
TIGRIS R.
EUPHRATES R.
Mosul
Tabriz
SYRIA
MESOPOTAMIA
Beirut
PALESTINE
Damascus
Alexandria
Haifa
Kirkuk
Jerusalem
TRANSJORDAN
Tehran
Cairo
SUEZ
CANAL
Baghdad
Ma'an
Kut-al-Imara
Aqaba
EGYPT
PERSIA
(IRAN)
Basra
HEJAZ (AL HIJAZ)
NAJD
PERSIAN GULF
SAUDI
ARABIA
NILE RIVER
Medina
Riyadh
ARABIAN
PENINSULA
ANGLO-EGYPTIAN
SUDAN
Jidda
Mecca
Taif
OMAN
N
RED SEA
ASIR
HADHRAMAUT
San'a
YEMEN
ADEN
ETHIOPIA
Aden
ARABIAN SEA
0 MILES 400
0 KM 400
palacios

British high commissioner of Egypt, Sir Henry McMahon, in which the subject of Arab independence was discussed. Sir Henry supplied guarded promises with a sharp eye out for Britain's interests, "spheres of influence," and other concerns—one of which caused dismay and hatred throughout the Arab world. This was spelled out in a secret British-French agreement, the Sykes-Picot Agreement, of May 1916, which provided for the postwar partition of the Ottoman Empire among the two powers. An undefined "Arab State" was mentioned, but France would take over much of the Levant, among other holdings, and the British would become the masters of Transjordan, northern Palestine, and a good portion of Iraq.

The Sykes-Picot note also mentioned an "internationalized Palestine." The Arabs were unaware of this agreement, which contradicted the veiled promises of the Husayn-McMahon letters, until 1917, when a copy was discovered by the revolutionary (Bolshevik) government of Russia, which published it after a defeated Russia withdrew from the war. The Arab revolt, which began in 1916, was based upon British and French promises no one seriously planned to keep.

Having ensured Arab aid in containing the Turks and their German ally in the Middle East, the British compounded the duplicity with the Balfour Declaration (1917). This communication, from the Foreign Secretary, Arthur J. Balfour, to the Parisian banker-philanthropist Baron Edmond de Rothschild, promised British support of a Jewish national home in Palestine, with the proviso that it would not violate the civil and religious rights of "existing non-Jewish communities" in Palestine. Since 1882 Rothschild had supported a Jewish settlement in Palestine, an idea first expressed by a Russian physician, Leo Pinsker, who appealed for a Jewish homeland in "the Promised Land,"

Zionist Archives and Library

Theodor Herzl, called "the father of modern Zionism," en route to Palestine in 1898. The idea of a Jewish state in Palestine had been formulated in 1881 by the Russian Jews Moses Loeb Lilienblum and Leo Pinsker, both of Odessa, in reaction to the vicious pogroms that year. Herzl turned to Zionism and wrote about it in his The Jewish State, *1896. As a writer and speaker, he brought wide attention to the idea, although he did not live to see his dream come true.*

Palestine, to escape anti-Semitism, specifically the pogroms of czarist Russia. An organization formed by students and young men of Kharkov had already formed themselves into a group called the "Lovers of Zion."

Their cause was greatly aided by a Viennese journalist, playwright, and administrator, Theodor Herzl, who had witnessed anti-Semitism at the infamous trial of Captain Alfred Dreyfus, in France, and experienced it himself in Austria and Germany. In 1896 Herzl published his paper *The Jewish State*. The next year, the World Zionist Organization met in Basel, Switzerland, to encourage the emigration of Jews from countries where they were being persecuted. Herzl could not obtain a charter from the Turkish sultan, or the British Government, to establish a Jewish homeland in Palestine. However, by this time, with Rothschild's financial aid, Russian Jews (Pinsker among them) had begun to buy property and to settle in Palestine as farmers and artisans.

By 1914, some ninety thousand Jews had settled in Palestine. The eruption of World War I and its subsequent horrors pushed the significance of this fact into the background. The Balfour Declaration meant one thing to world Jewry and another to Islam. It did not promise a Jewish national homeland in Palestine, merely the assurance that His Majesty's Government viewed it "with favour" and would use "their best endeavors to facilitate the achievement of this object . . ." Even King Husayn, when informed of the gist of the declaration (which remained secret until May 1919), was convinced that "the friendship of world Jewry to the Arab cause is equivalent to support in all States where Jews have political influence." The most powerful state to which the message alluded was, of course, the United States.

In the same message, delivered in 1918, Husayn was assured that the "Entente Powers are determined that the Arab race [sic] shall be given full opportunity of once again forming a nation in the world." He was not apprised of the Sykes-Picot Agreement of two years before, although in the wake of the Bolshevik takeover of Russia, Husayn became aware of it. He was promptly assured that it had been merely an exchange of points of view between the

Zionist Archives and Library

Vladimir Jabotinsky, a Zionist, writer, and soldier who served with the Jewish Legion; in 1917 he was a lieutenant in a British unit. After the war, Jabotinsky organized Jewish self-defense units in Palestine. One of his followers was a Polish immigrant, Menachem Begin.

Allies. Husayn had deep misgivings and began having doubts about his trust in the British.

Because of the spectacular slaughter on the Western Front and the uncertain fluctuations of battle on the Eastern Front, the Middle East was little more than a military sideshow to the belligerents. Still Britain was concerned with the Suez Canal and its oil supply in Persia and shipped troops and supplies that might have served better in Europe.

The Turks, with German cooperation and encouragement, were a problem in the East. To aid their ally Russia, the British devised what seemed to a bold plan to seize the forts guarding the approaches to the Dardanelles, in order to open up Allied shipping through the Bosporus at Constantinople into the Black Sea. Once cleared, arms and supplies could easily be transported to Russia. This produced the disaster known as Gallipoli.

The British began landing troops on the peninsula in April 1915 and encountered powerful resistance from the Turkish forces under the command of Mustafa Kemal (later known as the ruthless Kemal Atatürk), who enjoyed the counsel of the German General Otto Liman von Sanders. Gallipoli consumed British lives and supplies desperately needed on the Western Front, and eventually, and ignominiously, the evacuation of Gallipoli was begun in December.

In the same year, 1915, another fruitless venture was initiated in Mesopotamia (Iraq). The major British objective was to protect the oil supply funneling through the Tigris River at Basra, although Baghdad, farther north, was a tempting prize. Starting out from Basra, a British force led by Major General Charles Townshend reached the town of Kut al-Amara in September, took it from the Turks, and then found themselves prisoners inside the town. Relief attempts failed (especially during the rainy season, when floods made it impossible), and after a long siege, Townshend surrendered to the Turks in April 1916. Many of the ten thousand prisoners died through brutal treatment by the Turks. Kut al-Amara was not retaken until February 1917, by Lieutenant General Sir Frederick Stanley Maude, who then proceeded on to Baghdad.

The most successful contribution to the Allied cause in the Middle East was made by Husayn's Arab revolt. The British were nervous about the Turko-German threat to Suez and prepared for it with fortifications, troops, and rail extensions. Before the British commander, General Sir Archibald Murray, set off on his desert trek to Jerusalem, he was shaken by the approach of a small Turkish army, led by German Colonel Friedrich Kress von Kressenstein, pushing toward the canal. With his superior technology and shorter supply lines, Murray managed to turn the force around and, by December of 1916, was making his way slowly toward the Holy City.

By this time he was being aided by the Arab revolt. Husayn's son Faisal commanded this uprising, which, by June 10, had driven the Turks out of Mecca. In October, Husayn proclaimed himself King of Arabia and began looking forward to the day of independence from the Ottomans as well as the British.

The British were happy with the Arab revolt and its progress. Among others,

National Archives

Adviser to the Turks, German General Otto Liman von Sanders (center). He counseled the commander of the Turkish Fifth Army, Mustafa Kemal, who drove the British out of Gallipoli.

Culver Pictures

Turkish fort at the entrance to the Dardanelles, Gallipoli. The campaign, with Constantinople as the main objective, cost the British much and gained them nothing.

Culver Pictures

The historic—and dramatic—entrance of General Edmund Allenby into Jerusalem, December 1917. Allenby's victory, which ended Turkish power in the Middle East, had been expedited by Lawrence of Arabia and his warriors.

a British archaeologist who had studied the Arabs and spoke their language, T. E. Lawrence, was sent to act as liaison between the British and the Arabs. Like the Arabs, Lawrence of Arabia was inspired by the promise of Arab independence and was not privy to the behind-the-scenes Allied arrangements for postwar Arabia and Palestine.

Working closely with Faisal, Lawrence instigated hit-and-run raids on the Turks in Syria, especially against their supply lifeline, the Damascus-Medina railroad. Lawrence's camel-borne bands swept out of the desert to blow up bridges, tracks, and troop trains, and to harass Turkish troops. Their major function was to assist the progress of the British Palestine Army, under the command of General Edmund Allenby, in its conquest of the Holy Land. With Lawrence, a few Arab tribal chiefs, and a few hundred Syrian warriors, the motley band took the port town of 'Aqaba (at the northern end of the Red Sea, in today's Jordan). With the loss of only two of their greatly outnumbered force, the Arabs killed or captured twelve hundred Turks.

Faisal's Arabs engaged, beset, and otherwise harried some thirty thousand Turkish troops that might have otherwise been thrown against the British in Palestine. In December 1917, Allenby made a symbolic entry, on foot, into Jerusalem, a promenade expedited to a large degree by Lawrence and his unpredictable Arabs. In October 1918, the Arabs made their own symbolic entry, courtesy of Allenby, into Damascus; Ottoman Turkish rule over Arab lands was over.

But new complexities were taking shape.

When word of the fall of Palestine to Allenby was released, a leaflet in Yiddish was distributed to Austrian and German troops. It proclaimed, "Jerusalem has fallen! . . . Palestine must be the national home of the Jewish people once more . . . The Allies are giving the land of Israel to the people of Israel . . . Stop fighting the Allies, who are fighting for you, for all Jews, for the freedom of all small nations." The Arabs, with changes of a few words—"Damascus," "Syria," and "Arabs"—might have made the same declaration.

But once the war ended in an Allied victory—and among the victors was the United States—a war-weary world was confronted with an avenging, pledge-shattering Versailles Treaty. An idealistic President Woodrow Wilson was no match for the realistic French Prime Minister Georges Clemenceau and British Prime Minister David Lloyd George. In the Hall of Mirrors at Versailles, the Arabs, and the promises made to them, slipped into the background.

Although the treaty provided for the end of such secret arrangements as the 1916 Sykes-Picot Agreement in the future, its effects were a great betrayal in Arab eyes.

Turkey, which had sided with Germany, suffered the humbling occupation of some of its provinces by France, Britain, Italy, and Greece. Its economy, politics, and military all came under Allied control. To compound the humiliation, a Greek army landed in 1919 at Izmir (then Smyrna), in an attempt to regain a portion of its ancient Hellenic empire in Anatolia. The two great Euro-

National Archives

The Arab delegation to the Versailles Peace Conference, 1919. Prince Faisal, son of Husayn, sharif of Mecca, stands before the group. Lawrence of Arabia is behind, to Faisal's immediate left. Husayn was exiled from the kingdom of Hejaz in 1924, when the powerful Saud dynasty took over the major portion of the Arabian Peninsula.

pean powers, Great Britain and France, neither participated in nor condemned this military adventure.

In the face of an invasion by their traditional enemy, the Greeks, the national feelings of the Turks were aroused. Mustafa Kemal, the hero of Gallipoli, began to organize resistance to what he regarded as Allied-approved humiliations. In 1919, he formed an army based in the highlands of Anatolia and quickly attracted zealous followers willing to fight the "infidels" slicing up their homeland.

Kemal's resistance movement eventually grew from a primarily nationalist struggle into a revolution; his spirited army not only fought the Greeks but also the Turkish army of the sultan, who feared a nationalist party might eradicate the sultanate and provoke further Allied intervention. He was correct in one of these fears: the first.

Kemal soon established a provisional government at Ankara (at that time called Angora), from which he directed the double-edged war. His efforts impressed, rather than provoked, the outside world. The Russians, who had won their revolution, established friendly relations with the revolutionary Turkish forces; the Italians left their occupation zone in Anatolia; France arranged for a new treaty, modifying the frontier between Turkey and Syria (in Turkey's favor); and in September 1922, Kemal's army ejected the last Greek from Anatolia. In November, with the backing of the majority of Turks, who felt that the Ottoman government had not distinguished itself in the war with Greece, Kemal called for a separation of the offices of sultan and caliph. He then proceeded to abolish the sultanate.

Kemal declared a Turkish Republic in 1923 and moved the capital from Constantinople to his headquarters city, Ankara. The caliphate was abolished in 1924. By this time, Kemal had been in office for a year as the President of the new republic; he was, in fact, its dictator. Interested in modernization of the new Turkey (to Kemal, "modernization" meant Westernization), he initiated a series of drastic religious, cultural, and political changes. Believing that Islam's tendency to resist change and its insularity were partly responsible for Turkey's problems, Kemal organized a major program of secularization. This disturbed the more conservative Turks, especially the villagers, as opposed to the urbanized Turks, who took to Western ways more readily.

As an example: in 1925, Kemal outlawed the traditional fez and encouraged other modes of Western dress (the religious objection to the Western fedora was that the brim made it impossible to touch the ground with the forehead during prayers). He even banned the traditional veil for women. He replaced the Arabic script with Latin letters and, in 1934, decreed that all Turkish families must take a second (i.e., last) name. He himself then became Kemal Atatürk ("father of the Turks").

When he died, at the age of fifty-seven, in 1938, Atatürk had generally succeeded in making Turkey the most Westernized nation in the Middle East. He was succeeded by a fellow warrior, and political follower, İsmet İnönü, who adroitly continued the Atatürk form of dictatorship and good relationships abroad. Despite a preference toward the Germans because they were fighting the Soviets, İnönü managed to keep Turkey out of World War II—until 1945, when it was clear who would be the victor. Turkey declared war on Germany in 1945 and thus became a charter member of the United Nations.

In the Arab world, confusion, strife, and unrest were in sufficient supply after World War I. Faisal, the son of Husayn, the sharif of Mecca, and Lawrence's colleague in the Arab revolt, was crowned King of Iraq (a British mandate). Abdullah, with British blessing, became the emir of Transjordan (now Jordan) and worked to retain its independence from Palestine. However, when Faisal was elected king of Syria, he became the major spokesman for the Arabs in Palestine (and had begun to form an understanding and agreement with Zionist leader Chaim Weizmann). Meanwhile, Syria was under French rule, and the French dispatched an army to expel Faisal from Damascus.

Faisal raised a cry for Arab nationalism, in concert with Kemal's demand for Turkish nationalism, above and beyond the call of Islam. But it came to nothing. Faisal realized there would be no Arabia for Arabians in his world, at least not the one he had dreamed of with T. E. Lawrence.

That dream was ended by the rise in power of Saud, in central Arabia. With British aid, he began expanding his possessions and soon controlled the important trade routes in the southern Syrian Desert. He was often in conflict with Faisal and Abdullah. Husayn, their father, who ruled over the Hejaz, the region to the west of Saud's territory, declared himself the Caliph in 1924, presuming to be the leader of all Muslims. Saud's Wahhabi warriors challenged that proclamation and swept across the frontier, massacred the townspeople of Ta'if (southeast of Mecca), and laid siege to the Holy City's major port, Jidda.

Husayn abdicated, and his son Ali soon after surrendered, on January 8, 1926. Saud was not only king of the region of the Najd but also, more significant to Muslims, of the Hejaz. He convened an Islamic Congress in Mecca that same year, and promised not to interfere with the pilgrims who traveled to Mecca and to protect the holy cities of Mecca and Medina. Through diplomacy, he won recognition in the West, after he united his kingdoms into Saudi Arabia, in 1932. He even pacified Husayn and Abdullah in Iraq and Transjordan and made peace with Yemen, at the southern end of the Arabian Peninsula, which made him the ruler of Arabia. The Saudi dynasty was firmly established with the British present to lend a firm helping hand in the control of the oil deposits in Saudi Arabia and Iraq.

To the northeast, across the Persian Gulf, yet another Muslim country, Persia, also under the ubiquitous British eye, had begun its petroleum-based Westernization. The modern history of Persia—or more precisely, Iran—began with

(Left to right): Chaim Weizmann, General Allenby, and two of the chief rabbis of Palestine.

Zionist Archives and Library

Zionist Archives and Library

Chaim Weizmann, welcomed by British officers in a post-World War I visit to Palestine. In 1919, the Russian-born British scientist was head of the Zionist Commission to Palestine. An active Zionist all his life, Weizmann settled in the city of Rehovot, central Palestine, in 1936. There he established the renowned Weizmann Institute of Science. He was to become the state of Israel's first President (1948–52).

Copyright G. D. Hackett, N.Y.

Goldie Mabovitch as a schoolteacher in Milwaukee. Born in Kiev, Russia, in 1898, she came with her family to the United States in 1906. Early in her career as a teacher, she became involved in the Zionist labor movement. With her husband, Morris Meyerson, she emigrated to Palestine in 1921. Active in the labor movement and government in Palestine, she became Israel's Foreign Minister in 1956, when her name was Hebraized to Golda Meir.

Lord Balfour (standing in front row) and Chaim Weizmann (seated), Tel Aviv, 1925. Balfour had come to Palestine to participate in the ceremonies at the opening of the Hebrew University, on Mount Scopus, Jerusalem.

Zionist Archives and Library

Consulate General of Israel

European Jews en route to Palestine. After World War I and the Russian Revolution, the majority came from Eastern Europe in what is called the Third Aliyah (literally "ascent," i.e. immigration to Palestine) of 1919–1923.

the rise, in the early 1920s, of an illiterate army officer with a reputation for valor and leadership: Reza Khan. With British accord, he was placed in charge of the Persian Cossack Brigade (which had been trained and commanded by the Russians) when Allied troops began withdrawing from Persia, in 1921 (the Russians in 1921 and the British in 1924). The British commander, Major General Sir Edmund Ironside, had judged the tough, superpatriotic soldier correctly. In 1921, Reza Khan confronted the shah with his Cossacks in Tehran in order to establish a military dictatorship. He was appointed Prime Minister in 1923 and deposed the shah, Ahmed Mirza, in 1925.

This ended the Kajar (or Qajar) dynasty and, after Reza Khan was appointed shah and took the name of Reza Shah Pahlevi, he founded the ill-fated, and short-lived, Pahlevi dynasty. ("Pahlevi" was taken from the name of the language spoken by the Parthians, who ruled Persia after Alexander the Great. The new shah believed that this fused his dynasty with the true Persians, not the Turkic forebears of the deposed Kajars.)

Undoubtedly influenced by Turkish military-dictator-turned-national-leader Atatürk, Reza Shah began the modernization of Persia. He officially changed the name of the country to Iran in 1935 and initiated striking reforms, although he chose not to incite the highly influential, forceful mullahs, the Muslim clergy, and did not encroach upon the Shi'ite sect, which was predominant in Iran.

Consulate General of Israel

In 1929, Arab groups broke into Jewish dwellings, killing and destroying the possessions of a great number of Jews, particularly in the town of Hebron. The attackers appear to have spared Herzl's portrait on the wall.

Immigrants row to shore near Tel Aviv, 1939. Jews fleeing the Nazis were often denied admission to Palestine and often, as here, slipped into the country without permission from the British.

Zionist Archives and Library

This suited the shah's profound nationalist spirit, for the true Iranian monarchy was linked by legend and marriage to Ali, the son-in-law of the Prophet. Therefore, the Peacock Throne (seized when the Persians sacked Delhi in 1739) was intimately tied to this unorthodox offshoot of Islam. Of the major countries in the Middle East, Iran is the only one with a Shi'ite majority; the others cling to the more orthodox Sunni beliefs, based upon the traditions (Hadith), sayings, stories, etc., many attributed to the Prophet's widow, Aisha. Compilations of several Hadith have come down in the form of the common law of orthodox Islam called Sunna.

Although Reza Shah encouraged reforms that angered the Shi'ites (like Atatürk, he ordered the discarding of the veil and the formless dark dress of Iranian women), Reza Shah did not crush the clergy, as he did his political and military adversaries. This oversight would come home to roost at the Peacock Throne when his young son was placed there, in 1941.

Impressed with the technological and material progress of Europe, Reza Shah began his modernization of Iran by encouraging industry and education. During his reign, the University of Tehran was built; he also sanctioned study abroad (including for his son). His goal, within the strictures of a dictatorship, was the regeneration of Iran and an end to European dominance and interference.

Reza Shah was ambitious and despotic. In 1939, he had his twenty-year-old son Mohammed Reza marry Princess Fawzia (sister of King Farouk of Egypt; the son and the princess had never seen one another before the wedding). The Pahlevi name now enjoyed a touch of royalty. This union did not function as the shah had planned, for it produced no son and heir; Mohammed Reza had to wait twenty-one years and marry twice more, before his third wife produced a male successor to the throne.

Reza Shah acquired great wealth during his time on the throne, primarily through the appropriation of land—and the more than two hundred thousand peasants who inhabited it. They became his tenants, who owed him payment and services. These moves disconcerted the wealthy landowners, who saw this as a threat to their own holdings.

A U.S. Air Transport Command C-47 flies over the pyramids. Once Rommel's threat had been eliminated, Egypt was important to the Allies as a staging area for shipping supplies and aircraft to Soviet Russia and the Pacific.

U.S. Air Force

Culver Pictures

Sixteen-year-old King Farouk of Egypt succeeds his father on the throne, in 1936. Warmly greeted in the streets of Cairo, Farouk was eventually driven into exile because of the corruption of his regime and his own dissoluteness.

U.S. Army

An American Army camp, within sight of the pyramids near Cairo, 1943. The strategic Suez Canal was important to the Allies. German General Erwin Rommel, pouncing out of Italian-held Libya, brought his forces chillingly close to the canal in 1941.

His methods of controlling Iran were disturbing also to the intellectuals and the merchant middle class. Reza Shah's "reforms" and personal acquisitions were inconsistent with the Constitution, which had been so hard fought for and forced upon the dynasty he had deposed. He hinted at the threat of Soviet subversion to rationalize his strong-man tactics; if the opposition became too loud, he merely had them silenced.

Reza Shah's downfall resulted from the political philosophy he revealed during World War II. Not a diplomat, unfamiliar with the outside world, he made no secret of his admiration for another dictator, Adolf Hitler, and his method of dealing with his enemies. The shah's pro-German sympathies did not please the British, but they waited until Germany invaded the Soviet Union, in 1941, before acting. With their new ally, Soviet Russia, the British occupied Iran in August 1941. Reza Shah was forced to abdicate and went into exile in South Africa soon after, where he died in 1944.

Mohammed Reza Shah, aged twenty-two, succeeded his father on the Peacock Throne, a virtual puppet of the British and the Soviets. They were eventually joined by the United States, whose Persian Gulf Command was established to assure a system of transportation to and communications with the Middle East. American aircraft bound for the Pacific could be flown from the United States across the Atlantic and through the Middle East with stops en route at Cairo and Tehran, through which lend-lease aircraft and other supplies were sent to the Soviets.

Unlike some countries of the Middle East—Libya, Tunisia, Egypt—Iran did not become an active battleground. Iran remained neutral, and the young shah had the pleasure of seeing the issuance of the Tehran Declaration, signed by Great Britain, the U.S.S.R., and the United States, guaranteeing the independence and territorial integrity of Iran (1943). In time, the Swiss-educated, uncharismatic authoritarian would become notorious among certain American diplomats stationed in Iran as "Our Shah," whose policies and tactics would unleash an Islamic revolution in his country.

His then brother-in-law's country, Egypt, was not so fortunate. Since 1936, King Farouk reigned as a constitutional monarch; he succeeded his father, Fuad I, who had contended (as would Farouk) with both the British and the nationalist political party, Wafd ("delegation"). The Wafd was formed immediately after World War I, and its principal aims were independence from foreign domination for Egypt and demands for critical economic and social reforms. In his conflict with the Wafd, Fuad tried to cancel out the Egyptian constitution, which cost him his throne.

Farouk was initially hailed as a new hero, a handsome, slender young man who promised a new day for his countrymen. Instead he squandered millions on luxuries, while 80 percent of the *fellaheen* (peasants) of Egypt subsisted on the verge of starvation under unspeakable living conditions. Meanwhile the king bought yachts and jewels, collected rare stamps, and grew monstrously fat. Like Iran's Reza Shah, he agreed with Nazi Germany, which displeased the British, who saddled him with a pro-British premier.

The advent of the German Afrika Korps, under the command of Lieutenant General (later Field Marshal) Erwin Rommel—sent by Hitler to assist the floundering Italian Army in North Africa—rendered vast sandy wastes of North Africa into a great battleground for tanks. The British were most concerned about the Suez Canal; and when Rommel, who had arrived in Tripoli, Libya, in February 1941, battered the British back to El Alamein, Egypt, by July 1942, there was cause for alarm in the British camp. At the time, they were unaware of the exhausted state of the Afrika Korps, but they were concerned that Rommel's forces were roughly eighty miles from Alexandria.

The British shook up their command and sent Lieutenant General Bernard Law Montgomery to turn the Afrika Korps around. This he did, although not with quite the alacrity expected of him by his Prime Minister, Winston Churchill. At the delayed Battle of El Alamein (October 23 to November 5,

1942), Montgomery succeeded in breaking through the German-Italian lines and forced a general retreat. On November 8, when he set off in pursuit of Rommel, American-British forces began landing on the beaches of Morocco and Algeria, to the west.

Under General Dwight D. Eisenhower, the Anglo-American forces began squeezing Rommel's troops from the west as Montgomery closed in from the east. They merged in Tunisia, on the Mediterranean; by May 1943 North Africa was clear of Axis forces and became the base for the invasion of Italy.

The focus of the main war moved away from the Middle East, although the area was still occupied by the Allies. Preoccupied as they were with their own war and interests, they were unaware of the uneasiness and seething that surfaced from time to time. Problems arose as early as 1920, when Palestine, Iraq, and Transjordan were about to become British mandates after the defeat of Germany and the Ottoman Empire in World War I.

The mandate system was supervised by the League of Nations. The nations assigned mandates were given virtually complete military, political, and financial control over the fissured Ottoman Empire. For the peoples under this control, the mandate system was merely a continuation of the old imperialism under another name. Consequently there was a resurgence of local feelings of nationalism. While the League of Nations held out the promise of eventual independence from Western domination, it never came soon or pure enough. (When Iraq's independence was declared, in 1930, its advisers were British-chosen foreigners and it remained host to British air bases.)

Culver Pictures

King Farouk, in admiral's uniform, visits with President Franklin D. Roosevelt, who was on his way back from the Yalta Conference, February 1945.

A street scene in Damascus, Syria. Although the impact of World War II brought changes to the Middle East, many of the streets remained much as they had been for centuries.

American Museum of Natural History; photo by Philip H. Pratt

Department of Defense

Helicopters of the 101st Aviation Battalion, Rapid Deployment Force, near Cairo in 1980. Although Farouk was deposed in 1952, American presence in Egypt is even more potent today than during the World War II years.

Under the mandates, the League of Nations encouraged international trade in the Middle East. Under this rule of equal rights for all (except for the "natives," perhaps), American oil interests began moving into the area, first in Iraq and later in Saudi Arabia. The British were busy in the Persian Gulf, and the French (whose mandates included Syria and Lebanon) exploited the mineral deposits of North Africa. The full import of the Middle East oil wealth was not recognized immediately, due to dry holes and logistical problems. For example, oil was discovered in Iraq in 1927, but export in quantity did not occur until 1934, when pipelines to the Mediterranean were completed. For years after World War I, major exports from the Middle East were Egyptian long-staple cotton, Iraqi dates, and Persian rugs.

The significance of the British mandate in Palestine was not fully realized in the flush of Allied victory and dominance. The ambiguous promises made to both Arabs and Jews during the war festered with the coming of "peace." But there was no peace.

The British did not have an easy time in Palestine between the wars. The Arabs objected to the Palestine Mandate (1923), claiming that it was "framed unmistakably in the Zionist interest," that it left the Arabs' position there totally undefined, and that Jewish immigration would eventually overwhelm the Arab majority and completely dominate Palestine. Bloody riots broke out in 1929 and again in 1936, expanding almost into civil war; the Arabs were joined by sympathizers from Syria and Iraq.

Palestine was patchworked into a small Jewish area, divided in the south by an International Zone (in which the Holy City was situated, along with the port of Jaffa) and a larger Arab Zone. The Arabs did not accept this arbitrary (as they regarded it) division. When war came, in 1939, the disputes in Palestine were overshadowed by the larger events in Europe. But the treatment of the Jews by the Nazis brought demands for the immigration of Jews into Palestine, which served to exacerbate Arab resentment.

In Palestine, the Jews agreed to stop harrying the British about immigration for the duration of World War II, except for a splinter group of dissidents led by Abraham Stern. This "Stern Gang" was a terrorist group that frequently clashed with the police and attempted to assassinate British officials during

World War II. (They succeeded in murdering the British Secretary of State for the Middle East in Cairo on November 6, 1944.)

Because of the immigration restrictions imposed by a 1939 white paper, the Jews in Palestine blamed the British for the deaths of hundreds of thousands of Jews in German-occupied countries. The view of yet another extremist group, the Irgun, was expressed by its leader, Menachem Begin: "There is no longer any armistice between the Jewish people and the British and the British Administration in Eretz Israel which hands our brothers over to Hitler . . ."

Not only the British. In 1939 a ship carrying nearly a thousand refugees from Europe sailed along the American eastern seaboard for three weeks, during which they were denied entry into the United States. They returned to Europe. In December 1941 (the month of Pearl Harbor), the *Struma*, a yacht converted into a passenger carrier, arrived at Istanbul, Turkey, with 769 refugees. They were denied admission into Turkey. Later, the *Struma* was also denied a port in Palestine by the British. After extended negotiations, both the Turks and the British agreed to permit the children to come ashore at Palestine. Before this could be carried out, the Turks ordered the *Struma* out of their waters. On February 24, 1942, word came that the *Struma* had been sunk (probably by a German submarine); there was only one survivor.

The hapless British—their government offices burned and plundered, their shops looted, their police attacked—were caught in the middle, confronted by both the Jews and the Arabs, simultaneously.

Near the close of World War II, President Franklin Delano Roosevelt, only months before his death, invited King Saud to meet with him aboard a U.S. Navy warship anchored off Suez. This was shortly after the end of the Yalta Conference in February 1945, with the end of World War II in sight. The founder of the Saudi dynasty tried to impress the American President with Arab concern over the question of Palestine and Jewish immigration, which the British could not always keep under control.

Roosevelt assured the king that the United States would continue its policy already established in regard to Palestine: the United States would not make any basic changes without prior and full consultation with the Arabs and the Jews.

In May 1945 World War II ended its European phase with a victory for the Allies. The new American President, Harry Truman, wrote in August, when the Pacific war ended, to the new British Prime Minister, Clement Attlee. It was Truman's suggestion that Britain initiate a solution to the Jewish problem in Europe by authorizing the admission of one hundred thousand Jews into Palestine. Nothing came of this, the British being more sensitive to Arab views than the Americans. Confronting postwar problems of their own, war-weary, facing an uncertain future of policing two seemingly irreconcilable and powerfully resolute forces, the British eventually decided to turn the "Palestine Question" over to others, to the world. The world in the years 1939–45 had become a more dangerous place, an arsenal of sophisticated weaponry, and with the development of the jet engine for aircraft, a much smaller place.

3

Iran: Torch of Islam

His imperial majesty Mohammed Reza Pahlevi, King of Kings and Light of Aryans, after more than a quarter of a century as Iran's shah, officiated at an impressive ceremony in his magnificent palace in Tehran on October 26, 1967. He crowned himself and his third wife, Farah, Shah and Shahbanou (the first empress in the twenty-five-hundred-year history of Persia-Iran). Wearing the jewel-encrusted Pahlevi crown, his deposed father's pearl-covered cape, and an "all-conquering" sword encrusted with rubies, emeralds, and diamonds, the Shah formally placed himself on the Peacock Throne.

When he assumed the throne, in 1941, at the age of twenty-two, he believed that his country as his father, Reza Shah Pahlevi, had left it was not ready for an Emperor, or King of Kings. "It is no joy," he said, "to be the king of a nation of beggars." But since the end of World War II, with the development of the oil industry, Iran had, so far as he could see, prospered.

With the gold and red crown pressing heavily on his head, the Shah spoke with authority and promise. "My sole aim in life," he began his coronation address, "is the constant improvement of the welfare of Iran and the Iranian nation. My deepest wish is to preserve the independence and sovereignty of the country, to bring the Iranian nation up to the level of the most progressive and prosperous societies of the world, and to renew the ancient grandeur of this historic land.

"In this task, as in the past," he avowed, "I will withhold nothing, not even my life."

That past would return to haunt him. So would other words of his address: "For me it is a source of great pride and pleasure that there exists today between my people and me an unbreakable bond, and thus linked we are advancing together along the road that leads to greatness, prosperity, and the welfare of Iran."

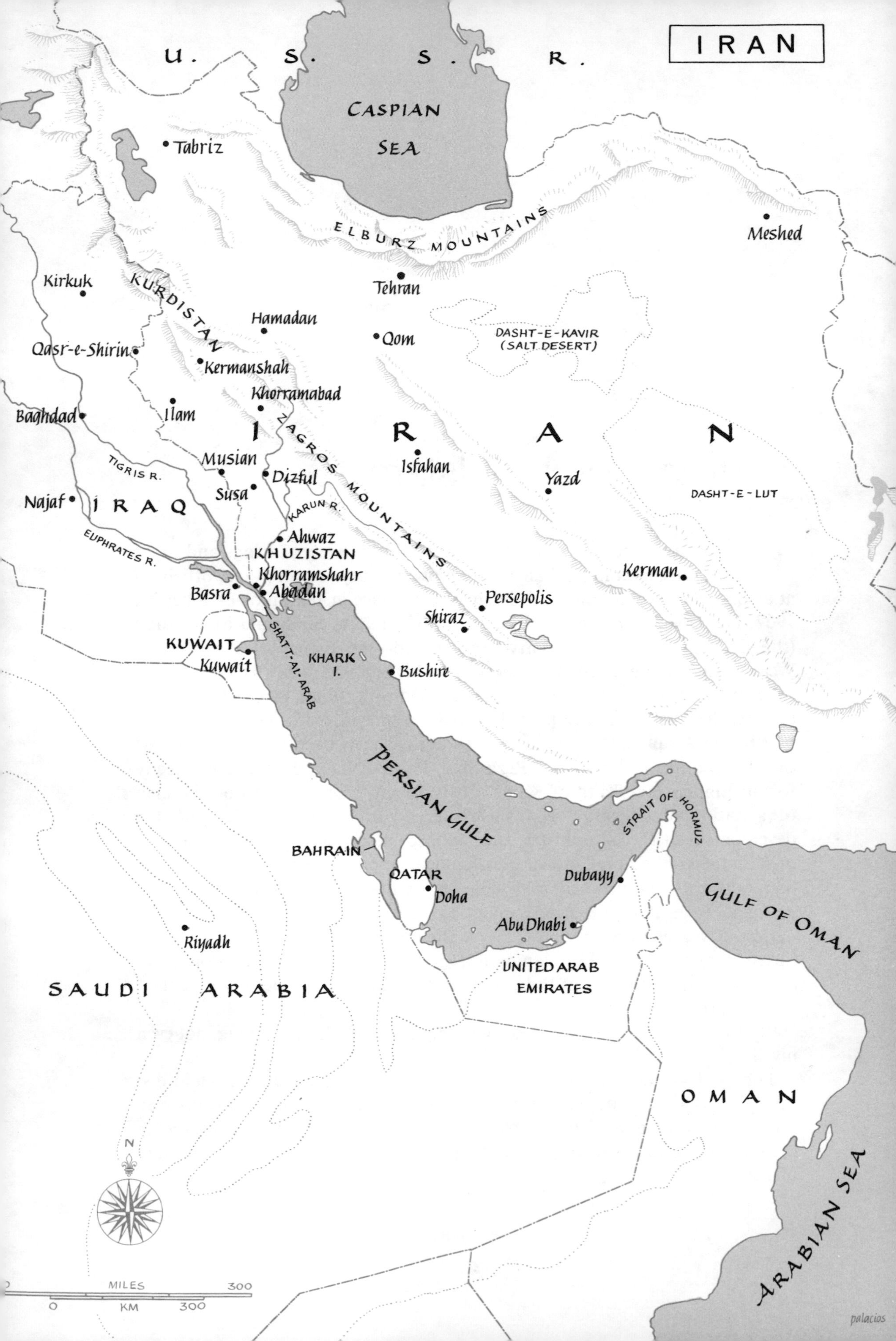

IRAN
U. S. S. R.
CASPIAN SEA
Tabriz
ELBURZ MOUNTAINS
Meshed
Kirkuk
KURDISTAN
Tehran
Hamadan
Qom
DASHT-E-KAVIR (SALT DESERT)
Qasr-e-Shirin
Kermanshah
Khorramabad
Baghdad
Ilam
ZAGROS MOUNTAINS
I R A N
Musian
Isfahan
Yazd
TIGRIS R.
Dizful
Susa
DASHT-E-LUT
Najaf
IRAQ
KARUN R.
Ahwaz
EUPHRATES R.
KHUZISTAN
Kerman
Khorramshahr
Basra
Abadan
Persepolis
Shiraz
KUWAIT
Kuwait
SHATT-AL-ARAB
KHARK I.
Bushire
PERSIAN GULF
STRAIT OF HORMUZ
BAHRAIN
QATAR
Doha
Dubayy
GULF OF OMAN
Abu Dhabi
Riyadh
UNITED ARAB EMIRATES
SAUDI ARABIA
OMAN
ARABIAN SEA
N
MILES 300
0 KM 300
palacios

United Press International

After twenty-six years of rule, Mohammed Reza Pahlevi installs himself officially as the Shah of Iran. His queen, Farah, is seated to his right, and their seven-year-old son, Crown Prince Reza, is on the Shah's left.

A dazzling parade followed, and a grand reception was held—five thousand guests from various nations were present—and thousands of athletes, marching bands, and motorcycle teams entertained the royal couple and their guests. At the torchlight tattoo by the Imperial Guards, the Shah, the Shahbanou, and guests observed a military unit march past, along with the Imperial Guards band. Most impressive of all were the ugly-snouted tanks of the Shah's army; they were American-made M-47s.

The first decade of the Shah's regime, 1941–51, was dominated by the British and American oil industry. These consortiums—paramount was Britain's Anglo-Iranian Oil Company—drained oil and profits from Iran as the economy of the Iranians deteriorated. As it functioned, Anglo-Iranian derived more profit from Iranian oil than the nation collected in royalties from these companies. Consequently, there was political and social turmoil.

The Tudeh Party, largely middle-class in makeup, with army backing (and left-wing prompting), joined with the more conservative, right-wing National Front Party to demand drastic changes in the system, including nationalizing the oil industry. While the Soviet Union remained strangely aloof, the Western powers (particularly Great Britain) viewed this with much alarm. There was reason: on March 15, 1951, the Iranian Parliament voted unanimously to nationalize the oil industry, and a month later designated the leader of the National Front Party, Dr. Mohammed Mossadegh, as Premier. The Shah had no choice but to wait and watch.

Britain simply refused to recognize Iran's right to take over the oil industry, and would not cooperate with the Mossadegh regime. The American interests, though less visible than the British, concurred. Oil production—and its income—virtually stopped. There were fears in the West that the turmoil would swing Iran into the Soviet camp, but unaccountably, the Soviets did not exploit the situation.

Years later it was learned (when classified State Department papers were made public) that at this same time there was concern by the U.S. Government over the monopolistic policies of certain American oil companies in Iran, as well as other nations in the Middle East. A Justice Department antitrust suit was voided in 1953 when the National Security Council invoked the Cold War phrase "national security."

By that year, Mossadegh's government was in disarray, although when the Shah tried to replace Mossadegh as Premier, rioting in the streets led him to reconsider.

Mossadegh's time in office was running out. His harsh dictatorship alienated the middle class; his nationalization of the oil industry achieved little except shrinking of the Iranian economy. He was wrong in his belief that the Americans, jealous of Britain's big stake in Iranian oil, would approve and support him. With his own party drifting away, Mossadegh depended (or seemed to depend) on the Tudeh Party; this raised the specter of communism.

In August 1953, the Shah, whose authority and integrity Mossadegh had systematically eroded for a year and a half, became concerned, especially about the loss of oil revenues. The Shah's sister, Princess Ashraf, had been driven into exile, because Mossadegh believed she was too great an influence on her twin brother and was endowed with a much sharper, scheming mind. Mossadegh had also begun to investigate the financial holdings of the Pahlevi family and had begun to weaken the army, the Shah's most potent instrument.

On August 16, 1953, the Shah sent his emissary Colonel Nematollah Nasiri, to inform the Premier that he was dismissed and would be replaced by Major General Fazlollah Zahedi. Mossadegh was infuriated by the news. He rejected the dismissal and publicly announced that the Shah had attempted to overthrow him. In response, people began rioting in the streets of Tehran, toppling statues of the Shah.

Wide World Photos

In a show of Islamic unity, the Shah of Iran visited King Saud of Saudi Arabia, shown holding one of his forty children, Prince Mashour. King Saud was deposed in 1964 and was succeeded by his brother Faisal.

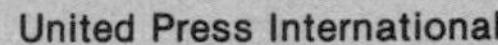

United Press International

Jordan's King Hussein during a state visit to Iran in 1970; he was royally and militarily greeted by the Shah at the Tehran airport.

At a military air base near Rome, the Shah of Iran inspects Italy's American-made North American F-86 "Sabre" jet fighters. American military aid would make the Shah's army the most formidable in the Middle East.

United Press International

The Shah and his wife—who had been packed and ready to leave for some time—first fled to Baghdad and then to Rome, where he frequented boutiques to buy presents that would console the Empress Soraya.

In Tehran, in the wake of the confusion caused by the Shah's flight, loyal troops, paid mobs recruited from the Bazaar (the very center of urban Iran), plus some help in the name of national security from the American Central Intelligence Agency ended Mossadegh's rule. Four days later, on August 22, 1953, the Shah returned to Iran. Mossadegh was arrested, charged with treason, sentenced to three years of imprisonment, and later, to house arrest in his country home for the rest of his life. (He died in 1967 at the age of eighty-six.) His Foreign Minister, Hussein Fatemi, was tried for the same offense as Mossadegh and was executed.

The Shah returned from his brief exile to what he called "a heartwarming, tumultuous welcome." Even more welcome was the promise from the American President, Dwight D. Eisenhower, of economic and financial aid amounting to $45 million. Now Mohammed Reza Pahlevi was even more determined to exert his authority.

He began by ending the oil crisis and clearing the way for foreign industries to profit from Iranian oil reserves. The military became the backbone of his regime. Eventually, as the Shah grew more powerful and subjected to vituperation from the mosques and the bazaars, he formed an elite miniature army (with the aid of his new, American friends), the secret police, Sazeman-e Ettala'at va Amniyate Khasvar, also known as SAVAK.

The Shah's plan was to forge a modern, Westernized state from his kingdom, rooted in oil and shielded by guns. Isolated from his people, the Shah set out to build a new Iran, heedless of the traditionalist objections from Islamic religious leaders. Since there was no true established church, in the Western sense, the Shah, mistakenly, chose to ignore the outcries. He did not realize that the voices of the mullahs (men of religion) reached the ears and hearts of more of his people, and with more force, than did his decrees and broadcasts.

The Shah quickly moved to crush political opposition; by March 1975, there was only one political party in Iran: the Shah's. He chose to ignore the Parliament, which did not agree with his Westernization. As the Shah later stated, his "main mistake, without a doubt, was to have made an ancient people advance by forced marches toward independence, health, culture, affluence, comfort." Very little of these enhancements filtered down to his subjects. However, the Shah, his family, and loyal henchmen prospered. Not that all of his reforms were not admirable; in fact, many of his most adroit decisions led some Iranians and Westerners, the CIA learned in 1976, to speculate that the Shah's policies may very well have been formulated by "a secret group of hired foreign advisers."

It was no secret that the Shah's powerful army was built up with American aid. It became the most potent military force in the Middle East, armed with sophisticated weapons, its troops trained by American advisers. The Shah's army was regarded as "the policeman of the Persian Gulf," the buffer against Soviet expansion in the Mideast, and "America's closest ally in the Third World." Goodly portions of Iran's oil revenues were invested in American tanks, aircraft, and other military equipment. From 1972 to mid-1976 the Shah spent $10 billion in the United States alone. (On occasion, when he wished to disquiet his American friends a little, the Shah also bought Soviet weapons.)

The acquisition of so much weaponry also disquieted the Shah's neighbors around the Persian Gulf. However, he explained that Iran's position in a most volatile region necessitated a massive army to protect its oil exports from interference (presumably Soviet, but Arab as well).

Some of the Shah's more enlightened policies—in regard to wider education for Iranians and the position of women in Islamic Iran—led to serious trouble. Students who could not afford to study abroad soon learned that their higher education must conform with the Shah's view of what he began to call his "Great Civilization." There was education, but no academic freedom, in short. Students of wealthy parents (often the Shah's allies) went abroad to study; if they returned, they brought back anti-Iranian ideas about constitutional government and democracy. (Some sixty thousand students formed the Confederation of Iranian Students Abroad to protest the Shah's repression and corruption.)

In January 1963 the Shah proclaimed his "White Revolution," a plan whose major points included land reforms and the enfranchisement of women. Since the mosques would lose some of their holdings in the redistribution of land, and the very thought of the equality of women was anathema to the clergy, the Shah had begun to stir up very serious opposition—which he chose to ignore, since there seemed to be no true organization of the mullahs.

In 1975, the Shah created a Family Protection Law, which gave women the right to divorce their husbands and even to challenge a husband's divorce action. While these changes, progressive in Western eyes, harmonized with the Shah's dream of a "Great Civilization," they were seen as a challenge to the clergy and a usurpation of the mullahs' authority in a Muslim society.

Among the most vociferous in his opposition to such modernization was the Ayatollah Ruhollah Khomeini, a respected holy man of some sixty years of age. Deeply religious, Khomeini believed that Islam was not merely a religious force, but also deeply moral and political. His arrest in June 1963 led to serious rioting in Iran, and the next year, to exile in the Shi'ite haven of An Najaf, Iraq. From there the Ayatollah continued his anti-Shah *jihad*.

Pahlevi disturbed even the more moderate members of the clergy when he initiated the modernization of the Holy Shrine of Imam Reza at Meshed. The memorial to the Shi'ite sect's eighth patriarch (who was poisoned in the ninth century) was regarded as the holiest of Iran's sanctuaries. To tear Meshed up with foreign bulldozers was sheer desecration—consequently, some of the bulldozers were put out of commission by bombings and vandalism. Another affront to the clergy was the Shah's official shift in 1976 from the Islamic calendar to the monarchic calendar based on the coronation of Cyrus the Great (thus placing the Pahlevi dynasty in immortal Persian company).

The rioting and mass demonstrations that this profanation incited were put down by the Army and SAVAK, and the significance of the protests was lost on the Shah and his supporters. Later that year, the CIA reported (in a secret document that appears to have been kept from the eyes of President Jimmy Carter) that "In the eyes of the religious leaders Mohammed Reza has betrayed an essential element of his role, protection of Islam. The present generation of religious leaders, moreover, seems to be convinced that the shah, as his father before him, is determined to destroy Islam in Iran."

There was another undercurrent that eluded the Shah's American supporters—politicians, oil dealers, the military, and arms merchants. Another CIA report informed Washington that "The secularism of the government and the religious conservatism of the clergy appear irreconcilable and there is no spirit of accommodation on either side.

"From the point of view of U.S. interests the important aspect of the problem is the hostility of a large influential group which has constant access to masses of population," wrote David H. Blee, intelligence officer for the Middle East, in his summary dated November 4, 1976. He emphasized an essential but little understood cultural reality: "Xenophobia is always just below the surface in Iran. Although masked by the Iranian tradition of hospitality to individuals, it has always been easy to stir up mob feeling against foreigners as an undifferentiated mass, and when this happened it has almost always had religious overtones."

One CIA secret report (which eventually fell into the hands of the Iranian

United Press International

Ayatollah Ruhollah Khomeini greets his followers from the roof of his home in Qom, Iran, 1979.

dissidents and then was widely published in paperback form) touched on yet another serious cause of discord: "The royal court has traditionally been a hotbed of byzantine scheming," it stated. "In the shah's family are an assortment of licentious and financially corrupt relatives, notably his twin sister Ashraf. . . . The periodic anticorruption campaigns which the shah launches would have greater believability if he saw fit to publicly reproach Ashraf." In the light of future events, it appears that no one in Washington was reading these summaries.

Meanwhile the Ayatollah, in exile, savagely attacked the Shah and recorded his diatribes on cassettes which were smuggled into Iran for distribution in the mosques and bazaars. He had begun to assume a mythical quality and to be regarded among the faithful as the "hidden Imam," the leader who would one day return to lead the Shi'ite faithful.

The Ayatollah was becoming troublesome and was stirring up religious protests inside Iran. He became more vocal after the mysterious murder of his son, Mostafa (generally attributed to SAVAK), on October 3, 1977. When the Persian daily *Etelaat* vilified Mostafa's reputation and placed the blame for the religious unrest in the country on him, theological students in the holy city of Qom staged a sit-in in their seminary the next day. Security forces moved in in early January 1978; after two days, at least seventy protestors were shot by security forces. In Tehran, students marched, demanding the end of the Ayatollah's exile. The Shah continued to scorn and dismiss the religious uprisings as "a lot of mullahs pining for the seventh century."

He himself, however, reminded His People of their lost former glory in 1971, when he led ceremonies honoring the ruins of Persepolis, which in the time of Darius was the ceremonial capital of Persia (circa 520 B.C.) until the arrival of Alexander. Like a loving, but uncompromising father, the Shah impressed upon the Iranians their uniqueness, their cultural contributions (their poets were active while Europe was still in the Dark Ages), their architecture.

While Iranians took pride in the civilization that Persepolis represented and could even feel superior to others of less advanced culture, Iran appeared to be dominated by foreigners. In the bazaars, among scholars, the clergy, and students, Pahlevi was scorned as the "American Shah."

The Shah's acquisition of American arms not only contributed to Iran's inflation (and serious unhappiness in the bazaars), it also brought in a great influx of foreigners, predominantly Americans. The very visible American—in uniform or out—was a galling, even hateful, presence to the urban Iranian and the embodiment of non-Islamic evil to the less educated, or uneducated, rural peasant. The Americans, more apparently than other foreigners (Frenchmen, Germans), stood for such desecrating Western depravities as alchohol, movies, rock music, whorish dress for women, cassettes, high rents, and the high cost of food. The engineers, military advisers, and operators of the Shah's costly electronics (complex radio systems, radar, etc.) were reminders of Iranian inadequacy and of the encroachment of Westernization on their culture.

In 1976 there were nearly twenty-five thousand Americans in Iran, most of

United Press International

Anti-American demonstrators gather around the American Embassy in Tehran; the tacit approval of Khomeini led to the ordeal of the American hostages.

them associated with the Shah's military preoccupations. The sophisticated technology required skilled personnel to train the Iranians in the use of such weaponry. As early as 1972, Secretary of Defense James Schlesinger cautioned President Richard Nixon against the sale of complex equipment to the Shah—such as the F-15 fighter, for example—which required special maintenance and spare parts. Schlesinger also warned against the presence of uniformed technical advisers in Iran. But this advice was not heeded, for the Shah—and his stockpile of arms and other equipment—was the buffer between the Soviets and the rest of the oil-rich Mideast. Rockwell International, for example, sold him an $850-million electronic surveillance system which could monitor the communications of his neighbors; but this sophisticated gadgetry demanded skilled technicians to operate it: Americans.

By 1977, the Shah faced more open unrest, abetted by increased unemployment and inflation. In the fall, in defiance of SAVAK, fifty prominent Iranians, some former associates of the deposed Dr. Mossadegh, signed an open letter to the Shah demanding the release of political prisoners. The Shah ignored them and the letter.

The Shah's standing among his people was also not improved when Presi dent Jimmy Carter visited him at the end of the year, as a sign of American friendship. In a toast as the New Year began, Carter said, "Iran, because of the great leadership of the Shah, is an island of stability in one of the more troubled areas of the world. This is a great tribute to you, Your Majesty, and to the respect and the admiration, and the love which your people give you."

A few days later, a Tehran newspaper published a letter accusing the Ayatollah Khomeini of conspiring with Communists against the Shah. The clergy and students at Qom again demonstrated, and security forces quelled the protests, but not until they had killed twenty of the demonstrators. During the traditional mourning period that followed, another protest occured, in Tabriz—a conservative but more secular setting. Thousands of voices were raised in the cry "Down with the Shah!" This was ominous, but ignored or misunderstood.

It was the beginning of the end for Mohammed Reza Pahlevi, not only as a monarch but also as a mortal. He was already suffering from the cancer that would take his life.

He also suffered through a year of strife, demonstrations, and fulminations from Ayatollah Khomeini (who in October 1978 moved to Paris at the request of the Iraqi Government). From Paris, the Ayatollah became even more vocal and critical of the Shah. Even the Shah's army could not put down every demonstration he inspired, and when it did, the overreaction and killings merely inflamed the people more. Also, stories about torture by SAVAK that began circulating not only infuriated Iranians but led to second thoughts about the Shah and his faltering regime among his Western patrons.

His attempts at compromise only brought new demands from the dissidents, whose membership ranged across the spectrum of the Iranian population. Emboldened by these numbers, the protesters staged mass demonstrations, crying out for reform and for the abdication of the Shah.

In June, Pahlevi promised free elections, but no one believed him; in August, nearly four hundred people were burned alive in the Rex Cinema, in the oil-refinery town of Abadan. Some believed that the disaster may have been caused by Muslim extremists who considered the movie theater a house of sin. Virtually all of Iran believed that the Shah's security forces had set the blaze to discredit Khomeini. Two days later, antigovernment riots erupted in Abadan.

When the disruptions spread and became difficult to handle, martial law was declared, in early September 1978. On September 7, twenty thousand dissidents assembled in Jaleh Square, in southern Tehran, to protest the law. When ordered to disperse, they refused, and the Shah's soldiers fired into the crowd, killing more than one hundred people. The enraged crowd rampaged through the city; they were pursued by the military, shooting into the mob, and by helicopter gunships firing down on them. The massacre ended around nightfall, with hundreds dead and thousands wounded.

On September 10, President Carter interrupted his peace talks with Sadat and Begin at Camp David to place a call to Pahlevi with a message of support. In Washington, D.C., and even at the top level of the embassy in Tehran, there was certainty that the Shah could handle the situation.

This was not so among the less senior members. Victor Tomseth, of the American Embassy, reported a few days after the Carter message that anti-American sentiment had risen sharply in Iran, and other officers hinted at "situations in which the U.S. could turn very swiftly into a scapegoat for Persian problems."

Tomseth summed up the situation in September 1978. Iranians were saying, "We have nothing against you personally, but Iranians dislike Americans because 1) you keep the shah in power, 2) American weapons kill our people, 3) you are a bad moral influence on our children, 4) you do not respect Islam, 5) you have caused inflation and shortages . . ." He added that "Several people, out of genuine concern for individual Americans they know, have advised that they leave Iran quickly lest something happen to them." (As a member of the embassy staff, the astute Tomseth did not leave.)

The Shah floundered from one inept solution to another. As a gesture to the protesters, he arrested General Nematollah Nasiri, head of the infamous SAVAK, and his own trusted Prime Minister of fourteen years, Amir Abbas Hoveida. No one took this seriously, for these men had been the Shah's faithful puppets; their capricious arrest, however, did not comfort his other loyal henchmen. Besides, these actions came too late. By the end of October, the protests had adversely affected the heart of Iran's economy with the strike of forty thousand petroleum workers.

Alarmed, the Shah formed a military government under a tough general, Gholam Reza Azhari, on November 6. Most oil workers were persuaded to return to their jobs by mid-month, but in December they left their jobs again, and oil production fell drastically. Sympathetic strikes in other fields—communications, transport, banks, import, and export—practically paralyzed the entire country. In desperation, the Shah made another gesture: he dissolved the military government, and on December 29, 1978, he appointed a former adversary, Shahpur Bakhtiar (formally of the National Front Party) as head of a new civil government. Unfortunately he was abandoned by his own party, which, despite its secular views, had begun to heed the voice of the Ayatollah.

Bakhtiar tried, but had trouble forming a cabinet. (No one wanted to be teamed with the Shah.) However, he did succeed in releasing some political prisoners and even disbanding SAVAK. Meanwhile, Khomeini, still in Paris, had appointed his own Premier, Dr. Mehdi Bazargan, and numbered the days of the Bakhtiar government by stating that "obedience to the Bakhtiar regime is obedience to Satan." Bakhtiar's home was fire-bombed, and portraits of the Ayatollah were defiantly placed on the gates of the Shah's Niavaran Palace.

On January 6, 1979, when the new Bakhtiar government officially came into power and one hundred thousand demonstrators rallied to protest it, the ailing Shah announced that he would "leave the country soon on a vacation."

On January 16, 1979, as he and his wife were driven to Tehran's airport, the Shah rationalized the decision in these words: "I was trying to convince myself that my departure would calm tempers, allay hatreds, disarm assassins." There were tears in his eyes—one of his soldiers had kneeled to kiss his foot—

As his fervent and faithful followers chant "Long live with Khomeini," the Ayatollah blesses a baby in the holy city of Qom.

United Press International

when he said, "I hope the Government will be able to make amends for the past [one of his rare moments of candor, when he actually admitted that mistakes had been made] and also succeed in laying foundations for the future." Once again he did not take the Ayatollah into account.

After he and his party boarded an airliner for Egypt, the cry of "The Shah is gone!" echoed through the streets of Tehran; there were celebrations, jubilation, and expectation. The Shah's people had rid themselves of a despotic, corrupt monarchy and had acquired a despotic, pietistic theocracy.

On February 1, 1979, Khomeini flew into Tehran and announced that "The parliament and the government are illegal . . . I will appoint a government with the support of the Iranian people." Ten days later, Bakhtiar was forced out of office by the Army and revolutionaries; the Ayatollah was now the government of Iran. He appointed Bazargan to serve as Prime Minister.

Tehran continued to smolder. On February 14, leftist guerrillas (whose underground leadership accused the Ayatollah of surrounding himself with reactionary religious leaders) stormed the American Embassy and held one hundred employees hostage until they were rescued by armed supporters of Khomeini. Four days later, PLO leader Yasir Arafat met with the Ayatollah and Bazargan, and declared that the Iranian revolution had turned the balance of power in the Middle East "upside down." On the same day, three generals and a former leader of SAVAK were executed.

In March, abandoning the secular capital, the Ayatollah moved to the holy city, Qom, where he vowed: "I will devote the remaining one or two years of my life [he was then 78] to reshaping Iran in the image of Muhammad . . . by the purge of every vestige of Western culture from the land. We will amend the newspapers. We will amend the radio, the television [both of which he and his followers exploited with quasi-Western-public-relations skill], the cinemas—all of these should follow the Islamic pattern.

"What the nation wants," he told the nation, "is an Islamic republic. Not just a republic, not a democratic republic, not a democratic Islamic republic. Just an Islamic republic. Do not use the word 'democratic.' That is Western and we do not want it."

What he wanted for Iran was a new kind of state. "The Islamic state," he continued, "is a constitutional state in the sense that those charged with running it are bound by the rules and conditions laid down by the Koran and Sunna." In short, the constitution of 1902 was canceled; it was "sinful," for its concepts had been adapted from "atrociously decadent societies" and were not fit for a pure Islamic state. So was the decadent idea that a system of laws would decree that one was innocent until proved guilty. By early March, the Ayatollah's firing squads had begun to deal with supporters of the Shah, ranging from members of the military, through governmental aides, to newspapermen. The Shah's former, but deposed, Prime Minister, Hoveida was granted a trial. It began at midnight, was held in a room in Qasr-e-Shirin Prison, and was presided over by five judges who had been imprisoned by the Shah. Hoveida, who had expected the trial to take place in the afternoon, was hardly alert; he had taken a sleeping pill. When he protested, he was informed that "Day or night makes no difference, because this is a revolutionary court."

Hoveida was accused of many crimes, ranging from smuggling heroin to the ultimate crime, "entering into battle with Allah and his emissaries." On April 7, 1979, he died before a firing squad, along with thirty-four other former officials of the Shah.

Only a week before, in a national referendum, Iranian voters approved Khomeini's "Islamic republic," which he proclaimed on April 1 as "the first day of the Government of God."

That government, it was demonstrated soon enough, dispensed its justice on the minor criminal as well as the major political offender. By the end of April, even Bazargan severely criticized the *komitehs* (committees of the Islamic Revolutionary Council) for their wholesale condemnations and executions, for conducting "a rule of revenge." The Ayatollah did not speak out and the executions continued; in May, the *komitehs*' death toll had reached two hundred and included members of the business community. On May 12, 1979, the leading independent newspaper ceased publication; the following day, the Shah and his entire family were condemned to death in absentia.

The new government operated with much the same chaos as had the Shah's; Khomeini remained aloof, making his decisions in saintly isolation in Qom. He revoked the Family Protection Law and abolished coeducational schools, while the *komitehs* administered his Government of God. Minorities—women, members of the Bahai sect, and Jews—were persecuted, their property confiscated or looted, and some were executed.

"Criminals," Khomeini exhorted, "should not be tried; they should be killed. I am sorry that there is still Western sickness among us."

During July of 1980 (to take a month of random examples), there was strict enforcement of the Islamic Code. On July 3, two women in Kerman were accused of prostitution. One man was charged with homosexuality; another, with the rape of a ten-year-old girl. Found guilty and condemned, they were then ceremoniously bathed, clothed in white from head to foot, buried in the earth up to their chests, and stoned to death by their fellow citizens, with the presiding judge of the Revolutionary Court casting the first stone. It was reported that the four prisoners, pelted with stones ranging in size "from walnuts to apples," took fifteen minutes to die.

This reintroduction of an ancient Islamic method of execution (the traditional punishment for sexual crimes and adultery) was questioned. A Kerman court official explained why it had not been employed before by other Revolutionary Courts: "Perhaps it's because they haven't been following the proper laws of Islam."

On the same day, seven others were killed by firing squads in other parts of Iran for crimes associated with drugs, sex, and murder. On July 14, firing squads executed twenty-six prisoners, among them one of the Shah's generals and two members of the Bahai sect, who were accused of espionage. Seven of the executions took place on a street in Tehran notorious for drug trafficking. The prisoners were taken into a former red-light district and shot because it was frequented by narcotics violators, one official explained, as a warning. On July 18, seven men and a woman were hanged in the same place for the same crime. In Paris, on the same day, an attempt was made on the life of the Shah's last Prime Minister, Dr. Bakhtiar. He escaped injury, but two people died (including a neighbor who happened to open his door to investigate the noise) and four were wounded. Two of the assailants were apprehended and two escaped. The assailants, according to their papers, were Palestinians from a group called Guardsmen of Islam, and may have had no connection with Iran.

Islamic justice traveled even farther on July 22, when an outspoken critic of the Ayatollah, one-time press attaché for the Shah, and leader of the Iran Freedom Foundation, Ali Akbar Tabatabai, was shot and killed in Bethesda, Maryland, a suburb of Washington, D.C.

The month closed with the death by firing squad of twenty-four men, eleven of whom were accused of plotting against Ayatollah Khomeini; also shot were three heroin dealers, a prominent Jewish hotel operator accused of "spying for Israel," and a former chief of Tehran's SAVAK. In August, Amnesty International, the London-based human rights group, estimated that from one thousand to twelve hundred people (the last figure is probably the more accurate) had been executed since the Shah had fled the country. This grisly news appeared on page 3 of the New York *Times*, but the eyes of most New Yorkers and the rest of America were following one of the most bizarre, frustrating episodes in American history. The Shah himself triggered the strange events that followed.

After his tearful flight to Egypt, in January 1979, the Shah became, literally, a man without a country. With unwonted foresight, he had provided for such a contingency by banking the bulk of his personal fortune (estimated as being in excess of a billion dollars) outside Iran. His known investments, including real estate, amounted to billions of dollars. (His Pahlevi Foundation Building, on New York's Fifth Avenue, was estimated as being worth more than $14 million in 1975.) The Shah did not want for money, only a haven for his wasting body.

From Egypt, he and his empress went to Morocco, where in March of 1979 he was informed by "a private emissary of the Carter administration" (a CIA agent) that he would not be able to come to the United States at the moment because of "the unstable relations between the U.S. and Iran."

The next stop was the Bahamas for a few weeks before the Pahlevis moved into a walled mansion in Cuernavaca, in central Mexico, noted for its gentle climate and splendid scenery. The setting was important, for the cancer that afflicted the Shah had worsened. When examined by an American doctor, the Shah was found also to have a fever and advanced jaundice. Pressure was put on the Carter administration to permit the Shah to come to the United States for treatment that he could not get in Mexico.

Although she did not know the Shah was suffering from lymphatic cancer, the Shah's twin sister wrote a letter to President Carter in August pleading for aid and informing him that the Shah had suffered a "quite noticeable impairment of his health in Mexico." The letter was answered with some coolness, since Carter had not been informed of the cancer either, despite the various intelligence-gathering resources of the United States in Iran. Even more powerful pressure was put on the Carter administration by such friends of the Shah as David Rockefeller and Henry Kissinger; undoubtedly some compassion was implicit, but the approaching 1980 political campaign was also a factor. How could Carter desert a friend in need, especially an ailing one?

Dr. Benjamin H. Kean was sent to Mexico to examine the Shah, and he recommended that further tests be conducted in New York, although he noted that the tests could be carried out elsewhere. On his return, the Carter administration finally learned that the Shah had cancer, among other complications, and now felt justified in admitting him—indeed compelled to admit him—into the United States. Dr. Kean also informed the Iranian Government on October 21, 1979, that Pahlevi was ill and would be hospitalized in New York. L. Bruce Laingen, U.S. chargé d'affaires in Tehran, and Henry Precht, in charge of the State Department's Iran task force, called on Prime Minister Bazargan and Foreign Minister Ibrahim Yazdi to advise them officially of the President's decision.

They did not believe that the Shah was as ill as claimed and suggested that an Iranian doctor be present during the tests (this point was dropped, for some unknown reason). They also promised protection for the American Embassy and its now-skeleton staff. Precht remembered that it was Yazdi who said ominously, "You're opening a Pandora's box with this."

The next night, the Shah's jet landed at La Guardia Airport and he entered New York Hospital. Twenty-four hours later, he underwent surgery (his gallbladder was removed along with gallstones), and he was treated for histiocytic lymphoma. Two days later, apparently recuperating, he celebrated his sixtieth birthday. He was still in the hospital nine days later, when, in Tehran, the Pandora's box blew open. (The Shah continued his wandering, sickly exile: further treatment at Lackland Air Force Base, Texas; unhappy with American hospitality, he attempted to return to Mexico and was refused entry; then he traveled to Panama, on March 23, 1980, and fled only twenty-four hours before the Khomeini regime filed extradition papers. Chartering a jet, he and his wife flew to Cairo, where they were welcomed by Anwar el-Sadat. More surgery followed, after which, somewhat improved, the Shah was sequestered with the empress in the Kubbeh Palace, once the abode of Farouk, at Heliopolis, near Cairo. He died in Cairo on July 27 of a massive internal hemorrhage.)

That death, so fervently anticipated—even prayed for, by some—did little for those who had been trapped inside Yazdi's Pandora's box, the American Embassy in Tehran, when it exploded.

On a bleak Sunday morning, November 4, 1979, Moorhead C. Kennedy, third-ranking official at the United States Embassy, stood at a second-floor window watching an angry, shrieking mob. They had been smoldering there since seven-thirty, as they had for the past two weeks, since word had come that the Shah had been admitted into the United States. Their chanting seethed with hate: "Death to the Shah!" "Death to Carter!" "Death to America!"

"I remember standing in a window and looking down on all the noise and anti-American anger," Kennedy later recalled, "and I wondered to myself what it would be like to die."

The demonstrators were youthful, probably students; they shouted, waved clubs, and carried posters of the Ayatollah Khomeini. Each day, Kennedy sensed, the protests had grown more malevolent, more virulent, more rancorous. By 10 A.M. many members of the staff were openly troubled.

Then, at around ten-thirty, a marine guard rushed into Kennedy's office and shouted, "Everybody downstairs! There's a break-in!"

As he hurriedly prepared to leave, Kennedy looked out the window again and "saw this sea of fanatical faces and heard their voices. They were like—they were lowing for death." He and fifty-one other Americans would, from that day, endure 444 days of abuse, torture, beatings, mock executions—not death, perhaps (although two of their number attempted suicide during the ordeal), but despairingly close.

Initially, about a hundred hostages were taken by the youthful zealots, more than sixty of them American. Only the Americans were detained. The militants demanded the extradition of the Shah in exchange for them. Some of the Embassy staff managed to slip out of the compound, situated in downtown Tehran. These six people found refuge in private homes and eventually in the Canadian Embassy, adjacent to the American Embassy. On February 1, 1980, they escaped from Iran by using Canadian passports.

The Iranians themselves, in a display of racism and sexism, released thirteen persons—five women and eight blacks—on November 19, 1979. The remaining black, communications technician Charles Jones, Jr., and two women, Kathryn L. Koob and Elizabeth Swift, it was explained, would stay, because they were suspected of spying. Koob was not even in the chancellery when the mob burst into the compound, but in her office at the Iran-American Society, along with William B. Royer, Jr., who taught there. They were eventually captured and returned to the Embassy.

Also absent at the time of the takeover were the chargé d'affaires, L. Bruce Laingen, the prescient Victor L. Tomseth (who had predicted what was now happening), and security officer Michael H. Howland. They had gone to the Iranian Foreign Ministry to discuss some diplomatic matters (with no success) and were prepared to return to the Embassy, about a mile away. Howland had heard of the break-in over the car radio, and the three men, upon hearing that the grounds were aswarm with howling Iranians, decided to return to the Iranian Ministry. The hope was to put some diplomatic pressure on to clear the Embassy grounds. They were not successful in this, either, even though the members of the ministry staff were embarrassed and sympathetic.

Foreign Minister Yazdi arrived to assure them that something would be done. The Revolutionary Council ruled that the three Americans should be given "protection" in the Iranian Foreign Ministry for the duration. They were the

Inside the American Embassy, November 4, 1979. A marine guard, wearing a gas mask, waits for the demonstrators to storm the offices of the embassy. No attempt was made by the Americans to fend off the militants with gunfire.

December 1979: as Christmas approaches, the hostages have been held for over a month and the American Embassy is firmly in the hands of the student militants. Inside the compound, two of them pose with pro-Khomeini, anti-Carter posters.

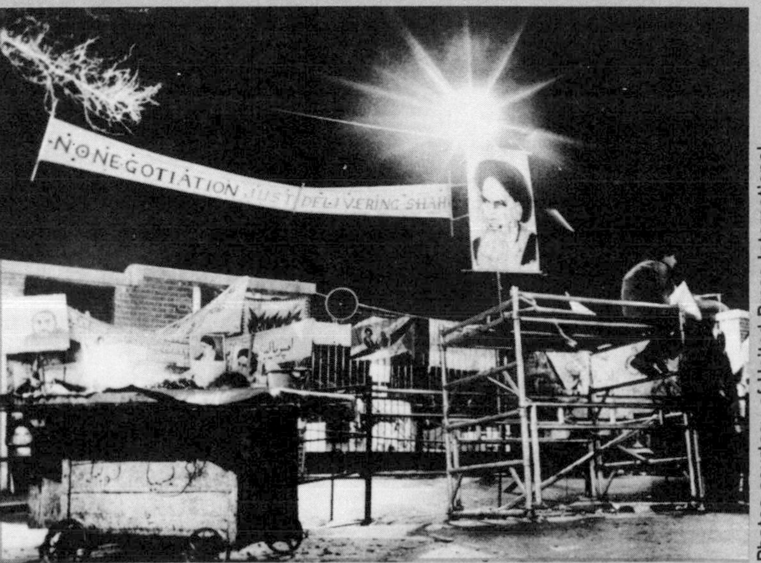

January 1980: after a New Year's demonstration, the militants leave the watch at the embassy to a television crew who had filmed the day's angry protests.

Photos courtesy of United Press International

best-treated of the fifty-two hostages, until just before their release; they spent the last few days of their captivity in a Tehran jail.

One other hostage was released, after two hundred fifty days, Vice-Consul Richard I. Queen, who was in Tehran on his first foreign assignment. After his release, in July 1980, for medical reasons (diagnosed as multiple sclerosis), Queen revealed something of the treatment he and the other captives experienced. In what they came to call "the night of the Gestapo Raid," Queen had been brushing his teeth when a gunman in a white mask burst into his room and shouted, "Go! Move!"

He was pushed into an assembly room, where he saw twenty-one other hostages and a dozen more masked gunmen. They ordered the prisoners to lie down, but naval Commander Donald A. Sharer refused, saying that they would have to shoot him standing, not lying down.

The rest of the hostages also remained standing while the gunmen clicked their rifle bolts.

"I knew that was it," Queen said, "my last moment. I just tried to give myself last rites." But nothing happened and the hostages were led away. The object was simple torture.

Elizabeth Swift had a similar experience. A guard put the muzzle of his gun to her head. "I heard the trigger click, but nothing happened," she later said. "They only wanted to torture us. The torture was prolonged with threats of the return of the men in white masks."

One of the women who was later released, Elizabeth Montagne, Laingen's secretary, got a frightful preview of what was in store for the Americans soon after the Embassy was overrun. A gunman seized her and ordered her to give him the combinations of the safe. When she told him that she did not know any combinations, the man placed a single bullet in his pistol and jammed it into her chest.

"He went click," she recalled, "and the bullet went up one chamber—I could feel it go up."

"I'm a very good judge of character," the gunman told her, "and I know you're lying to me."

"If you think I'm lying you're a lousy judge of character," she snapped back, "because I'm telling you the truth. I can't open those safes."

Click.

There was further dispute over the kind of information that she might have access to, followed by another click.

"Is this worth dying for?" he inquired.

"No, it's not," she replied.

Click.

"And . . . ," she told an NBC News reporter, "this little game must have taken about four, five minutes, it seemed an eternity—and I can remember my mind being very, very clear, and very, very sharp. I remember my heart trying to jump out of my chest. He kept pointing the gun at me, and the last—there was one click to go."

Photos courtesy of United Press International

A view from inside the embassy grounds, surrounded by armed and alert militants.

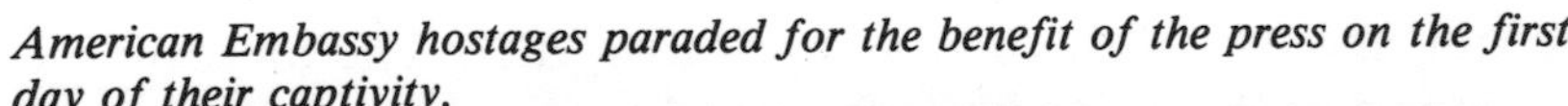

American Embassy hostages paraded for the benefit of the press on the first day of their captivity.

The gunman asked, "Do you think I'll pull the trigger?"

She did not answer but thought, "I wonder what it would feel like to have bullets go through my chest. Then I thought, well, it can't hurt for long."

"We stared at each other, and then he—he put the gun down."

"O.K."—he shrugged—"so you don't know the combinations."

After he left, Elizabeth Montagne "kind of collapsed."

When the predominantly youthful rabble had cut through the embassy gate and swarmed screaming into the Chancellery, they acted spontaneously, and even they did not expect the occupation to last for more than a few days. Senior officials in Washington felt the same. In fact, the occupations of several other Western embassies were also expected. (The British Embassy was occupied for a while the next day.) But the Ayatollah ordered the rampaging militants to stop, although he blessed their seizure of the American Embassy. The immediate political outcome inside Iran was the resignation of the Bazargan government, on November 6.

What escalated into an international crisis actually began as a student protest against the American treatment of the Shah and, as originally planned, was to have lasted for three days, maybe five. In the beginning, about four hundred angry young Iranians calling themselves "The Students Following the Imam's [i.e., the Ayatollah's] Line," advised by a militant young clergyman, Hojatolislam Ashgar Moussavi Khoeni, were actually students. Fully aware of their plan "to make an action so that the cries of our oppressed people could reach all the world's ears," as a student put it, was Hojatolislam Ahmed Khomeini, the Ayatollah's son and principal aide. The takeover was not a spontaneous demonstration but was carefully planned and discussed by the participants. It merely grew beyond their expectations and got out of hand.

Once they had broken into the compound and forced their way into the chancellery and past the few marine guards (who could only deter them with tear gas, having been ordered not to shoot), the students occupied the building and waited. They expected to make their gesture and be expelled by the police or the Army. But this did not happen. Foreign Minister Yazdi tried, but he and Bazargan were quickly dismissed from their offices. The students just as quickly realized that they had become politically powerful.

A student grasped the significance of their sit-in when mobs of Iranians flocked to the Embassy. He told New York *Times* reporter John Kifner that he "saw people coming, crowds coming. They were calling by telephone, sending messages of support. We realized our action was something great! Yes, something really great! It was like a bomb burst, and we realized then that we had to keep going."

That began one of the most bizarre episodes in diplomatic history: drawn-out, frustrating, aggravating, cruel, and at times, for its victims, hopeless and boring. Even the initial militants, motivated by religious beliefs and hatred for the Shah and the United States, became, in the phrase of John Kifner, "hostage to the hostages."

Treatment of the Americans varied, ranging (especially in the first days of the occupation) from cruelly harsh to sympathetic. The hostages, often forbidden to speak to each other and cut off from news from the outside world (even sunlight from that world), felt isolated, abandoned, forgotten. Besides fear and apprehension, they lived with monotony and ennui. They had little idea of what their captivity stirred up in the United States.

The importance of television during their 444 days of torment was paramount. When the television cameras focused on the Chancellery, they also provided the militants with a worldwide stage. Their parading the blindfolded hostages before the cameras, burning the American flag (or using it as a garbage collector), burning President Carter in effigy, and chanting "Mar Bar Amerika" (Death to America) angered and unified the American people. The plight of the hostages rallied the country and brought demands for actions.

The Carter administration considered every possibility, including a military move early in the seizure, but, as Secretary of State Cyrus R. Vance recalled, after the idea had been brought up on the first day, "The Joint Chiefs reminded us that downtown Tehran was not the same as Entebbe Airport." When a request was made of Israeli intelligence to study the situation, Defense Minister Ezer Weizman informed the Administration that they saw no way that a successful rescue operation could be carried out. The idea was set aside for the moment; unfortunately it would be raised again.

"There was no way," Vance concluded, "to get a rescue team into the middle of the city, with thousands of demonstrators milling about, without getting the hostages killed in the process." Not to mention Iranians. Besides, once he recognized the value of the students to his revolutionary theocracy, the Ayatollah would have welcomed such carnage. "This is a war of Islam against blasphemy," he declared. He also stated that he did not fear the military might of the United States and that most of the Iranian population was "looking forward to martyrdom."

A military solution to the problem in this light was not feasible, so the Carter administration attempted other approaches, diplomatic and economic. The President himself called dozens of world leaders, from close allies to supporters of Khomeini, asking them to put pressure on Iran. A few tried but little came of their efforts. One group of Iranian clergymen came to the State Department with an offer to go directly to the Iranian people and stir up public opinion to the degree that the hostages would be released. For this, the clergymen asked for $20 million. If the hostages were not freed within twenty days, the mullahs promised, the money would be returned. The State Department rejected the plan.

Among the economic sanctions Carter imposed was the ending of oil imports from Iran and freezing all Iranian assets in American banks. The State

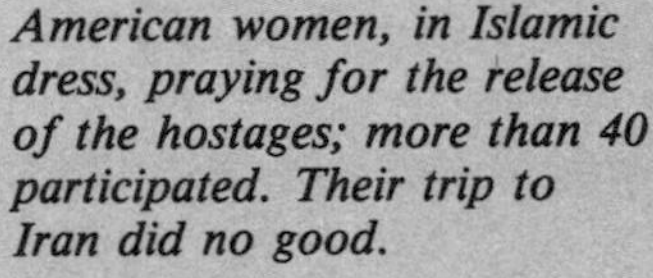

American women, in Islamic dress, praying for the release of the hostages; more than 40 participated. Their trip to Iran did no good.

Photos courtesy of United Press International

The attempts of U.S. Secretary of State Cyrus Vance (left) and UN Secretary General Kurt Waldheim to negotiate the release of the hostages was no more successful than the effort by the American women who had traveled to Tehran.

Department followed that with the expulsion of 183 Iranian diplomats from the United States. Many Americans questioned why they weren't taken into custody.

Carter was proceeding cautiously; his was not an easy task, for it was difficult to know who truly represented Iran: the chaotic government, the students, the Ayatollah? Often he said nothing; other times he rescinded official government decisions that appeared to be soft on the hostages; at times he praised the captors, thus giving them his sanction. Obviously Khomeini was the key figure, and he would not confer with "The Great Satan," the United States. He would not even recognize the United Nations.

On December 31, 1979, the UN Security Council adopted a resolution calling on Iran to free the hostages by January 7 or face sanctions. Secretary General Kurt Waldheim arrived in Iran on January 1, 1980. He was back in New York by January 7 but brought no hostages with him. Khomeini refused to see him, and his automobile was harried by protesters. When Waldheim returned, on that day, he foresaw "no quick solution" to the crisis. Later in the month, Carter, in his State of the Union address, stressed that the United States would have "no basic quarrel with Iran" once the hostages were released.

Inside their mad prison, the hostages were not aware of the efforts being made to set them free. They were led to believe that nothing was being done; their mail was kept from them; and when Christmas came, they felt they were being exploited for television cameras (some refused to participate). Some resented the efforts of the American clergymen to cheer them up and to impress the people back home with their "kind" treatment by the Iranians.

Moorhead Kennedy later recalled that on their first Easter in captivity one of the clerics turned to a hostage and said, "I sure would like to spend, say, twenty days with you fellows. It would give me a chance to meditate."

"Well, not long before that," Kennedy commented, "we had been stood up against that wall [in a mock execution] and we all said to ourselves, you know, we'd very much like to have had him with us."

In November 1979 an event occurred that momentarily diverted attention from the hostages. Close to five hundred fanatical Muslims attacked the Grand Mosque in Mecca and held it for a few days. This was an unheard-of sacrilege in the Muslim world—and was attributed to the machinations of "The Great Satan." When the Mosque was retaken, some three hundred of the insurgents were killed and one hundred seventy were taken prisoner. The uprising was led by an admirer of Khomeini who had been financed by Muammar al-Qaddafi—a theology student known as Mahdi ("the guided one," who claimed divine enlightment). His given name was Mohammed al-Quraishi.

The heavily armed, well-trained (by Cubans and Yemenis in Aden) insurgents were members of a splinter Muslim sect in opposition to the leadership of Saudi Arabia. Taking the holy shrine and holding three hundred of their brothers hostage seemed a dramatic but pointless gesture and they were dealt with ferociously: the prisoners were beheaded. The direct effect on the American hostages of this supposedly American-inspired desecration was hardly noticeable, for in the early weeks their general treatment by their captors was harsh: hands tied even while they slept, they wore hoods even while moving from one room to another in a building they knew well; they could not communicate with one another and they were roughed up (never seriously) now and then.

Another trouble spot that attracted worldwide attention but had little effect on the hostages' fate was Afghanistan, which the Soviet Union invaded on Christmas Day. This put the Soviets in threatening contiguity to Iran.

Meanwhile, midnight raids and what promised to be death by firing squad seemed to come at random for the American hostages, although the raid by the white-masked gunmen may have been triggered by the escape of the six Americans via Canada. Another, called "the panty raid," in which the men were lined up against a wall and stripped to their underpants and searched, may have been inspired by a suicide attempt by one of the hostages. When they returned to their cells, they found that their razor blades had been confiscated.

After one of the mock executions, Colonel Charles W. Scott found that he lost the fear of being killed. Eventually, many hostages feared being shot by mistake, rather than design. It was evident that their young guards were not overly familiar with their automatic rifles and machine guns. As twenty-two-year-old Sergeant James Lopez put it, he found this "slightly nerve-wracking because we had all these little kids running around with shotguns."

Not all of the hostages' captors were "students." During the 444 days, guards came and went. Charles Jones felt that the "majority of the so-called students were young unemployed kids [unemployment of Iranian young men had reached 70 percent]. Many of them call themselves students because they have no better names to call themselves."

With the coming of spring 1980, life inside the compound settled down to the usual boredom. There was some hope with the arrival of the Swiss Red Cross and a plan formulated to fly the hostages out. However, that plan was quashed when the Ayatollah insisted that the decision be made by the Iranian Parliament, which did not really exist at the time. The hostages did not know this; then, on April 25, the relative serenity was shattered.

"Something had gone down," Sergeant Lopez assumed. "We did not know what.

"All of a sudden there's running up and down the hallways. There's vans being backed in, the door kicks open, and they tell us, 'Pack, you will be leaving soon'. They were very frazzled, they were very nervous, which made us nervous because these clowns were running around with automatic weapons, fingers on triggers, locked and loaded."

No one was injured, although many believed they were going to be taken out and shot. The hostages were dispersed throughout the Iranian countryside, to Qom, Isfahan, Shiraz, and Tabriz. The three captives in the Iranian Foreign Ministry were lucky; they merely lost the use of their table-tennis privileges.

April 25, 1980, was a bleak day for President Jimmy Carter. After months of fruitless attempts at negotiations to free the hostages, after considering such punitive military measures as a naval blockade of Iranian ports and bombing Kharg Island and Abadan, two major oil targets, from the air, and rejecting these measures, the President made a decision. Under pressure, political and popular, to "do something," Carter approved the plan to rescue the hostages.

According to the few details that have since been revealed by some of the participants, that plan had never really been abandoned, but studied and discussed in deep secret. As the negotiations got nowhere, and at times it appeared that the lives of the hostages were in jeopardy (there were threats to put them on trial as "spies," and intimations of executions one by one), Carter went ahead.

All but one of Carter's advisers who knew about the planning of the rescue felt certain that it would work: Secretary of Defense Harold Brown, national security adviser Zbigniew Brzezinski, CIA director Admiral Stansfield Turner, General David C. Jones, chairman of the Joint Chiefs, and the Vice-President, Walter F. Mondale; the lone holdout was Secretary of State Cyrus R. Vance, who, when he was informed of the decision, resigned his post before the mission took place (although his resignation was not made public until after the attempt).

A special commando unit made up of Army, Air Force, Navy, and Marine Corps personnel underwent special training and rehearsals for the mission. Initially only the Army and the Air Force were involved; the Navy and the Marines were introduced later, a concession to interservice rivalries. If the Big Mission of the year was to come off, all branches would have to be represented. Some military analysts have suggested that this may also have contributed to some confusion in command.

The plan called for six C-130 Hercules transports, carrying rescue teams and fuel, to take off from bases in Egypt and fly a circuitous route skirting Arab radar, to land at a former SAVAK air strip in the Salt Desert near the town of Posht-e-Badam, in Iran, about two hundred fifty miles southeast of Tehran. At about the same time, on April 24, eight Sikorsky RH-53D "Sea Stallion" helicopters took off from the carrier USS *Nimitz*, in the Arabian Sea. The helicopters were to rendezvous at Desert One (as the base was code-named) with the rescue teams, for an early-morning mission. The plan called for a minimum of six helicopters to bring the teams (some two hundred men) into Tehran and to get them and the hostages out. The first Sikorsky aborted its mission at the beginning of its flight. The formation had flown about eighty miles when one of the Sea Stallions was forced down in the desert with rotor-blade trouble. It was abandoned after its crew and all pertinent documents were picked up by another helicopter.

Continuing on toward Desert One, the formation ran into a series of sandstorms, which no one had detected although they were expected. One of the helicopters lost its navigation and flight instruments; the pilot turned around and headed out of the sand and back to the *Nimitz*.

The six remaining planes landed, though behind schedule, at Desert One.

United Press International

The charred remains of the Hercules transport and its American crew at Desert One after the failure of the rescue attempt.

The mission then suffered another unfavorable incident: a bus carrying more than forty Iranians, a fuel truck, and a pickup truck drove onto the scene during the rendezvous stage. No one had counted on such a contingency, although the planners were aware of the road near the SAVAK base.

When the vehicles did not stop, the Americans fired warning shots. The bus halted, the fuel truck caught fire, and its driver raced to the pickup truck, which sped away. No pursuit ensued, for it was decided that the men were smugglers and would raise no alarm. The forty-three bus passengers were detained. (There was even talk of taking some of them as captives, but that was vetoed.)

Then came the penultimate calamity. A third Sea Stallion, which had suffered a partial hydraulic failure in flight, was eliminated from the mission, leaving five helicopters, one less than the original minimum. Air Force Colonel James Kyle, in command of the helicopters, consulted with the commander of the Army's rescue team, Colonel Charlie Beckwith. They agreed: abort the rescue mission.

It was afternoon in Washington and 3 A.M. in Iran the President heard the difficult but indisputable decision made by the commanders in the field. He agreed, put down the phone, and, as Brzezinski has written, "He then put his head in his arms and cradled it on his desk for a few seconds." At that very moment, the mission suffered its final disaster.

As the helicopters refueled from fuel-carrying C-130s in preparation for the return to the *Nimitz* and the C-130s readied for the return to Egypt, the bus and its passengers were released. Desert One was clouded with fine desert sand. At his position in a Hercules transport, Sergeant Joseph J. Beyers waited for takeoff. "We had all this dust coming down from the rotors and all our dust comes right up at them from our engines . . . there was just too much dust and stuff flying around."

There was no visibility in the morning dust. The pilot turned, Beyers remembers, but "in the wrong direction . . . that's when he hit us."

One of the rotors sliced into the fuselage of Beyers' C-130, and instantly both aircraft burst into flame. Although something fell on him and knocked him down, Beyers reached the crew door and, to those watching, he appeared to be "catapulted out." Unconscious and severely burned, he was pulled away from the blazing wreckage. Ammunition inside the planes began detonating, making it dangerous to attempt any rescues. five men died in the Hercules and three in the Sea Stallion. Eight dead: the fiasco had become a tragedy.

The burned bodies and the four remaining Sea Stallions were abandoned, and the Americans left Desert One. Hours later, Iranian Air Force F-4 Phantoms shot up the charred wreckage, killed one of the Iranian guards, and wounded two others. Ayatollah Sadegh Khalkhali appeared soon after to supervise the removal of the bodies, which were eventually returned for burial in the United States. In Tehran, where there were no longer any imprisoned Americans, masses of enraptured Iranians gathered around the Embassy to celebrate the latest in humiliations of the United States.

Jimmy Carter not only suffered personally, but diplomatically and politically as well. TASS, the official news outlet for the Soviets, suggested that Carter had been willing "to sacrifice for his election interests." Some Western nations, friendly to the United States, were critical of not being informed of what many regarded as a military action. Carter insisted that the mission had been designed as a rescue attempt, not a military strike.

Most political rivals subdued their criticism; many Americans sympathized with the harried President, for he had satisfied their need for some kind of decisive move after five months of what appeared to be inaction. Before the mission, presidential aspirant Ronald Reagan himself had called for action; he and fellow Republicans intimated that, in office, they would do something—but presented no rescue plan of their own. After the failure, he kept quiet. Another aspirant, Edward Kennedy, said, "Whatever our other differences, we are one nation in our commitment to the hostages, our concern for their families, and our sorrow for the brave men who gave their lives trying to rescue their fellow citizens."

The families of some of the hostages were not so restrained. "He's trying to kill them," Sara Rosen sobbed to newsmen after the failure of the mission. Her son, Barry, was one of the hostages. Bonnie Graves, wife of hostage John Graves, said the attempt "endangered not only the lives of the hostages but

Photos courtesy of United Press International

In Tehran, just outside the gates of the occupied embassy, Iranians, civilian and military, celebrate the news of the failed rescue mission.

Ayatollah Sadegh Khalkhali, a judge in the Revolutionary Court, observes the uncovering of the body of one of the Americans killed in the failed rescue attempt. The bodies were put on display in the embassy.

A distressed President Jimmy Carter after the failure at Desert One. The setting is San Antonio, Texas, where Carter visited four of the servicemen injured in the mission. Congressman Chick Kazan stands at Carter's right.

the peace of the entire world." George Holmes, Sr., father of one of the Marines killed at Desert One and an attorney in Pine Bluff, Arkansas, probably spoke for him when he said, "It was a risk worth taking."

If the rescue mission had succeeded, it is possible that Carter would have been reelected—which led one senior Democratic senator to say, "The whole thing has heavy political overtones . . . no one would have done it who was not running for the presidency." Perhaps its most positive effect, as pointed out by Brzezinski, was to relieve "public pressure for a large-scale American military action against Iran and thus permitted the resumption of our diplomatic efforts, reinforced by sanctions, to obtain the release of our people."

On April 25, the Ayatollah had the last word, when he threatened to have all the hostages slaughtered if Carter attempted another "silly maneuver."

The maneuver cost Carter dearly: relations with Western Europe and Japan (his most faithful allies) were strained; the attempt had raised questions about American military readiness (already in disesteem after Vietnam) and American technology. Finally, although the Soviets had not actually moved into the area, their position in the Mideast was strengthened (Moscow offered to come to the aid of Iran if the United States initiated a blockade); the adversary relationship between Islamic Iran and Russia had begun to thaw.

For whatever reasons, Carter had gambled and lost. If the helicopter debacle had not occurred, what might have happened? What if there had been more helicopters? What if someone had thought to provide them with dust filters? What if they had gotten to Tehran? No one will ever know, but some analysts conclude that the body count would have been considerably higher than eight.

The hostages, unaware of the failed attempt to rescue them, were bewildered by their dispersion; many were moved more than once, and they rarely knew where they were, since they were blindfolded and manacled in the vehicles. After the debacle, negotiations between the United States and the several Iranian governments (if they could be called that) virtually ended. The hostages faced another nine months of torturous, threatening captivity. One group, imprisoned in a jail, heard the cries of Iranian prisoners being tortured by the Ayatollah's faithful followers and dispensers of Islamic justice.

Possibly knowledge of the release of Richard Queen for medical reasons, on July 11, 1980, might have given them some hope, but their captors did not inform them of it. (They learned of it later, when they were given an expurgated copy of a newsmagazine; the militants had ripped out the news section but had neglected to cut out the table of contents.) Nor did the death of the Shah, on July 27, improve their lot; death had cheated the Iranians of their vengeance and they felt frustrated and thwarted.

In characteristic language, Tehran Radio opened its announcement of his death with: "Mohammed Reza Pahlevi, the bloodsucker of the century, has died at last." This was followed by a musical interlude.

"Behold how history repeats itself," the report continued. "The treacherous Shah dies next to the tomb of the ancient Egyptian Pharaohs and in the asylum of Sadat in disgrace, misery and vagrancy, in the same state of despair in which the Pharaoh and his army were drowned in the sea . . . Upon the orders of God, Pharaoh's body was thrown out of the sea so that it may serve as a lesson to future generations, and a symbol of Satan and all that was Satanic . . ."

The broadcast closed with a threat: "Those who ignore the divine words of God, are none but the Pharaohs of our time like Carter, Sadat, Begin, and Saddam Hussein [Iraq's president], who do not seem to take a lesson from such dark dooms."

The first real break in the stalemate came in September, when the former West German ambassador to Iran, Gerhard Ritzel, via sources in Iran, informed the State Department that the Iranians were ready to end the hostage crisis quickly. This surprising switch was verified on September 12, when the Ayatollah himself made a radio address in which, after castigating and vilifying the United States, set forth conditions for the release of the hostages:

1) The return of the Shah's wealth in American banks;
2) Cancellation of financial claims against Iran;
3) Ending the freeze on Iranian assets in the United States;
4) Guarantees of no U.S. interference in Iranian affairs.

While Deputy Secretary of State Warren Christopher met secretly in Bonn with the Germans' Iranian contact (believed to be Sadek Tabbatabi, brother-in-law of the Ayatollah's son), another complication muddied the negotiations. On September 22, war between Iran and Iraq broke out, with the bombing by Iraqi aircraft of ten airfields in Iran. By the following day, the major oil center at Abadan was in flames and Iraqi troops began moving into Iran.

The hostages learned that something was happening when they heard, ironically, the strains of the Sousa march "Stars and Stripes Forever" blasting through the streets. The prisoners still in Tehran also heard about the bombing of Tehran Airport on the opening day of the war. The outbreak canceled a second meeting between Christopher and Tabbatabi.

Iranian president Abolhassan Bani-Sadr blamed the invasion on America and warned that "if the international situation gets worse, it could get worse for the hostages." As commander-in-chief of the Iranian Army, Bani-Sadr made a point of visiting the battlefront, rather than remaining in potentially explosive Tehran. He left the negotiations to Prime Minister Mohammed Ali Rajai (who would replace Bani-Sadr as President in July 1981). Bani-Sadr eventually sought refuge in France, and Rajai was assassinated in September 1981. Foreign Minister Sadegh Ghotbzadeh was executed by firing squad, for plotting the death of Khomeini, in September 1982. It was obviously safer at the front.

With the distraction of a war with Iraq, the hostages became more burdensome to the Iranians. Some of the students left to go to the front, where some eventually died. While the newly formed Parliament debated the hostages' fate,

Iran announced that Algerian representatives would serve as intermediaries in ironing out the conditions for their release. Two days later, on November 4, 1980, former film actor Ronald Reagan was elected President of the United States. In the week that followed, Warren Christopher was in Algeria to work with the Algerian negotiators. Most of the talk, curiously, did not touch on philosophy, culture, or principles, but money.

The hostages noticed some change. Their captors were defensive, but less hostile. Some of the bolder Americans predicted defeat for Iran in the war with Iraq and that their preoccupation with holding them hostage had left them open to invasion from their traditional enemy to the west.

They took heart, too, in noting that the American trade sanctions were having an effect: long blackout periods were in force in Tehran, food and kerosene were more scarce.

The convoluted negotiations dragged on, and the trapped Americans spent their second Christmas in captivity; two days before, when talks broke down, the Iranians threatened to put them on trial after new Secretary of State Edmund Muskie called a revision of the conditions, a demand for $24 billion, "unreasonable." (Iran finally settled for $7.9 billion.)

By mid-January 1981, the refractory Iranian Parliament authorized the Iranian Government (whatever that was at the moment) to continue to bargain for the release of the hostages. Hopeful rumors spread among them. On January 19, a familiar figure reappeared, "Mary, the Terrorist," who had interviewed hostages in the early weeks of their captivity. With her was a man who informed them that "candidates for freedom" would be interviewed for television. Good words would hasten their release, it was implied. A number of the hostages were certain it was just another media event "to build up America's hopes and dash them again."

On January 19 an agreement was officially announced; the next day marked the inauguration of President Ronald Reagan. Obviously the date was set to render one final humiliation to "the great Satan Carter." He could not greet the freed hostages as President and also attend the inaugural. The Ayatollah fixed it so that when he did meet with these people whose freedom he had worked for and anguished over, he would be Jimmy Carter, ex-President, from Plains, Georgia.

As the hostages, almost in disbelief, geared up for their release, there was a final hitch; this one, however, was contributed by the American bankers involved in the complex negotiations. Under Secretary of the Treasury Robert Carswell managed to eliminate the two technical additions which incensed the Iranian negotiators, chief of whom was Behzad Nabavi. On January 20, all the monies due Iran were placed in the Algerian escrow account in the Bank of England, and eighteen minutes after Ronald Reagan was sworn in as President of the United States, the hostages—after 444 days—were set free.

Prime Minister Rajai proclaimed the entire incident a great "victory" for Iran. But Bani-Sadr's newspaper, *Islamic Revolution*, printed an editorial which questioned this. "Why make such a noise about victory for Iran and announce it to the world when what we got from the United States was what belonged to us in the first place? Besides, many of our demands were not met. Out of all the Shah's money which rightfully belongs to the people, they didn't even throw us a used dollar bill."

Such quibbling did not concern the hostages. They could not quite believe that they were going home—their captors had lied to them before. But when, that evening, they were being given comprehensive medical examinations by a team of doctors who introduced themselves with "We're the Algerians," they believed it.

They even believed the Iranian who told them, "O.K., it's time. Everybody's going home."

It might be noted that the Algerians took certain precautions while in Tehran. When their Air Algérie 727s were being refueled at Mehrabad Airport, they carefully checked the fuel; they accepted no food from the Iranians, but bought their own in Tehran, and, once aloft, switched the refueling stop from Ankara to the U.S. Air Force base near Athens.

Like Carter, the hostages were treated to a final humiliation by the Iranians. They were blindfolded, stacked into buses and trucks "like cordwood," and driven to the airport. There some were roughed up and verbally abused and heard the chant "Bad, bad, America's bad!"

Aboard their 727, they continued in a state of incredulity; this was exacerbated by their long stay on the runway before the craft was cleared for takeoff.

End of an ordeal: the former hostages land at Rhein-Main Air Force Base, Germany, after being flown out of Iran to Algiers. Next stop for these returnees will be home, the United States.

United Press International

(A second 727 carried Algerian guards and, supposedly, the hostages' luggage, but that was stolen en route to the airport.) It was a long, tense wait, and it was not until they heard the engines turning over that they were ready to believe it was all true.

The released captives were flown to Algiers and turned over to their own countrymen, then flown to Wiesbaden, Germany, for further medical checks. It was in Algiers, when they were to have appeared on television, that the first inkling of their treatment and the bitterness it engendered surfaced. Embarrassed Algerians, Islamics themselves, turned off the cameras when one of the hostages said, "I hope Allah never answers their prayers."

In Wiesbaden, before they were flown home, many continued to speak out. Malcolm Kalp, who had spent 373 days in solitary confinement after a failed escape attempt, said, when he heard the Iranians had received $8 billion in what he saw as ransom money, "I'd give them $8 billion worth of bombs." Army medic Donald R. Hohman, whose West German wife was a nurse at Wiesbaden, spoke for many when he said, "All I want to see is a scorched-earth policy in Iran."

Their bitter comments led to demands that the agreement with Iran not be

On January 27, 1981, the national Christmas tree, at the White House, is lighted for the first time since the hostage captivity began. Fireworks also celebrated the safe return of the fifty-one Americans.

United Press International

honored, in reprisal. But Reagan refused to cancel the accords with Iran. There were sensible reasons: it would embarrass the government of West Germany and the Algerians who had worked so hard to achieve the release. Intensified estrangement would jeopardize the flow of oil and Iran's strategic position in the Persian Gulf (i.e., virtual invitation for intercession by the Soviets). In addition, U.S. banks and commercial firms with holdings or outstanding claims against Iran would suffer.

So the hostages, fifty-one embassy personnel and one businessman, Jerry Plotkin, trapped inside the building during the takeover, were joyously received as heroes by their fellow countrymen. Their inhuman ordeal was over, but long-range effects, emotionally, would take their toll. Some were strangers to their children; marriages were strained; some, who appeared to have cooperated with their captors, felt guilt and were shunned by fellow sufferers. It would not be easy, but the worst was over. They conveyed little affection for the Iranians and Iran.

When budget officer Bruce W. German was asked if he would be willing to return to Iran, his answer was a simple and rancorous "Only in a B-52."

With the hostages home safe, Americans followed the war between Iraq and Iran with grim satisfaction during the first several weeks of the fighting. Strong man, dictator, Iraqi President Saddam Hussein, however, was no friend of the West and, when it suited his purposes, was an unabashed client of the Soviets. A protégé of Nasser, he, like Libya's Qaddafi, hoped to become the leader of the Arab world one day.

With Egypt isolated from the rest of the Arab world after Sadat's recognition of Israel, Syria in constant quasi-civil war, and Iran in disarray over the hostage crisis, Hussein saw his opportunity to fill the vacuum in the leadership in the Persian Gulf, even all of the Middle East.

Iran was the thorn. If the Ayatollah spread his Islamic revolution, it would be most troublesome for Hussein. Although Iraq's majority was Shi'ite, his ruling party was Sunni. Khomeini harbored scant affection for Iraqi rulers, who had banished him after fourteen years of exile. Hussein's contention with Iran dated back to the reign of the Shah. In 1975, in a humiliating agreement, Iraq agreed to relinquish control of the eastern half of Shatt-al-Arab, the combined estuary of the Tigris and Euphrates, leading into the Persian Gulf; in exchange, the Shah promised to stop supporting Iraq's Kurdish rebels. As secretary and second in command to the President (Major General Ahmed Hassan al-Bakr), Hussein was a disgruntled signatory to the despised accord.

It was known by then that Hussein was the man behind the man, and after Bakr resigned ("ill health"), in 1979, Hussein became President. He then bided his time. He slackened his Soviet ties, subdued the Kurds, and began shopping the Western markets for weaponry with Iraq's petroleum money. Hus sein's relations with the United States were not cordial, based on the United States' support of Israel and its nonrecognition of the PLO.

On September 17, 1980, it was announced by Hussein before Parliament and broadcast over Baghdad Radio that the border treaty was "null and void." He cited the Islamic rulers of Iran's "violating good-neighborly relations" since the Shah's overthrow, in 1979. Actually border clashes and air strikes had been reported as early as September 2 on a three-hundred-fifty-mile stretch from Qasr-i-Shirin (Iran) in the north to Basra (Iraq) in the south. Iraqis had reported that they had taken some ninety square miles, which, it was claimed, should have been returned to Iraqi sovereignty at the time Hussein and Pahlevi signed the border agreement.

In his address, Hussein stated that there was little difference between the regimes of the Shah and of the Ayatollah. "Both," he said, "engaged in expansionist designs against Iraqi and Arab territory [reminding his listeners that Khomeini was Persian, not Arab]." He charged, too, that the Ayatollah was merely using Islam to shield "Persian expansionist ambitions."

Hussein soon took action after abrogating the border agreement. On September 22, 1980, the border skirmishing flared and burst into real war.

Before he unleashed the attack, Hussein let some of his Arab neighbors know what the objective was. Iraq would reimpose its sovereignty over Shatt-al-Arab, would seize more than three hundred square miles around the town of Musian (adjacent to the oil-producing province of Khuzistan), take over a portion of the Abadan refinery, and occupy three barren islands (of strategic value) in the Strait of Hormuz that the Shah had taken in a move of military expansion in 1971.

The early headlines brought comfort to those who wished the Ayatollah's Iran ill. The initial air strikes, made by Iraqi pilots in MiG 25s and 27s, left a shambles of burning Boeing 707s and 747s. Two MiGs strafed Mehrabad Airport, east of Tehran, concentrating on the military section, and shot up an Iranian Air Force 707, one of the Shah's legacies. Other strikes in the vicinity of the cities of Shiraz, Bushire, Dizful, and Ahwaz, among others, left a trail of black smoke columns rising into the air.

Iran responded with a call for mobilization, which the Iraqi Revolutionary Council described in these words: "The Persian racists have announced a general mobilization and closed Iranian air space, thus affirming they have expanded the circumference of the military conflict and brought the situation to total war." Soon after, it was claimed that Iraqi troops had taken strips of land on the east (i.e., Iranian) bank of Shatt-al-Arab and had moved toward, and surrounded, Abadan and nearby Khorramshahr. Abadan had been bombed and shelled.

The Iranian Air Force, in their still-flying McDonnell F-4 Phantoms, replied in kind, striking with rockets at the capital, Baghdad, and several Iraqi oil centers. At Basra, across Shatt-al-Arab, just inside Iraq, the air attack killed four Americans and four Britons.

The United Nations swung into action and urged the two nations to stop and settle the issue by negotiation. The United States, although accused of being behind Hussein's actions, declared neutrality and continuing concern for the fate of the hostages. However, most of the world concern was over the oil supply, for two of the most prolific oil producers had begun destroying one another's facilities.

Although not exactly caught off guard, the Ayatollah's Iran was handicapped by self-inflicted problems. Khomeini acted with dispatch by suspending the trials of the military accused of plotting against his revolution. Old soldiers came out of retirement, and even the Shah's son and heir, nineteen-year-old Crown Prince Reza, a fighter pilot, offered to return to Iran. He was not encouraged to do so.

The Ayatollah went on radio to deny Iraqi reports of his death and informed the once-despised soldiers that he appreciated the activities of the reawakened Iranian Army and assured them "that if you are killed, you will go to heaven."

To the majority of Shi'ites in Iraq he said, "If you kill Saddam before we execute him, stab him in the back. Paralyze the economy. Stop paying taxes. This is a war between Islam and blasphemy." His own soldiers, expecially the Shi'ite Muslims in the Khorramshahr area, fought with unexpected intensity, causing one Iraqi major to comment that his men were fighting against "fanatics." The less-inspired, more-professional soldiers in the vicinity of Ahwaz pinned down Iraqi troops with artillery fire. Claims and counterclaims were issued from Baghdad and Qom-Tehran, generally canceling one another out. Khorramshahr was taken, and then it wasn't; Abadan fell, and then it didn't. Attempts at mediating were rejected by Khomeini.

By early October the fighting in Khuzistan Province around Dizful, Ahwaz, Khorramshahr, and Abadan seemed to be stalemated. Military analysts predicted a long "war of attrition." The stiff fighting by the Iranian Army had evidently been further stiffened by zealous revolutionary guards sent to the front to assure their dedication to the Ayatollah's war against Hussein. Despite the deadlock, Khomeini vowed that Iran would not only take back the territory that the Iraqis occupied but would continue on into their country and "punish the Criminal Baath regime for its crimes."

Around this same time, the ominous news came that King Hussein of Jordan had gone to Baghdad to meet with Iraqi officials and to assess the Iran-Iraq situation. He was the sole Arab leader who then supported Iraq, and during the visit he pledged to "provide military support to Iraq if needed." (In February of the next year Hussein kept his word; Libya had already come out in favor of Iran, but the support was mostly verbal. Syria later countered the Jordanian move by filtering Soviet arms into Iran.)

The curious nature of the war was illustrated on October 8, 1980, when Iranian troops shelled and set fire to five ships, sinking three, in the port of Khorramshahr. Iraqi sources had claimed the city to be under their control days before. At least twenty crewmen were lost in the shelling and sinking. The three ships that went down were registered in India, China, and Panama.

Later in October, Prime Minister Mohammed Ali Rajai came to New York to address the UN Security Council to put Iran's case before the world. He refused to discuss the subject of the hostages and, when he did speak, charged that his nation was the victim of American-inspired aggression.

Two days later, on October 19, word came from Tehran admitting that Iraqi forces had sealed off Abadan and had made gains near Khorramshahr. Baghdad joyfully announced expected "good tidings" during the Muslim feast of Id al-Adha (commemorating the willingness of Abraham to sacrifice his son at the command of God). Although the Koran prohibits the spilling of blood during the four-day holiday, neither side observed that holy edict. Nor were the peacemaking attempts of the UN envoy, Olof Palme, former Prime Minister of Sweden, of any avail.

A war without any foreseeable resolution and with few highlights, the Iran-Iraq conflict moved off the front pages and into the inside pages of the newspapers. There were reports of casualties, but, like the victory claims, they were not reliable. The numbers were not dramatically substantial, and the fighting was sporadic, measuring gains in yards. To most Americans, the fate of the hostages was more newsworthy than the vaunting of belligerents, each claiming a direct line to Allah. The Iran-Iraq war appeared to be a personal quarrel between Khomeini and Hussein.

However, by the end of the year Iraq claimed a "qualified victory," since its forces occupied most of the town of Khorramshahr and encircled the oil-refining city of Abadan and the capital of Khuzistan, Ahwaz. Large forces were involved with minor military action. Iraqi commanders were not ready for a major head-on confrontation, and the Iranians were content to fight a kind of guerrilla war. As the rainy season came, both sides dug in, and now and then exchanged artillery fire.

The new year—1981—brought little change. UN envoy Palme paid a second peacemaking visit to the two warring countries, but without results. The headline-producing news of the month was the release of the Americans from their long imprisonment in Iran.

That development had little effect on the war, although it led to further

United Press International

At the right, Abolhassan Bani-Sadr, President of Iran during most of the hostage ordeal and at the time the war with Iraq erupted. Although he had been one of Khomeini's favorites, Bani-Sadr fled to France when he fell out of favor with the Ayatollah.

disarray in the Iranian Government, which eventually toppled President Bani-Sadr. (In July he hijacked an Iranian Air Force plane and fled to Paris.) The frustrating stalemate finally came to a head in Iraq. A leading member of the Revolutionary Command Council, Tariq Aziz, announced a change in Iraq's war aims. Instead of merely taking back its territories, Iraq would seek the dismemberment of politically unsettled Iran. A heavy spring offensive was intimated and, Aziz made clear, Iraq would lend all possible support to dissident minorities inside Iran, notably the Kurds and Arabs. (Iraqi soldiers had for some time been assisting the Kurds fighting the Iranians in Kurdistan, in northern Iran, and Arabs in the oil-rich Khuzistan Province, in the South.)

That Iran was in trouble was evidenced by the allocation of $200 million "to buy kerosene, gasoline, and motor oil from abroad," an unusual action for the world's second-largest petroleum exporter. Khomeini attributed this chaos, and the fact that Iran had not conquered the invading Iraqis, to Iran's political bickering, Bani-Sadr's more rational secular followers versus the mullahs.

Awaiting the end of the rainy season as an artillery duel boomed overhead, an Iraqi colonel told Washington *Post* reporter David B. Ottoway, "Khomeini is a dodger and a liar . . . We will cut the Iranians' throats. We will hang onto their land until they recognize our rights [control of Shatt-al-Arab]."

The war dragged on; after one full year, making it the longest Middle East conflict (if the Arab-Israeli War is subdivided into five) in contemporary history, it was still a standoff. Western newsmen found it a confusing conflict to report (American journalists were excluded from the war zones), particularly since contradictory communiqués about the same places were issued by both sides. It was unlike any war in memory.

"This is an oriental war," a Jordanian minister to Baghdad commented, "not a war that can be interpreted by the analytical standards of the West. It is not economics and military equipment that will determine it as much as it is the determination, and survivability, of the two men leading Iraq and Iran."

However, Western analysts estimated that in the first year Iran had lost some $100 billion in oil income, and Iraq about $50 billion; this would have an adverse effect on the living conditions of their peoples. Inside Iran, thousands of people rallied at Freedom Square, Tehran, to mark the first anniversary of the war. (Iraq celebrated it on September 4, claiming that it had begun on that day, not the twenty-second, when Iran shelled the border town of Khanaqin.) The Iranians carried banners emblazoned with "Death to America" even as firing squads eliminated seventeen more dissidents, members of the People's Mujahedeen Party, which opposed the Ayatollah. No one mentioned, in either Tehran or Baghdad, that the first year of the war had cost each nation more than ten thousand lives.

A surprising development occurred only days later (it was denounced as a lie by Iraq), when Iran announced that it had broken the siege of Abadan and had pushed Iraqi troops over the Karun River, north of the town. Iraq conceded that its forces had made a "tactical withdrawal" of ten miles under pressure of Iranian troops, probably the highly motivated Revolutionary Guards. No journalists were permitted in the area, so that, yet again, the communiqués did not correspond: Iraq claimed 118 Iranian dead and 23 of its own; Iran claimed 1,000 Iraqi dead, 70 Iranian dead, and 1,521 prisoners.

The battle was not confined to Abadan; there was also fighting in the streets of Tehran and executions of the guerrillas in that city and in Isfahan. Fifty-seven members of the People's Mujahedeen, the Islamic underground group opposing Khomeini's fundamentalist regime, were executed in Tehran and more than 50 in Isfahan (these executions raised the death toll to over 1,350 since the fall of Bani-Sadr, in June). The announcement of the pullback at Abadan did not end the skirmishing in the streets of Tehran. Also from Tehran came word that Iranian forces were poised to begin their drive on battered Khorramshahr.

The tide of the sluggish war had turned to Iranian advantage. Despite financial aid from Saudi Arabia, beginning in January 1982, Jordanian volunteers pledged to join in the defense of "Arabism and the Arab nation" to gain battlefront experience in preparation for "the number one enemy of the Arab World, Israel," and Iran made crucial advances along the 380-mile front. By the end of 1981 their forces claimed to be inside Iraq on the northern end of the front, at Qasr-e-Shirin; in this they were aided by Kurdish rebels. During the last months of the year, Iranian artillery barrages increased, because Iranian factories had become more active, with Soviet supplies filtered through Eastern Europe and even Israel. The zeal of the Revolutionary Guards, according to an Iraqi dissident who had fled to Iran, was "unbelievable . . . They are fanatic." He had viewed battle film in which he saw the youthful Guards clear a minefield for advancing troops by simply charging through, blowing up the mines—and themselves. Other sources noted that the earlier tensions between the fervid Revolutionary Guards and the more professional Iranian Army officers had lessened, so that the Iranians operated more cohesively and effectively.

Neither combatant made much use of air power, but relied on artillery exchanges primarily, and infantry pushes. Neither wished to raise the issue of bombing cities with civilian populations or even major attacks on oil installations. In this area, Iran had the problem of a shortage of replacement parts for the American-made Cobra helicopters and the F-4 and F-14 fighters and fighter-bombers. (One estimate, in January 1982, said about nine of the original seventy-seven F-14s and about fifty of the ninety F-4s were still serviceable.)

By March, the Iraqi Government admitted that Iranian attacks on the Basra facilities west of Khorramshahr on Shatt-al-Arab, as well as offshore oil facilities in the Persian Gulf, were costly. Iraqi Deputy Oil Minister Abdul Monem Samouri estimated that repairing the damage might require more than five years, an unusual admission in a war in which no one admitted setbacks.

At the end of March, Hussein admitted that the Iranians had forced his troops out of the Susa-Dizful area. In nine days of hard fighting, Iranian troops pushed the Iraqis back twenty-four miles, within ten miles of the border. In this push, Tehran Radio announced that three Iraqi brigades had been "completely destroyed" (twenty-five thousand dead or wounded, fourteen thousand prisoners) and that a "glorious victory for Islam" had been gained. The Iranians were so certain of victory that they broadcast the attack in advance on the same network, ordering the Revolutionary Guards to be ready to move at 3 A.M. and "to attack the last bunkers of the enemy and take back from them all the land and villages and towns, and so that you can define the country's borders." This was not quite achieved, but even Hussein had to concede the "victory."

There was more intense fighting and on May 24 the startling news that Iranians had retaken Khorramshahr, claiming that all of the thirty thousand Iraqi troops surrendered and that their commander, Colonel Ahmed Zaidan, had been killed. (The communiqués from Baghdad reported only that there was fighting in and around the port city and nothing about casualties or captivity.)

This major defeat for Hussein brought more petrodollars from Saudi Arabia and other oil-producing countries opposed to Khomeini's revolution. Strangely, Iraq's nominal friend and chief source of weapons, the Soviet Union, provided Iran with large shipments of arms via Syria. Hussein's desperation was revealed in his willingness to accept aid from Egypt, with which he had broken since its peace treaty with Israel. The word for him from Tehran was not good: not only did a cease-fire depend on a complete withdrawal of all Iraqi troops from Iran, but there would be no peace without Hussein's downfall.

Hussein got the message, but soon learned that Khomeini had read it differently. On June 20, Hussein announced the beginning of the withdrawal from Iran. Khomeini went on Radio Tehran the next day and countered with a declaration that the evacuation would not end their war. There were three other conditions demanded by Iran: an international commission to be formed to assign war guilt, an assessment and assurance of payment for war damages (said to be $150 billion), and the return to Iraq of some 120,000 Iraqi refugees of the Shi'ite sect and of Persian descent in Iranian exile. It appeared that Hussein was surely at the end of his rule except that, only ten days before, the Arab world had been thrown into shock and dismay by the Israeli invasion of Lebanon. To topple a strong Arab leader, despite his failure in the war with Iran, would only have upset the Persian Gulf situation even more. Hussein continued to have important Arab backing, and so his faltering government faltered on.

Even as the fighting went on, Iran made a curious request: passage through Iraq for Iranian troops so that they could fight Israel in Lebanon. This was accepted on the condition that it be followed by an Iraqi-Iranian cease-fire. Iran rejected the condition and the fighting continued.

Then on July 14 came the announcement that Iranian troops had overrun "the first bunkers of the enemy." The Iranian invasion of Iraq had begun in the South. The official word from Iran was that the invasion had been launched "to perfect" their defenses and to prevent "further Iraqi and other United States lackeys' aggression." Within hours, word had come through that the Iranians had penetrated into Iraq, in the vicinity of Basra, to depths of from six to ten miles. In retaliation, Iraqi aircraft attacked the cities of Ilam, Bakhtaran, and Khorramabad, east of Baghdad and southwest of Tehran. Casualties were reported in "the hundreds."

Khomeini went on Radio Tehran, calling on Iraqis to rise up against the "blasphemous regime" of Hussein. Meanwhile his troops moved into Iraq on a fifteen-mile front, within five miles of Basra, Iraq's major oil city. Some Western analysts sensed that the invasion was only the first phase of a drive through Iraq in an attempt by Iran to assist Syria and Lebanon in a war on Israel. In the East a Shi'ite victory, and a new government in Baghdad, would disrupt the Sunni-dominated Arab governments of Saudi Arabia, Jordan, the United Arab Emirates, Kuwait, and Egypt.

Severe fighting brought heavy casualties—although figures, as usual, were contradictory. An advance by the Iranians was announced by Iraq as a "planned withdrawal" and the setting of a trap. The Iranian commander of ground forces, Colonel Sayyad Shirazi, in an interview with a reporter of the Tehran *Ettelaat*, said that their objective was Baghdad and the overthrow of Hussein. "Our attention and target is to find him," he concluded, "and also find an overland route to reach Jerusalem."

That was in mid-July 1982, after which the Iraq-Iran war bogged down again. By the fall of the year, Iranian troops had neither found Hussein nor reached Baghdad. As for the "overland route" to Jerusalem: mere military fantasy. Both nations celebrated the second anniversary of their war in characteristic fashion—on different dates and with conflicting official statements. On September 22 a parade was held in Tehran in celebration, the beginning of a "war week."

Iranian sources dramatically announced that on that day Iranian fighters had driven a lone MiG-25 out of Iranian skies before it could bomb Tehran. During the ceremonies, Khomeini's son read a message from his father mocking Hussein for his failure to cripple Iran's oil production. The Iraqi leader had declared Kharg Island, a loading point for oil tankers, a war zone, the intent being to keep foreign shipping away (it did not work). Iraqi aircraft also bombed the island five times during the two years of war, causing heavy damage but no stoppage.

Also, the Iraqis would not admit that they even had MiG-25s in their air force. So the vaunting, fantasy war (with its realistic toll of lives) dragged into its third year.

In the Middle East, it would seem the most elusive fantasy is that of peace. How apposite is the observation by Tacitus: *Ubi solitudinem faciunt, pacem appellant* ("They make a desert and call it peace"). A vast desert was there from the beginning, but its dwellers appear to be intent on expanding it throughout their world—to the globe itself.

4

Terrorism: The Clandestine War

During the June 1982 incursion into Lebanon to seek out and extirpate the Palestine Liberation Organization, Israeli dispatches invariably referred to PLO members not as guerrillas or Palestinians, but as "terrorists." In the West the word had a grim, frightful connotation: sudden, bloody, seemingly senseless and random attacks on airports, airplanes, buses, busy streets, embassies, department stores—anywhere the innocent mingled with whomever the assailants regarded as the enemy.

The Western democracies were particularly alarmed in the late 1960s when a series of apparently unrelated bombings, kidnappings, and assassinations occurred in Western Europe and North America. Common to these assaults were the disconcerting presence of Palestinians and Arabs in the attack teams and the employment of Soviet weapons. When captured and "encouraged" to talk, it was learned that the terrorists had received training in such far-flung places as Cuba, Libya, Beirut, and South Yemen. What manner of soldier—man or woman—were these disturbers of the international peace, these zealous assassins?

Assassin is derived from the Arabic word *hashshashin*—"hashish eaters"—a band of dedicated murderers who belonged to a Shi'ite Ismaili sect that operated out of the mountain fortresses of northern Persia (now Iran), Iraq, and Syria. The word was Latinized and introduced into the English language by the crusaders. Legend has it that these killers were primed for their missions with hashish (a narcotic produced from the hemp plant) as well as more fleshly pleasures (as a preview of the eternal delights awaiting them if they were killed while carrying out their assignments). The sect flourished from around 1090 until 1256, when the Persian branch was wiped out by the Mongols, the Syrian branch by Egyptian Mamluks; the few survivors scattered.

While the organized assassins were annihilated and dispersed, their philosophy of death in a holy (but often political) cause and their modus operandi survived in folklore (e.g., "The Old Man of the Mountain," the legendary story of Hasan Sabbah, the founder of the sect) and practice through the ages.

Clearly, political assassinations were nothing new. Americans were familiar with such historically significant assassinations as that of Abraham Lincoln, the Archduke Franz Ferdinand (which most believed had led to World War I), the mass murder of the Russian Czar, his family, and four other members of the royal household, which marked the dawn of Bolshevism in Russia; Leon Trotsky, exiled from Soviet Russia, was killed in 1940 by a young assassin; the pacifist agitator Mohandas Gandhi was shot in New Delhi eight years later; also in 1948, peacemaker Count Folke Bernadotte was ambushed and killed in Jerusalem.

That mysterious part of the world, the Middle East, had only begun to impinge on the American consciousness with the founding of the State of Israel, in 1948, and certain political-business initiatives that seemed so naturally to flow out of the American experience in the area during World War II—when Iran served both as a conduit and as a buffer between the Soviet Union and the United States. Bernadotte's murder was followed by what appeared to be a rash of assassinations in that troubled, incendiary—and to Americans, remote—corner of the world. In 1951 King Abdullah ibn Hussein of Jordan was slain; in 1958 Iraqi rebels killed King Faisal and his uncle, Crown Prince Abdul; the day after, Premier Nuri as-Said—but all this was in a faroff place, of little concern to the average American.

The full impact of the assassin struck home with the shooting of President John F. Kennedy, in 1963; a haunting, protracted trauma ensued. Bordering on a paralyzing preoccupation, the Kennedy assassination (not to mention an incomprehensible war in Southeast Asia) turned whatever slight attention the average American may have spared to the Middle East, to soul-searching. Meanwhile an Iraqi government had been overthrown and its hapless Premier shot by a firing squad (a more formalized kind of assassination); Nasser was meddling in Syria and in Yemen; Iraq was dealing with its rebellious Kurdish population; Israel and its neighbors Jordan and Syria exchanged accusations and gunfire.

Then, early in 1965, Iranian Prime Minister Hassan Ali Mansour was shot by a student in Tehran.

Fanatical, perhaps drug-crazed individual zealots willing to die for some cause were comprehensible, especially in the arcane, fomenting Middle East.

But when the twentieth-century "terrorist," the urban guerrilla, came on the scene, the tale took a jolting turn. The hit-and-run killings that had flourished in Baghdad, Tehran, and Cairo began to occur in London, Paris, Rome, and eventually, in 1980, Washington, D.C. This was the beginning of the mindless war on the noncombatant, the stroller who just happened to be passing by when the interior of an embassy was blasted into the street or an automobile disintegrated without warning, or who chanced to board the wrong airliner.

The urban guerrilla who studied the Fatah pamphlet entitled *The Revolution and Violence, the Road to Victory* (circa 1967), was imbued with the glory of vengeance and violence. "Violence," he or she learned, "liberates people from their shortcomings and anxieties. It inculcates in them both courage and fearlessness concerning death . . . Violence will purify the individuals from venom, it will redeem the colonized from inferiority complex, it will return courage to the countryman."

Al Fatah was a movement formed, after the occupation of the Gaza Strip in 1956, to continue the fight with Israel. "Fatah" is the reverse acronym of the Arabic name for the group, *Harakat al-Tahrir al-Watani al-Filistini,* namely the "Movement for the Liberation of Palestine." The leader and one of the founders was an ex-engineering student turned guerrilla, Yasir Arafat.

The platform of Dr. George Habash's Popular Front for the Liberation of Palestine makes it clear that "the conflict between the guerrillas and those who strive for a peaceful solution [to the Palestine question] is unavoidable . . . The Arab bourgeoisie and world imperialism are trying to impose a peaceful solution . . . but this suggestion merely promotes the interests of imperialism and Zionism . . ."

On a Soviet-weapons-shopping tour of North Korea, Habash explicated further when he said: "No frontier, be it political, geographic, or moral, can resist

Leaders of the Arab world who reject any kind of peace with Israel: Dr. George Habash, of the Popular Front for the Liberation of Palestine; Libya's Muammar al-Qaddafi; the Palestine Liberation Organization's Yasir Arafat; and Basan Abu Sharif, spokesman for the Popular Front.

United Press International

the action of the people. Nobody is innocent, nobody can be neutral in the world today." Later, upon returning to his home base in Beirut, he announced that "Palestine has joined the European Revolution." His guerrillas, in short, would combine with the "destabilization" (i.e., government-disrupting) forces of the murderous Italian Red Brigades, Germany's Red Army Faction, and other clandestine terrorist groups in a war *for* the people, with those people all too often serving as, in Habash's view, "guilty" bystanders.

The "war in Europe" opened in the summer of 1968, and although Habash was languishing in a Syrian prison at the time, his hand was in on the operation—his good right hand. Another graduate of Beirut's American University, Dr. Wadi Haddad, had dropped out of medicine to join with Habash in an Arab Nationalist Movement, which went underground in 1963. (The two had operated an eye clinic in Amman, Jordan; it also served as a front for their political activities.) After the Six Day War, they formed the Popular Front for the Liberation of Palestine, with Habash as leader and Haddad as operations officer. Driven out of Jordan, they moved to West Beirut, where they set up to continue their war on Israel.

It was Haddad who planned the first strike in Europe, in the summer of 1968: the hijacking of an Israeli El Al plane, in Athens, carrying more than twenty Jewish passengers. They were then transported to Algiers and held hostage—while the world watched—for five weeks. It was a modest beginning, but it worked as a public-relations venture. The incident captured worldwide attention. The El Al hijacking had not resulted in any killing, but its press coverage had been most gratifying to its planners. And the job had been carried out with disciplined precision.

However, Habash and Haddad (and their sometime collaborator Ahmed Jibril, who was probably in on the operation) could not have carried out such a venture without expecting an Israeli response in kind. The shape of things to come should have impressed them after another guerrilla attack occurred on an Israeli airliner at the Athens airport, on December 26, 1968, in which the plane was left burning. Two days later, in retaliation, an Israeli task force demolished thirteen Lebanese airliners at Beirut International Airport. Since Habash commanded his war out of a private domain in West Beirut or Tripoli, Lebanon suffered for his war.

One of Habash's most complex attention-getting actions, on September 6, 1970, involved four airliners, carrying more than six hundred people. All were hijacked (with one exception) over Europe en route to New York. The exception was an Israeli El Al Boeing 707. Two of Habash's commandos, a woman and a man, ran through the aisle brandishing pistols and hand grenades shortly after takeoff from Amsterdam. Their objective was the cockpit, but stringent El Al security policy required that the cabin door be locked.

It was all over very quickly; a steward, Shlomo Wiedler, tackled the male hijacker and was joined by some of the passengers. In the scuffle the commando was fatally wounded and Wiedler was shot and seriously wounded. The woman commando, Leila Khaled, too, was intercepted by the passengers and wrestled to the aisle of the plane; in desperation, she pulled the pin of her hand grenade, which did not detonate. She was overpowered, bound with neckties, and found to be carrying a second grenade.

Captain Uri Bar-Lev then set the plane down, with its 148 passengers, at a London airport. The male commando was already dead; his companion, although injured, was taken into custody. Wiedler was rushed to a London hospital and was later reported out of danger. Two passengers with cuts and bruises, also hospitalized, were reported in satisfactory condition.

The fates of the other three airliners were not so satisfactory. A Pan American 747 with 170 passengers and crew was hijacked shortly after taking off from Amsterdam and, finally, low on fuel, touched down at Beirut International Airport. The hijackers threatened to destroy the plane and everyone in it if a rescue attempt was made. Another American plane, a TWA 707 (with 145 people aboard) was taken over after leaving Frankfurt, and a Swissair DC-8 and its 155 hostages were seized after leaving Zurich. These two planes ended up on an abandoned World War II airfield at Mafrak, in northern Jordan. Not only did the hijackers of the Popular Front for the Liberation of Palestine claim the aircraft, they also assumed control of Mafrak, stating that the area was theirs. This was an affront to Jordanian sovereignty, which was already unhappy with the presence of the Palestinian guerrillas. The threat to blow up the planes and their human cargo involved the Jordanian police and military, as well as attracting television crews and the world press.

Three days later, a BOAC VC-10 was hijacked and joined the 707 and the DC-8 at the Mafrak airstrip. From time to time a few hostages (non-Jewish) were released in groups, until fifty-four hostages remained as insurance for the guerrillas. Their demands for the release of guerrillas imprisoned in Switzerland, West Germany, and Great Britain were met (the hijacking of the VC-10 obtained the release of Leila Khaled). The remaining hostages were then released, and all three of the airliners at Mafrak and the Boeing 747 at Beirut were destroyed—in a blaze of revolutionary glory.

Soon after the planes were destroyed, King Hussein of Jordan decreed martial law, and his new military government was to "restore order and impose the State's authority." Thus was initiated the bloody "Black September" for the Palestinian guerrillas in Jordan and their flight to hapless Lebanon.

In 1972, Arafat's Fatah proclaimed "a challenge on the land of confrontation": Israel itself. The demand was for the freeing of Palestinians imprisoned in Israel for terrorist activities.

The confrontation occurred at Tel Aviv's Lod Airport; the plane was a Belgian Sabena 707. Four hijackers, two men and two women, seized the airliner on the ground, holding its ninety passengers and crew of ten hostage for twenty-three hours.

Israeli Defense Forces soldiers, masquerading in the white coveralls of ground crewmen, were driven to the plane, which had been on the runway overnight and well into the day (May 9, 1972). As members of a Red Cross team passed

Habash's most spectacular hijacking, September 1970. The BOAC VC-10 at "Revolution Air Base," as it was called by the Palestinian guerrillas; in the middle, the American TWA 707; on the right, the Swissair DC-8.

Photos courtesy of Wide World Photos

Palestinian guerrillas (left) joking with Jordanian soldiers in the early phase of the hijacking of the three jet liners. Subsequently they would fight in the "Black September" confrontation unleashed by King Hussein in the wake of the hijacking.

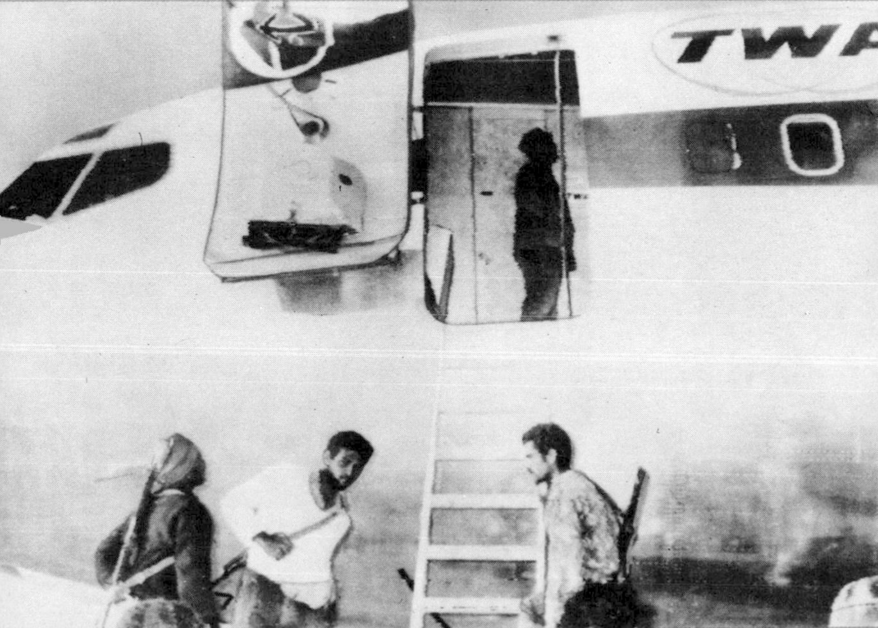

Guerrillas guarding the TWA Boeing 707.

Black September prelude: While Palestinians and Jordanian troops exchange fire around "Revolution Air Base," passengers from the hijacked airliners take refuge in a hotel.

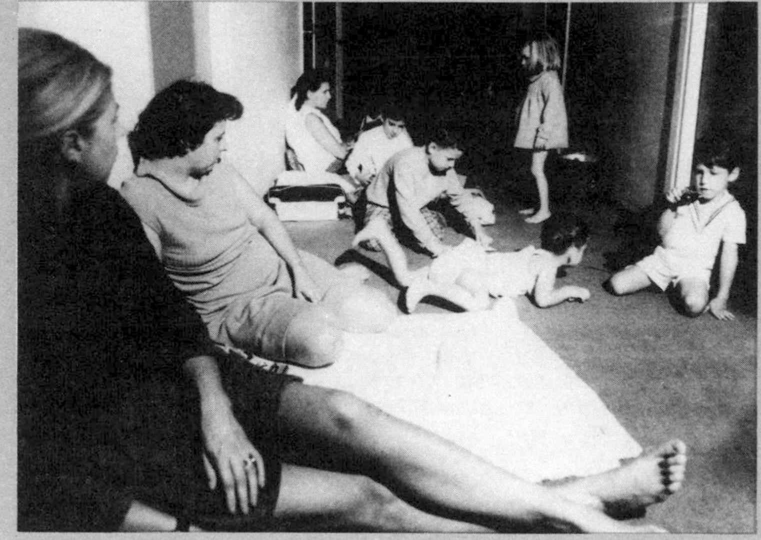

Photos courtesy of Wide World Photos

The burning wreckage of the TWA 707 after being blown up by the Palestinian guerrillas. All passengers were safely evacuated before the explosion.

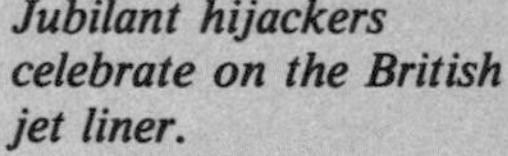

Jubilant hijackers celebrate on the British jet liner.

food and drink into the plane's cockpit, about eighteen soldiers approached it in two airport trolleys. They moved around the Boeing as "mechanics," checking the engine, the wings, and the tires, which had been deflated during the night, making it impossible for the plane to take off.

"This [the work of the false ground crew] went on for about five minutes and we photographers were taking shots," David Rubinger, of the Jerusalem *Post,* reported.

"Suddenly, apparently at a given signal, the 'mechanics' ran for the doors. We stood astounded for a few minutes. Then the next thing we saw was a woman passenger sliding down the wing."

The Israelis rushed the plane with guns drawn, and a brief exchange of shots ended the long ordeal. As passengers dived for the floor, the Israelis shot and killed the two male hijackers and seriously wounded one of the women before she could activate what appeared to be a small bomb. The fourth hijacker, a woman who appeared to be second in command, was captured. Several passengers were also seriously wounded in the shooting. In two minutes the ordeal was over. An Al-Fatah spokesman accused the International Red Cross and the Belgian Government of "deceiving" the hijackers and threatened reprisals against Belgian interests. Fatah also claimed that "several enemy soldiers were either killed or wounded" in the shootout; in fact, three Israeli soldiers were injured, none seriously.

The sequel took a gruesome international turn at the end of the month. Dr. Habash had established a guerrilla training camp at Baalbek, Lebanon, where Japanese "freedom fighters" were treated to courses in the handling of assault rifles, submachine guns, and other weaponry. Three men were chosen to carry out the next foray of the Popular Front for the Liberation of Palestine. They left Lebanon and flew to Frankfurt, then to Paris, where they boarded an Air France jet for Rome. They were met there by the professional revolutionary "Carlos the Jackal" (the well-off son of a Venezuelan doctor, he had been born Ílyich Ramírez Sánchez and was "politically" trained in Cuba and Moscow). "Carlos" provided the Japanese guerrillas with Czech-made VZ-58 assault rifles and hand grenades, which they checked through in their luggage.

The plane set down at Lod Airport around 10:30 P.M. and the three men patiently waited for their luggage in the airport's customs hall.

Suddenly the airport resonated with machine-gun fire and the crack of bursting hand grenades as the three men raked over the crowded arrivals hall with the VZ-58s and lobbed grenades into the throng. As the terrified passengers fell to the floor or tried to take cover, the three men began firing, on the people who were waiting, through a glass partition in the terminal building. The terminal was filled with smoke from the shooting and grenades—and the screams of the wounded.

Within minutes, airport security forces closed in on the guerrillas, who ran onto the airfield, tossing a grenade at a Scandinavian Air Lines plane, damaging an engine. One of the assailants slipped through the security forces net,

Wide World Photos

Jordanian troops carrying off bits of destroyed BOAC, TWA, and Swissair planes as souvenirs. Soon after, King Hussein declared martial law and drove the Palestinians out of Jordan and into Lebanon.

but one was captured (Kozo Okamoto, who received a life sentence for his part in the shootings), and the other committed suicide.

Their brief intrusion had left a carnage of misery in its wake. Lod Airport was closed down, and all operating rooms at Tel Hashomer Hospital were needed to treat the wounded. As maintenance crews sifted through the broken glass, shattered luggage, and blood-stained debris, the first count of casualties to be published accounted for twelve dead and fifty wounded. The final figures were twenty-six dead and seventy-two wounded. Among the dead were sixteen Puerto Ricans who had flown in to visit the birthplace of Christ.

The purpose of this senseless mission was described in the Popular Front's publication *Al-Hadaf* by a spokeswoman for the Japanese Red Army, Fusako Shigenobu. It had been done, she said, "to consolidate the international revolutionary alliance against the imperialists of the world." This curious alliance had already begun to disrupt the governments of Europe, with Italy as one of the main focal points.

The next most devastating airliner attack occurred at Rome's Fiumicino Airport on December 17, 1973. Obviously staged as a protest or an attempt to block the approaching Arab-Israeli peace talks in Geneva after the Yom Kippur War, the target was a Pan American airliner. The Arab guérrillas, it was later learned, had been provided with the funds, weapons, and explosives by Libya's generous Colonel Muammar al-Qaddafi (although he denied it). The five-man hit team attacked the Pan American plane with incendiary bombs, killing thirty-one passengers, who burned to death. They then hijacked a West German plane and ordered the pilot to fly to Athens. There they demanded the release of two Palestinian guerrillas held by the Greek police and, when the authorities did not comply, killed one of the Italian hostages aboard the plane. They took off again and, on December 18, landed in Kuwait, on the Persian Gulf. The hijackers surrendered to the police, and the surviving twelve hostages were freed. Three days later, the Arab-Israeli peace conference convened as planned.

Not all of the spectacular aerial attacks occurred on the ground during the Habash-Haddad campaign for world attention. When, on September 8, 1974, a TWA 707 blew up in flight and crashed into the Ionian Sea, off the coast of Greece, killing all eighty passengers aboard, the Palestinians claimed responsibility for it.

Such mindless killings, in fact, were causing worldwide consternation and not contributing much to the liberation of Palestine. By 1974 it seemed that the Popular Front was turning its attention away from hijackings and concentrating more specifically on the Israelis and the Arab bourgeoisie, though continuing to use Europe as the battleground.

The date was September 5, 1972; the unlikely setting was the international Olympic Games in Munich. Teams from the various countries participating, literally from all over the world, were housed in a specially built Olympic Village. Although patrolled by guards, it was relatively easy to enter the village simply by wearing what appeared to be an athletic uniform or sweat suit.

While the planning of the games proceeded, so did another: a Black September attack on the Israeli team. The European administrator of this guerrilla unit was the personable, well-mannered Hassan Salameh, who operated out of Switzerland and was well known in the international set. (What was not well known was that he was Yasir Arafat's cousin; he had lost his father in a Haganah bombing in 1948.) Through the international revolutionary arms network, Salameh provided his Black Septembrists with guns and ammunition for the Olympics venture. It is very possible that some members of the hit team had worked in and around the site of the games, including Olympic Village, and were familiar with the environment, security, and where the Israeli team was quartered.

Before the games began, veiled threats of possible trouble had circulated. Since there were Arabs, Israelis, Russians, Americans, Finns, et al., some friction was expected; the West German police believed they could handle it.

Early in the morning of September 5, a guard saw some men slipping over the fence into Olympic Village, but he simply assumed they were fun-loving athletes breaking training.

Olympic Village, Munich, West Germany, September 5, 1972. A member of the Palestinian Black September group peers from the balcony of the building in which the Israeli Olympic teams are housed, during what came to be called the Munich Massacre.

West German police attempting to negotiate with a leader of the group holding nine Israelis prisoner (after killing two).

West German police move into Olympic Village; negotiations with the Black Septembrists have been unsuccessful.

Photos courtesy of Wide World Photos

The Black September team consisted of eight men; when they burst into the building housing the sixteen members of the Israeli team, they killed two of them. In the confusion, while wrestling referee Yosef Gottfreund held a door shut, eighteen Israelis managed to escape into the night. Nine others were seized by the Black Septembrists, and were bound hand and foot. Then the negotiations began. Word went out that unless Israel released some two hundred imprisoned guerrillas, the hostages would be killed at regular intervals.

West German Federal Interior Minister Dietrich Genscher tried to negotiate with the guerrillas—he even offered himself and other West German officials, including the chief of police and a former mayor of Munich, to take the place of the Israeli captives—but to no avail. Permitted into the room where the athletes were tied and under submachine-gun guard, Genscher realized the impossibility of attempting to storm the Israeli quarters without causing the hostages to be killed.

When no word came from Israel about the release of the two hundred Palestinian prisoners, the guerrillas demanded transportation to the nearest airport and a jetliner. Their first destination was to be Cairo, but the Egyptian Government refused to accept them. (Egypt had already withdrawn its teams from the games.)

On Wednesday, September 6, the Jerusalem *Post* (as did other newspapers in Israel and Europe acting on a late bulletin from Munich) published the gratifying news that the ordeal was over. The report stated that a team of West German marksmen had killed "four terrorists" and had freed the nine captive Israelis. There was joyous celebration in Israel and a collective sigh of relief from much of the rest of the world that had observed the crisis on television.

Thursday's news was appalling. Because Israel refused to bargain with the terrorists, as did several Arab governments, the solution to the confrontation remained in the hands of the West Germans. After nearly fifteen hours of seemingly hopeless talk, an agreement was reached. A Lufthansa 747 was to be provided for the terrorists and the hostages to take them from Olympic Village to nearby Fürstenfeldbruck Airport. Departure time was to have been about 7 P.M., but the helicopters did not take off from Olympic Village until 10 P.M.

In the darkness, five hundred West German troops encircled the brightly lit airport. Closer in, near the 747, were five snipers with orders to shoot the Arabs. The Israelis, they saw, were blindfolded and tied together; the Arabs never exposed more than four of their number at any time.

Two of the Arabs remained with the helicopters and stood guard over the pilots; another stood on the tarmac, his Kalashnikov ready. These three Arabs were picked off by the snipers, unleashing a wild shooting match and, for the Israelis, massacre.

Once the shots were fired, the five remaining terrorists riddled the control tower, slaughtered five of the Israelis with bursts from their assault rifles, and

A West German policeman, in an athlete's uniform, position two floors above the room (bottom right) where the Palestinians are holding the Israelis.

United Press International

A border-patrol helicopter hovers over Olympic Village; the West German Government has agreed to supply the Palestinians with transportation for them and their hostages to the airport in order to board an airliner for the Mideast.

Wide World Photos

United Press International

The plan to apprehend the Black Septembrists and release their Israeli prisoners went awry during the night of September 6. West German police snipers' firing at the Palestinians resulted in a general shootout in which nine Israelis, five Palestinians, and a policeman died. Four Israelis died in this helicopter when a hand grenade was thrown into the cockpit.

incinerated the remaining four by tossing a hand grenade into their helicopter, which burst into flame. Manacled as they were, the Israelis had no chance.

When the skirmish ended, all nine of the Israelis were dead, as were five Arabs and a policeman who had been on duty in the buildings that the terrorists had blasted with their Kalashnikovs. Three of the Arabs surrendered. (They were released the next month when a Lufthansa airliner was hijacked en route to Frankfurt and threatened with the destruction of plane, crew, and seventeen passengers. The Arabs, ranging in age from twenty to twenty-five, were given a hero's welcome in Tripoli, Libya.)

The 1972 Olympics shootout focused worldwide attention on the Palestinian cause, but the general reaction was revulsion. The chief celebrant of the exploit appears to have been Libya's Colonel Qaddafi, who dispatched a plane to the scene to bring the bodies of the dead gunmen to an Arab land for an "honorable burial." When the three survivors were freed after the Frankfurt hijacking, he treated them to a celebration and a press conference at which the three young men vowed to "fight on." It was also reported that he rewarded PLO leader Yasir Arafat some five million dollars for the Black September action—which, indeed, enabled him to fight on.

An aroused, mourning Israel was not prepared to turn the other cheek. On Thursday, September 7, a boxed item appeared on the first page of the Jerusalem *Post*; it was headed "Speculation on reprisal." It was, in turn, predicated on statements issued after an emergency meeting of the Cabinet, attended by chief of staff David Elazar. The statement called upon "the nations of the world to take effective measures to wipe out Arab terrorism." Israel, it continued, would persevere in its struggle against the terrorist organization and "would not exempt those who aid them from responsibility for the acts of the terrorists."

On September 8, Israeli jets in sweeping waves lashed out at targets in Lebanon and Syria. One attack struck the Fatah youth-training center at Mahr el Bared, north of the Tripoli at the northern end of Lebanon. This was followed, a few days later, by an invasion of southern Lebanon by the Israeli Defense Forces in a thirty-six-hour incursion resulting in the destruction of houses and other buildings occupied by the Palestinian commandos. Although no accurate figures are known, about three hundred died in the attacks, not all of them Palestinians. This led to the setting up of checkpoints along the Lebanese-Israeli border by the Lebanese Government; an agreement was reached between Premier Saeb Salem and Yasir Arafat that would keep the PLO, or any of its various guerrilla units, from attacking Israel from Lebanon. Neither of these expedients held for long; the Palestinians had virtually taken over all of southern Lebanon, and the government of Lebanon was in disarray.

The Israelis did not stop at reprisal raids in the Middle East to avenge the Olympics massacre. Mossad, Israel's international intelligence agency, formed a special team called the "Wrath of God" to seek out those responsible for the killings at Munich. Although Hassan Salameh eluded them for a while, Mossad caught up with Mahmoud Hamshari, the PLO representative in Paris, in early December 1972. While one agent, posing as an Italian journalist, "interviewed" Hamshari in a café, another slipped into his apartment building to make an impression of the lock on the door. During a second "interview" the agent used a key made from the impression and entered the apartment. Working quickly, he placed an electronically controlled bomb in the base of the telephone. They were now ready.

The next day, with Hamshari's wife and daughter absent at the time, the telephone rang in their apartment. Hamshari answered, and as soon as the Mossad agent was assured that he had the PLO leader on the phone, it blew up in his face. He died soon after.

In Paris, on June 28, 1973, members of Mossad placed a pressure bomb under the driver's seat of the automobile of Hamshari's successor, Mohammed Boudia; it detonated as soon as he slipped into the seat. Thus ended the life of one of Europe's most active terrorists and a graduate of Moscow's Lumumba University, where he had befriended the infamous "Carlos."

The Mossad continued its pursuit of the mastermind Salameh (whom they regarded as the most responsible for the Munich slaughter), and in July 1973 thought they had found him, in Lillehammer, Norway. But they were unaccountably wrong and killed a Moroccan waiter instead. Several of the men in the assassination team were arrested and, as far as the Israelis were concerned, this ended their war against the Palestinian guerrillas on foreign soil. Salameh declared that the Palestinians and the Israelis had agreed to stop killing one another except on their own home grounds.

The month after the bungled attempt on Salameh, a renegade group of Palestinians shot up and grenaded a TWA airliner in Athens, killing five passengers and wounding fifty-five. In September, on a tip from Mossad, Italian police arrested five Arabs in an apartment house near the Rome airport. They were armed with two Soviet-made SAM-7s, with which they had intended to shoot down an El Al jetliner as it settled into its landing path over their apartment house. The portable SAM-7 was an innovation to the Western democracies and was studied with great care.

Mossad stayed out of Europe, as promised, as Salameh went about his bloody business. Seven years after Munich, in January 1979, the Mossad found Salameh in Beirut, now one of the most active centers of Palestinian activity. He was blown to bits in a Beirut street by a car bomb.

These deaths did not end the operations of the revolutionaries cooperating with the PLO in Europe. After Boudia died in the automobile explosion, his successor was his former classmate at Moscow's Lumumba University, Ílyich Ramírez Sánchez, code-named "Carlos."

Educated in the techniques of urban guerrilla warfare in Cuba, Moscow, and the Middle East, Ramírez had connections with the Palestinians as well as with Baader-Meinhof revolutionaries in Germany. Vain, egocentric, Ramírez seems to have had little in the way of political conviction; he cooperated with both the Right and the Left—and even managed to get them to cooperate. The unifying element was simple violence.

Carlos, to use his popular name, had a rather bizarre career as gunman and terrorist before he "retired" (Libya, perhaps). The target of one of his first assassination attempts was the London Zionist and president of the Marks and Spencer clothing chain Joseph Edward Sieff. When the butler opened the door on Queen's Grove Street, he was ordered by the lone gunman to lead him to the owner of the house. The sixty-eight-year-old Sieff was number one on Carlos the Jackal's London hit list. (Playwright John Osborne and violinist Yehudi Menuhin were also listed.)

"I ordered the butler to take me to his master, who was in the bathroom," Carlos told an interviewer. "I fired three times, but only one bullet hit him, on the upper lip. Generally, I fire three bullets, which kill instantly. But this fellow was lucky. Only one bullet got him, and his teeth checked the shock. So he escaped death." The unsuccessful assassination also ended Carlos' London venture.

Carlos' chief aide, Michel Moukarbal, a protégé of Dr. Wadi Haddad, was not so lucky. When Paris police came across Carlos while tailing Moukarbal on a trail that had led from Beirut, the Jackal reacted like a true urban guerrilla. Not only did he shoot two unarmed officers of the *Défence de la Sécurité du Territoire* and wound another, but, mistakenly believing that he had been betrayed by Moukarbal, shot him to death. "He stood before me," he obligingly informed an interviewer. "I shot into his eyes, he fell to the ground, I shot once more into his temple. I was calm . . . and walked away as if nothing happened." He even remembered that the weapon he had used was a Russian Tokarev 7.62. Carlos later informed an Arab interviewer from the weekly *Al Watan Al Arabi,* "I am not a professional killer. It isn't easy to shoot somebody in the eyes when he's looking right at you . . ."

Another of Carlos' Parisian exploits was to toss a couple of hand grenades into the chic boutique-rendezvous Le Drugstore, killing two and injuring a dozen people. (This purportedly was in sympathy with Japanese terrorists occupying the French Embassy in The Hague.)

The shooting of the French security police and the execution of Moukarbel finally blew Carlos the Jackal's cover (the police at the time had no idea who he was), and he left for the more hospitable ambiance of the Middle East. When he returned to Europe, Carlos executed his most spectacular operation.

Leading a team of six—two Lebanese, one Palestinian from Dr. Habash's Popular Front for the Liberation of Palestine, and two members of the Baader-Meinhof Gang (also known as the Red Army Faction)—Carlos shook up both the West and the Arab world.

The setting was Vienna and the target was the headquarters of the Organization of Petroleum Exporting Companies where a meeting had been called, attended by eleven Arab oil ministers and their staffs. The objective was to impress upon the delegations the dangers of dealing with the West. Why would Arabs join in an attack on their own brothers? Dr. Habash provided the rationale when he told interviewer Oriana Fallaci that among the most detrimental to the Arab cause were the "Arab reactionaries." He indicated as an example ". . . Saudi Arabia, where the majority of oil wells are in American hands. Or Lebanon, with its rotten government. Then there is Jordan, whose king is ready to recognize Israel . . ."

On December 21, 1975, Carlos and five others burst into OPEC headquarters, armed with pistols and hand grenades carried in their Adidas bags. Carlos and the male member of the Baader-Meinhof duo, Hans-Joachim Klein, also carried an Italian-made Baretta submachine gun. The others were armed with Russian-made Tokarev automatic pistols, whose maximum effective range is fifty-five yards. Klein's partner, and possibly second-in-command, was chic Gabriele Kröcher-Tiedemann. When the assault began, she asked an elderly plainclothesman, dashing for the elevator, if he was a policeman. When he answered "Yes," she shot him in the back of the head with her Tokarev from a distance of about four yards. She then pushed him into the elevator and pressed the DOWN button. When an Iraqi security guard seemed menacing, she shot him in the stomach. (Both the Austrian and the Iraqi died.)

Carlos dressed for the occasion in a dashing trenchcoat; he also sported dark glasses and a beret (the headgear of revolutionaries). He had lost some weight (his favored nickname among some was "Il Gordo," which can be translated "Fatso") and had grown a sparse beard. Carlos encountered trouble from a senior member of the Libyan delegation, who attempted to wrestle him to the floor. In the scuffle, Carlos shot him dead.

Klein also encountered trouble. He threw a hand grenade at a guard and received a blast of return fire. The bullet struck his Baretta, fragmented, and seriously wounded Klein in the stomach. The three participating Arabs apparently stayed out of the action—and it was soon over.

"I killed two of them," Kröcher-Tiedemann told Carlos.

"Quite right," he replied. "I killed one."

Kröcher-Tiedemann then asked to have Sheikh Zaki Yamani, Saudi Arabia's Minister of Petroleum and Mineral Resources pointed out to her, no doubt anxious to use her Tokarev. But Carlos had other plans for the eleven hostages: money. Another important captive was Iran's Dr. Jamshid Amouzegar.

The Austrian Government acceded to Carlos' demand for a jetliner to take his captives to some safe spot in the Middle East, where a suitable ransom could be negotiated. If this fell through, then Kröcher-Tiedemann could exercise her Tokarev.

Their departure for Algiers with the eleven OPEC officials was thoroughly covered by television cameras. Aboard the plane, Carlos, having made it clear that he was the infamous "Carlos the Jackal," spent a good deal of time with Sheikh Yamani. "You will have heard of me already; I am Carlos," he said with characteristic humility. "You can tell the others."

Yamani was impressed with his "intelligence" and apparent ability to meld disparate factions into an operating unit of some potency. Carlos expounded on the subject of his power in the revolutionary movement and sexual exploits, but Yamani was also struck by his lack of political commitment. Carlos, Yamani said after he and the others were ransomed, was "not a committed communist" and did "not believe in the Palestinian cause or Arab nationalism . . ." It was the mayhem he reveled in.

With the release of the hostages, Carlos slipped away from the international scene. The PLO coffers were richer by some $2 million and Carlos himself by $2 million (a gift from an appreciative Colonel Qaddafi). The wounded Klein was rewarded by Qaddafi with two hundred thousand dollars, and he, too, dropped out of the movement, "nauseated by the demented action of the international terrorists." After he had recovered, Klein and his two companions flew to Aden, South Yemen, where Dr. Haddad ran his revolutionary training schools. Klein was reprimanded by Haddad for not killing anyone, as had his companions. It was enough for him; he got out. Carlos, too, went underground, but for different reasons; whether he blended into the protective embrace of Qaddafi, in Libya, or returned to Moscow is not known.

A year later, in 1977, Gabriele Kröcher-Tiedemann, stopped at the Swiss border for a border check, pulled a pistol from her handbag, and shot two Swiss guards (one of whom was invalided for life). Her trial was a media event—with hundreds of armed policemen, some with machine guns, helicopters circling the courthouse, and protesting Swiss sympathizers shouting slogans against "the boredom and air-conditioned misery of capitalism." The diminutive, seemingly vulnerable, young terrorist was sentenced to remain in jail until 1993.

Going international, exporting the Palestinian cause to Europe, had not truly succeeded; in fact, such ventures as the Olympic Games killings and the Pan American bombing in Rome, as well as others, had backfired. The press coverage was extensive, but it was often unfavorable. It also encouraged Israeli retaliation.

Even as the hijackings, bombings, and kidnappings alarmed, even intimidated, several European governments, the various factions of the Palestinian organizations made their bloody sweeps into Israel.

The "Target: Israel" incursions were not at all like the theatrical, televised Carlos exploits. They were on a small scale, furtive and impossible to evaluate or analyze militarily, for it would be difficult to state what these attacks achieved. They made little, but ruthless, sense.

An organization calling itself the Popular Front for the Liberation of Palestine—General Command had been formed in 1959 by a Syrian Army captain, Ahmed Jibril, ostensibly to wage war on Israel's citizens. After the early hijackings, it ventured into that activity in Zurich in February 1970. Some of its agents persuaded some young women to carry what appeared to be harmless packages aboard a Swissair jet bound for Tel Aviv. The aircraft detonated in mid-air, killing all forty-seven people aboard.

Wide World Photos

Major General Mordechai Gur, chief of the Northern Command, bordering on Lebanon, inspects the interior of a school bus that had been ambushed by terrorists striking out of southern Lebanon. Firing small arms and bazookas, the Palestinians killed ten riders, half of them children.

In May, Jibril turned again to Israel. A team of his *fedayeen* (these generally comprised some three to five men) slipped over the border between Israel and Lebanon and took a position along a highway. They were armed with an 82-mm. rocket launcher. From their hiding place they observed a military patrol pass by, then saw the bright yellow school bus from the Israeli farm cooperative Avivim approaching. As the driver slowed to make a turn, the guerrillas shot three rockets into the bus. The driver and two teachers died, as did three passengers ranging in age from five to eight; twenty were injured. Jibril's group quickly made certain that they received "credit" for the exploit.

The Popular Front for the Liberation of Palestine—General Command was also responsible for another hit-and-run raid into Israel from Lebanon, although the three Arab participants did not, in the end, return to fight another day.

During the night of April 10, 1974, three of Jibril's men, heavily armed, slipped across the border and made their way toward nearby Kiryat Shmona, in northern Galilee. Two of this so-called "suicide squad"—a Palestinian, Monir Moghrabi, and a Syrian, Ahmed e-Sheikh Mahmoud—were twenty years old; their companion, an Iraqi, Yassin Mousa el-Mouzani, was twenty-seven.

Traces of their entry into a block of apartments were found by a border patrol. The police of Kiryat Shmona were alerted, and units of the Israeli Army raced to the settlement. Early in the morning, the battle was ignited when a two-man police patrol was fired upon from the apartment building. Immediately after the three men entered two ground-floor apartments, they had shot five people; they then systematically moved through the building, shooting everyone they saw. On the top floor, the fourth, they found a vacant apartment, from which they began sniping at people in the street.

After taking hostages, the three men demanded the release of one hundred Palestinian prisoners held by Israel, including the Japanese survivor of the Lod Airport massacre, Kozo Okamoto. By this time, the Israeli Army had arrived on the scene. When the troops stormed the building, the guerrillas detonated the explosive belts they wore, killing themselves along with their hostages. The final death toll for Israel was eighteen, two of them soldiers. Of the sixteen dead civilians—the youngest of whom was two-and-a-half and the oldest sixty—half were children, five were women, and three were men. Sixteen wounded were taken to Government Hospital in Safad, south of Kiryat Shmona.

Again the Popular Front for the Liberation of Palestine—General Command took "credit" for the assault; Jibril, in claiming it, announced that his splinter group, which had broken away from Habash's PFLP, was inaugurating a "new school of struggle based on the highest degree of revolutionary violence." But his group became less visible after Kiryat Shmona and made no other claims. Others would continue such bloody attacks.

Within a month, perhaps "inspired" by Jibril's raid, Naïf Hawatmeh planned a similar operation. Hawatmeh led a group of Palestinians even more Marxist-Leninist than Jibril's, and who had also broken away from Habash's PFLP.

With degrees in philosophy and social sciences from the University of Beirut, Hawatmeh formed a splinter group called the Democratic Front for the Liberation of Palestine. Except for some fighting in the streets of Beirut and Amman between his faction and that of Habash, until broken up by Arafat's Al-Fatah, he had not brought off any notable military action.

But "military" is hardly the word for what occurred. On May 15, 1974, three of his group infiltrated the village of Maalot, in northern Israel, near the Lebanese frontier. This time they took over an elementary school, demanding the release of twenty-three Israeli-held prisoners. The fact that this ploy had never worked before did not deter them; the Israeli Army quickly moved in.

Hawatmeh's guerrillas were killed in the attack on the school, as were twenty-two children; some seventy children were wounded. Hawatmeh, who professed to favor a political solution—as opposed to a military one—in the Israeli-Palestinian struggle, lost whatever following he may have attracted among sympathetic Israelis that infamous day. The attack also initiated a week of reprisal raids from the air and sea by the Israeli Defense Forces on Palestinian camps in Lebanon, with reported casualties of more than sixty persons. One more bloody but fruitless raid, on an apartment house in the village of Beth Shean in November, ended Hawatmeh's ventures into terrorism.

Such attacks—blowing up buses, planting bombs in shopping areas, etc.—continued through periods of war and "peace," but it remained for Arafat's Fatah to mount one of the most ruthless of the anti-Israel raids and to incite one of Israel's most potent responses, a portent of things to come. The World War II-like commando raid occurred even as peace talks between Egypt and Israel were transpiring.

Sometime in the early afternoon of March 11, 1978—a Saturday, the Jewish sabbath—two rubber dinghies carrying thirteen Palestinians were dropped from a supply ship of "undisclosed nationality" off the Mediterranean coast north of Kibbutz Ma'agen Michael, about midway between Haifa and Tel Aviv. All had not gone well for the commandos. They had shipped out of Tyre, Lebanon, on March 8, and because of some "wrong directions" had tossed around offshore for two days, not quite knowing where they were. Finally spotting some lights, they made for shore, paddling toward what appeared to be a deserted beach. The surf was high and strong winds swept the shore. One of the boats capsized; two of the guerrillas drowned and all the equipment in their boat was lost. Once ashore, the eleven remaining members of the squad swiftly moved into a wooded nature preserve; they rested, had some food, and shared a bottle of whiskey. They then proceeded through the preserve. (The mystery of this landing is how the group managed to slip past the sophisticated Israeli coastal defense network of radar, patrol boats, and shore patrols, as well as air reconnaissance.)

Moving inland through the forest, armed with Soviet-made rockets and launchers, submachine guns, and hand grenades, the squad came upon a nineteen-year-old woman and shot her; a German tourist couple in a rented car were also gunned down. Among the first victims identified was an American nature photographer, Gail Rubin, also shot inside the preserve. The little band then cut through a chain link fence and were now on the Haifa-Tel Aviv coastal highway.

A pickup truck approached from the direction of Haifa. Some of the party tried to signal the driver to stop; suspicious at seeing a band of men carrying what appeared to be weapons, twenty-two-year-old Maya Shoshinsky stepped on the accelerator and veered sharply to the left lane, away from the men. When the truck raced by, they opened fire and shattered glass flew through the interior of the truck. Though cut by the glass, as was her aunt who was seated next to her, Shoshinsky sped away from the gunmen; in the back seat lay the bodies of her dead parents.

The guerrillas managed to commandeer a Mercedes (the fate of its passengers is unclear); one group got into the car and headed south toward Tel Aviv; the other remained in ambush alongside the road. When the regular Tel Aviv-Haifa bus came by, they sprayed it with automatic fire, hitting several of its forty passengers. The commandos boarded the bus and ordered the driver to turn around and follow the southbound Mercedes. As the driver began his turn, a station wagon approached from the north. The bus stopped to form a roadblock across the highway and two gunmen left it, took position, and opened fire. The driver of the station wagon was Hanoch Tel-Oran, the distinguished flutist of the Jerusalem Symphony. He swerved around the bus, but in the fusillade he was wounded, as was his wife, Sharona; their fourteen-year-old son, Imri, was killed.

Meanwhile the other group had abandoned the Mercedes and had taken over a tour bus crowded with passengers: thirty-one adults and thirty-two children. In their attack on the bus, the Palestinians shattered the windshield with machine-gun fire—killing five-year-old Na'ama Hadani and wounding several others. The driver continued on for a few yards, then stopped the bus

Guerrilla incursions into Israel inevitably invited retaliaiion; Israeli border police set out on a search for terrorists.

Consulate General of Israel

Consulate General of Israel

A bomb planted in a bus detonated and killed six passengers in Jerusalem.

and opened the door; more than twenty passengers managed to escape into nearby fields. The terrorists forced the rest to remain in the bus. The nine-year-old sister of the dying Na'ama was one of the escapees. Her father was wounded, and her mother carried her dying sister in her arms.

Soon after, the other bus arrived and all the hostages and terrorists boarded the tour bus and sped south. The hands of the male passengers were tied; the rear window of the bus was smashed to enable the terrorists to fire at passing traffic and pursuers. The gunmen, and one woman, chanted slogans—"No Begin, No Sadat!" "To Tel Aviv, to Tel Aviv!"—and sang songs. They also shot through the roof of the bus from time to time.

By this time the Israeli police and the Army had been alerted; a wounded driver called in from a highway emergency phone, and soon after, two jeeps joined in the chase at Netanya. Armed only with pistols, they were forced, by machine-gun fire, to keep their distance. Farther south, alerted by radio, two policemen and two policewomen parked their jeep across the southbound lane and took firing positions on the side of the road. The bus, coming on at high speed, swung around the roadblock, drove over the island, and raced on, spraying gunfire from the rear window and hitting one of the policemen in both legs.

Just north of Tel Aviv, near the Country Club, the police had placed a roadblock: two Cortinas over both lanes of the highway. Policemen and border police took positions in ditches. When the bus slowed down for the roadblock, the police opened fire, puncturing all the tires of the vehicle.

One of the passengers, Avraham Shamir, remembered that moment. "There was a bedlam of shooting and we all crouched on the floor. Suddenly a terrorist next to me was hit. He slumped over and his head hit my shoulder. I grabbed his pistol and managed to shoot two other terrorists who were standing in the front of the bus.

"Just then, I turned my head and spotted another terrorist behind me. We both fired simultaneously. I think he got me too—or my daughter who was next to me—in the shoulder. One of the terrorists pulled out a hand grenade from his overalls and pulled the pin. I grabbed his hand and managed to throw the grenade out the window. It exploded and I think it was then I was wounded in my eye."

The bus had begun to fill with smoke, and Shamir shouted to everyone to make a run for it. He got out and took cover in the brush alongside the road.

Once the tires of the bus had been flattened, several Palestinians left the bus and began firing rockets and light mortar shells at the police. As Shamir had noted, there was a bedlam of shooting and throwing of hand grenades, one of which set the bus ablaze. As the Palestinians ran from the burning bus, six were cut down by Israeli guns. Two more were killed by "an officer of an elite combat unit" who happened to drive upon the scene of the conflagration armed. He found the guerrillas hiding in the brush and shot them before he himself was wounded in the shoulder.

Two were taken alive as they attempted to slip away in the dark; one, at least, eighteen-year-old Hussein Ibrahim Mahmud Fajad, surrendered voluntarily.

Since it was by then known that there had been eleven guerrillas that had left a thirty-mile trail of carnage along the highway and only eight were accounted for after the shootout, a great manhunt was initiated. For the first time since the end of the British mandate, in 1948, a curfew was imposed over a large area of northwestern Israel, affecting some three hundred thousand people. That Saturday night, more roadblocks were set up and helicopters circled overhead as search parties, police, soldiers, border guards, civilian volunteers, and trackers with dogs combed the brush and sand of the beaches along the highway. Businesses and schools were closed throughout the area as well as in Tel Aviv, since many employed in the city could not leave their homes in the affected area. Only television and radio kept the thousands entrapped in their homes informed of developments.

On Sunday night the massive manhunt was called off; interrogation of the two prisoners revealed that three of the terrorists had died in the bus explosion. Nine of their number had died in their murderous rampage. But before they died and the two were captured, they had killed thirty-seven civilians and wounded more than seventy—the largest civilian toll since Israel became a state.

From Lebanon, a Fatah spokesman took responsibility for the raid, stating that its objective had been to "torpedo President Anwar Sadat's peace initiative." He also admitted that the PLO camps and enclaves in southern Lebanon were put on the alert "in anticipation of a violent Israeli response." In the latter instance, he was right.

Just before midnight of Tuesday, March 14, 1978, a four-pronged infantry attack, supported by tanks, aircraft, and even ships firing from the sea, moved across the Lebanese border. Although great numbers of Palestinians had already fled north, the Israelis encountered resistance in some pockets. Known PLO camps were shelled by artillery and bombed from the air. Once the Israelis crossed into Lebanon, they were joined by units of the Christian militia, com-

Shambles after a terrorist spree on the Haifa - Tel Aviv highway. The result was this burned-out bus and thirty-four fatalities.

Photos courtesy of Consulate General of Israel

manded by Major Saad Haddad. He greated the Israelis with "I've been waiting for this night for a long time." Haddad's troops, tanks, and artillery combined with those of the Israeli Defense Forces to drive the PLO out of southern Lebanon. Lebanese soldiers also served as guides for the Israelis.

By Wednesday afternoon, after only sporadic resistance, the fighting was virtually over. The Palestinian camps were overrun—many of them already abandoned. The Israelis fought ferociously, spurred by the savagery of the gunmen's rampage on the coastal highway. Chief of operations Aluf Rafael Eitan, in briefing his senior officers before the attack, quoted Israeli poet Chaim Nahman Bialik: "Revenge for the killing of a small child has not yet been invented by the devil."

As the infantry, followed by tanks, pushed northward toward the Litani River, beyond which Syrian "peace-keeping" troops were positioned, Israeli jets bombed and strafed the port of Ad Damur, south of Beirut. It was from Ad Damur that the Palestinians had set out for their Saturday killing spree. The single Syrian reaction to the invasion was to fire, without result, at the Israeli aircraft. Prime Minister Begin had made it clear in his various radio broadcasts that Israel was hunting the PLO and planned to drive it out of southern Lebanon only; he had no intention of tangling with the Syrians and assured the world that the invading forces would stop short of crossing the Litani River.

Aircraft, however, operated north of the river line, and when Palestinian reinforcements were observed moving across a bridge and south in the northeastern sector, the Israeli Air Force bombed the bridge. Meanwhile, Israeli naval craft intercepted attempts to reinforce and supply troops in the South along the Lebanese coastal road. By Thursday, March 16, only mop-up operations continued in the hard-fighting pockets in Bint Jubayl, near the southeastern border, and Taibeh, also in eastern Lebanon and just south of the Litani River.

An uneasy calm settled over the area, broken from time to time by rocket and artillery fire. Even from north of the Litani, the Palestinians could strike at villages with Katyusha rockets. On Friday, March 17, rockets were fired into Galilee (which also came under artillery fire), killing two Israeli civilians and wounding two others. (The Katyushas were also used to fire into the Lebanese Christian settlements of Klea and Marjiyoun.)

Immediately before he left for the United States to confer with President Jimmy Carter and to appear at the United Nations (which was clamoring for a troop withdrawal), Begin authorized the final thrust into Lebanon. (Initially, he had assured a penetration of only six miles or so.) The next day, Sunday, March 19, the Israelis made a surprise lightning thrust to the north and west, encountering scant opposition. When the day ended, the Israelis occupied nearly all of southern Lebanon. They controlled all the highways, roads, and trails into the South, as well as the strategically critical Akiya Bridge (within easy artillery range) over the Litani River. Tyre, a major PLO stronghold and supply artery, was cut off from the sea by Israeli missile boats and from the south and east by infantry and artillery.

The six days of fighting had cost the Israeli Defense Forces seventeen killed and more than fifty wounded. Estimated Palestinian dead was announced to be about three hundred, but was likely much higher. Large numbers of prisoners were sent to Israel. The Lebanese who had not fled to the North, perhaps a hundred thousand, became the Israeli Army's responsibility; food, medical supplies, and other necessities—including barracks to replace destroyed dwellings—were provided. Voices were raised in Israel and the United Nations questioning Israeli motives, now that southern Lebanon was secure. Begin continued to promise a withdrawal when the Israelis could be certain that the PLO stayed out of southern Lebanon, within artillery range of Galilee.

On March 21, Israel declared a unilateral truce, and UN troops began moving in to enforce the cease-fire. On April 11, Israel began to withdraw from Lebanon; and on May 24 PLO leader Arafat pledged to the government of Lebanon that he would keep his guerrilla forces out of southern Lebanon. June 13 dawned, and with it came the final withdrawal of Israeli troops from Lebanon—and the beginning of PLO infiltration back into their old hideouts and camps across from vulnerable Galilee.

In an interview given on the Sunday that the Israelis carried out the final push in Lebanon, the youthful terrorist Fajad, who had voluntarily surrendered after the bus explosion, commented that he believed that the "operation had been a mistake." He also admitted that the civilians were deliberately selected as victims. He could not say whether or not the mission had in any way advanced the Palestinian cause. When asked, "How many people do you think you killed?" he replied, "I don't remember."

Both he and the PLO operations officers who had planned the mission would long remember the forceful reaction to the coastal highway attacks. Less than two years before—at a place few had ever heard of, Entebbe—it had been demonstrated that the Israelis would move swiftly and with determination.

Code-named by its Israeli planners "Operation Thunderbolt," this remarkable exploit was an education in what could be expected when Israeli citizens were taken hostage. If its lessons had been learned and its impact grasped, bloody incursions such as those carried out by zealots like Fajad might never have occurred. It would have spared a good deal of Palestinian and Lebanese blood. The raid on Entebbe, although it occurred not quite two years before the Sabbath bloodbath (and is therefore out of chronology with the other terrorist raids in this section), deserves its own special treatment.

Dr. Wadi Haddad's last in his series of aircraft hijackings was also his ultimate fiasco. Assisting on the planning was an Ecuadorian guerrilla, Antonio Dages Bouvier, who had been an instructor of Carlos the Jackal in Havana and his colleague in London, where the two had compiled a list of notable Jews for assassination. After the OPEC Munich operation, Carlos went underground and his mentor collaborated with Habash's Popular Front for the Liberation of Palestine in planning a Munich-like combined operation. He and operations commander Dr. Haddad contrived an elaborate airline hijacking that would require the services of members of the PFLP's Arabs, Germans from the deteriorating Baader-Meinhof Gang, as well as one of the world's most ruthless and murderous dictators.

Air France Flight No. 139, which had originated at Ben-Gurion Airport, Tel Aviv, had flown uneventfully to Athens, where it touched down to refuel and to let off and take on passengers. With 245 passengers aboard (plus a crew of 12), the pilot, Captain Michel Bacos, lifted the plane off the runway at about noon. At twelve-ten an Israeli medical student, Moshe Peretz, noted in a diary he had decided to keep of his trip: "A few moments after taking off I suddenly heard a terrible scream. My first thought is someone's fainted. I see two persons rush forward. One is a long-haired youth wearing a red shirt, gray trousers, and a beige pullover. The other has a thick mustache, wears long trousers and yellow shirt. They are running toward the first-class compartment."

They were headed for the cockpit. Flight attendants, "frightened and hysterical," came out of the first-class section and, though trembling themselves, attempted to keep the mystified and nervous passengers calm.

"A minute later, we hear the excited voice of a woman over the plane's internal comunications system. Speaking English with a foreign accent, she informs us that the plane is under the control of the 'Che Guevara Group' and the 'Gaza Unit' of the Popular Front for the Liberation of Palestine . . . The hysterical voice over the loudspeaker announces that all passengers are to raise their hands above their heads and not move.

"At the entrance to the first-class compartment there stand two terrorists holding drawn guns and hand grenades without safety pins."

Flight 139 was flying over Greece when contact was lost with the aircraft, in the early afternoon of Sunday, June 27, 1976. Israeli intelligence, monitoring all radio activity in the Mideast, was instantly concerned—because the flight carried many Israelis. By 1:30 P.M., Prime Minister Yitzhak Rabin had been informed. The first message was not clear about whether the plane had been destroyed, or had been hijacked and forced into radio silence. There was silence, too, in Athens and in Paris, where family, relatives, and friends awaited the arrival of the Air France airbus.

Nor were the passengers aboard the plane, at that moment, any better informed; they had no idea of their destination or of their ultimate fate. They had cause for alarm, however. The leader of the group, who called himself the "captain" of the aircraft, was Wilfred Bose, former colleague of Carlos the Jackal and a member of the Baader-Meinhof Gang. He appeared to be reasonably calm and reassuring. A youngish woman who had boarded the plane with him in Athens, after an early-morning flight from Bahrain, was Brigitte Kohlmann.

Diarist Peretz described her as "the sort who gets things together fast. Anyone who wants to go to the toilet lifts a finger, she shouts an order to go; in one case, when two passengers get up at the same time to go to the toilet, she screams like a veritable animal." Her frenzied, strident conduct during the hijacking was later attributed to the death of another Baader-Meinhof Gang member, Bernard Hausman, who had been blown up, along with a woman security guard, at Ben-Gurion Airport the month before. She had been told by the Palestinian high command that the Israelis had killed Hausman; in fact, he had unknowingly carried two booby-trapped bags aboard the Austrian Airline plane. When asked by the suspicious officer to open his luggage, the unsuspecting Hausman did so willingly, and the two died in the explosion. Hausman had not realized that Dr. Haddad had sent him on a mission as a walking bomb. Nor did the agitated Brigitte Kohlmann know this; all she knew was that the Jews had murdered her friend and she hated them.

During the first three hours in flight, the hijackers searched the passengers for weapons; they found none.

Bose, who had a map, had ordered Bacos to take a southerly course; this brought them to their first stop, Benghazi Airport, Libya. In Qaddafi's anti-Israeli nation, many of the passengers had reason to be apprehensive; during the unexplained wait of more than six hours, they were served a cold supper (obviously they had been expected), and the plane was refueled.

In Benghazi, too, their luck took a good turn, although no one realized it at the time. Patricia Heyman, although a resident of Israel, also held a British passport. She was also in a stage of advanced pregnancy. Because she felt ill, she was permitted off the plane and subsequently persuaded her captors to free her. They put her on the next Libyan Airlines jet to London. Even before her former fellow passengers left Benghazi, Mrs. Heyman had talked to Scotland Yard, which immediately reported to Israeli intelligence. They now knew that the terrorists included a German woman and man, plus two or three Arabs, all armed with guns and grenades, and bound with their captives for a land "friendly to the terrorists." That memorable Sunday closed with the Israelis in Jerusalem and Tel Aviv speculating on how to meet the emergency—politically or militarily—and the hostages in the night sky speculating on their destination.

At around 3:15 A.M., Captain Bacos landed the plane at Entebbe Airport, Uganda, within sight of Lake Victoria. This was indeed a country friendly to the terrorists, the terror-ridden domain of "His Excellency al-Hajji Field Marshal Dr. Idi Amin Dada." President Idi Amin, admirer of Adolf Hitler and his works, had once been a friend of Israel. The Israeli Defense Forces for nearly nine years (April 1963 to March 1972) had helped to build his army and air force, and built modern additions to Entebbe Airport. When word came that the Air France jet had landed there and that the kidnappers were making demands over Uganda Radio, Defense Minister Shimon Peres and chief of staff Mordechai Gur already had models of the airport, its buildings, and runways at their disposal in case a military solution became necessary.

The Israeli-Uganda agreement had ended acrimoniously when Israel refused an invitation to join Amin in an invasion of Uganda's southern neighbor Tanzania. The landing of the plane at Entebbe compounded the problem for Israel. The jet had been hijacked over Greece; it was the property of Air France, and therefore of French concern. Before acting, the Israelis would have to wait to see what occurred on the political/diplomatic scene and whether the United Nations might provide a solution, since the plane carried citizens of nations other than Israel.

While the military began searching for some means of freeing the hostages, the Israeli Government pursued, in public, the diplomatic route. Called into service in what was the most bizarre aspect of the Entebbe adventure was Colonel Baruch Bar-Lev, soldier turned shopkeeper and once an associate and friend of Uganda's dictator. From his shop in a suburb of Tel Aviv, Bar-Lev phoned Amin in Kampala at the request of the Israeli Government, who told him nothing of their plans except to keep Amin talking. On Monday, the second day of the hijacking, working on Amin's vanity, Bar-Lev tried to get the all-powerful dictator—now basking in the worldwide limelight—to free the hostages; after all, it was his country and a mere handful of terrorists faced his army. All too quickly, it became clear that Amin was cooperating with the hijackers.

That was obvious to the hostages as soon as Amin appeared at the airport, in resplendent and bemedaled uniform (and a small son in tow wearing a miniature replica of the uniform), embraced the leaders of the hijackers, and placed the jet under the guard of his soldiers. On meeting the hostages, he was smiling and introduced himself, complete with titles, his military medals, and the announcement that he had been "appointed by God Almighty to be your saviour."

The hostages were then moved out of the plane and imprisoned, under the eyes of the hijackers, in the old, abandoned terminal building. To reinforce the kidnappers, Ugandan soldiers surrounded the building.

On Tuesday, June 29, the official demands were broadcast over Radio Uganda and the situation for some of the hostages took an ominous turn. The price for liberation was the release of fifty-three jailed terrorists (forty in Israel, six in West Germany, five in Kenya, and one each in France and Switzerland) by noon of Thursday, July 1. This was followed by a separation of passengers with Israeli or dual-nationality passports from the non-Jewish captives. Then forty-seven of the non-Jews were flown to Paris. Clearly the Israelis were the target of the operation. When Amin appeared after this segregationist turn (which reminded many of its victims of the Nazi death-camp roll calls of World War II), he blamed their plight on the "fascist Israeli Government." It was well established even before the hijacking that Israel did not negotiate with hijackers; he knew it and the Palestinians knew it.

By Wednesday evening, after the released passengers had arrived in Paris and were interrogated, the Israeli Government leaders were certain that the diplomatic route would accomplish nothing. Bar-Lev continued to engage a preening Amin, intimating that he had no real control over the hijackers—who had been joined by others after the landing in Entebbe. One of the newcomers, who apparently took over command of the operation from Bose, was

United Press International

Idi Amin Dada, Uganda's "President for Life," who served as host to the passengers of the French airliner—as well as to their West German and Palestinian captors.

Wide World Photos

Genial host Idi Amin graciously chats with freed hostages on their way home; by this time the Israeli decision to carry out Operation Thunderbolt had been made.

Dr. Haddad; he was accompanied by his lieutenant, Bouvier. The bemused hostages found the intense little man with a peculiar slouching walk and a drooping mustache more a figure of fun than menacing, and referred to him, with naïve amusement, as "Groucho." They had no idea who this rather nondescript man was, nor were they aware of the fact that Amin was not actually negotiating for their release (as was realized in the Ministry of Defense in Jerusalem). If something was not done soon, the dumpy little figure of fun would become their ardent executioner.

And so Bar-Lev maintained his curious dialogue with Amin, who hammered away at the belief that it was the stubbornness of the Israeli Government that was the major threat to the hostages. However, because Amin was to fly to Mauritius, a tiny island in the Indian Ocean, east of Madagascar, for a meeting of the Organization of African Unity, he took credit for postponing the deadline until after his return on Sunday, July 4. This gleam of hope was dimmed when one hundred and one hostages, most of them with French passports, were released, leaving ninety Jews behind (forty-five men, thirty-four women, and eleven children). Captain Bacos and the crew of the plane refused their freedom and chose to remain with the now predominantly Israeli captives.

The hostages, however, had yet another glimmer of hope when it appeared that the Israeli Government had decided to concede to the Palestinian demands. This was a ploy, for from the moment that the Jews were separated from the non-Jews, Rabin, Peres, and their staffs and advisers were driven by the certainty that the remaining hostages were doomed unless they moved swiftly and militarily. It was believed that would not occur until Amin's return from his meeting in Mauritius.

While "Track A," diplomacy and discussion, proceeded publicly, "Track B" was turned over to chief of staff Gur. Since the hijacking, intelligence information from several sources—West Germany, Canada, Britain, France, and the United States, as well as Mossad agents operating out of Kenya—came in and was examined. The freed hostages contributed to the knowledge of the numbers of hijackers and Ugandan soldiers involved, the disposition of the hostages, and other vital information. Even psychological information on Amin and the known hijackers was consulted.

By Friday, July 2, rehearsals for "Operation Thunderbolt" were underway. The audacity of the plan, worked out by paratroop commander Brigadier General Dan Shomron and Air Force chief of staff Benny Peled, was striking. The operation would be under the command of American-born Harvard graduate Lieutenant Colonel Yehonatan ("Yonni") Netanyahu. He would lead a team of commandos into Entebbe and, if all went as it did during the desert rehearsals, out again in one of the most daring rescue operations ever attempted. In all, about 500 men and women were involved; of these, 196 were soldiers—commandos, aircrews, etc.

Within hours, a delicate flight plan was evolved, portions of which were designed to deceive some of the personnel at Kenya's Nairobi Airport. While the Nairobi government was sympathetic, it seemed wise not to implicate it directly in Thunderbolt. Some of the aircraft that were to take part in the mission appeared in civil colors and registrations.

The twenty-five-hundred-mile flight to Entebbe would have to elude Arab radar and avoid violating the airspace of Arab nations as well as neutrals. Therefore, most of the flight after takeoff from Israel was done over the central Red Sea. At the southern end, the planes turned on a southwestward course,

ENTEBBE
THE RESCUE
Frankfurt
GERMANY
POLAND
Munich
Vienna
AUSTRIA
Zurich
U.S.S.R.
Odessa
ROMANIA
ITALY
YUGOSLAVIA
Rome
BULGARIA
BLACK SEA
CASPIAN SEA
GREECE
SICILY
IONIAN SEA
Ankara
TURKEY
Tunis
Athens
MEDITERRANEAN SEA
SYRIA
Tehran
LEBANON
Tripoli
Baalbek
Beirut
IRAQ
IRAN
Tripoli
ISRAEL
Haifa
Tyre
Baghdad
Benghazi
Ma'agen Michael
Mafrak
Tel Aviv
Amman
Lod
Jerusalem
JORDAN
Cairo
KUWAIT
PERSIAN GULF
LIBYA
BAHRAIN
EGYPT
Medina
Riyadh
SAUDI ARABIA
Mecca
RED SEA
CHAD
Khartoum
YEMEN
S.YEMEN
SUDAN
Aden
N
Addis Ababa
ETHIOPIA
SOMALIA
Entebbe Rescue Mission
UGANDA
Kampala
Entebbe
KENYA
INDIAN OCEAN
MILES
0
600
KM
LAKE VICTORIA
Nairobi
palacios

flying over Ethiopia, and approached Entebbe from Kenya, in the south, over Lake Victoria. To avoid detection over the Gulf of Aqaba, the airborne units would have to skim the waters at low altitude. Flying time was estimated to be seven hours.

There was little margin for error, and before Rabin's Cabinet agreed to set Thunderbolt in motion, they agonized over it for hours. All realized that one small slip would jeopardize the mission and hundreds of lives. The rescue itself would be an intricate process depending on surprise, speed, and precise timing. Realistically, it was expected to cost thirty lives and fifty wounded—provided that there were no air accidents and that the Ugandans, as well as the Palestinians, were not alerted.

About 2 P.M., Saturday, July 3, Operation Thunderbolt got off the ground fifteen minutes before it had actually been approved by the Israeli Cabinet. If time were wasted, the schedule might go awry at Entebbe. If for some reason the Cabinet voted against the mission, the planes could return to Israel.

The first plane to take off was a Boeing 707, in El Al civil markings; it carried the Air Force's General Peled and deputy chief of staff Yekutiel Adam. This plane was to serve as a flying command post. It flew, as would any other commercial airliner, to Nairobi, where only a few people (among them the airport's chief of police) actually knew what its purpose was. The command plane was followed by a second 707, a hospital ship, which would remain at Nairobi to receive the casualties. All of the jets could also be refueled in Nairobi for the flight back to Israel.

These aircraft were safely on the ground in Kenya when the other planes began taking off, at 3:30 P.M. The tiny armada consisted of four Lockheed C-130s (the Hercules transport was affectionately called the "Hippo" by the Israelis) and eight McDonnell-Douglas F-4E Phantoms providing high cover. The Hippos were timed to land at Entebbe at short intervals: the first carried mission commander General Shomron, a special unit of Netanyahu's commandos, and a Mercedes limousine repainted to appear like the one Amin used. Once the Hippo had landed, the Mercedes, with the commandos crammed into it, would be driven to the hostage area to deal with the hijackers.

The second Hippo carried more commandos, a hospital team, and equipment; the third also carried equipment, plus a special team to destroy the thirty or so MiGs deployed around the airport. The last Hippo brought a team of specialists, fuel, and replacement parts; like the preceding plane, it would land on the old military runway near the new terminal, where the Soviet jets were parked. This plane would remain on the runway throughout the operation and pick up any stragglers. The two leading Hippos were to set down on what was called the International runway, adjacent to the old terminal, the prison of the hostages.

The planes' flight, in complete radio silence, was not an easy one; there was much turbulence and each plane was gingerly flown through the night, tossing and pitching. "There were times when we flew them like combat planes," a pilot recalled. "We did everything but dogfight. We made sharp turns to

U.S. Air Force, Department of Defense

The Lockheed C-130, the "Hippo," four of which were used in Israel's Operation Thunderbolt, the raid on Entebbe, Uganda.

Wide World Photos

Chief of staff Lieutenant General Mordechai Gur at a press conference in Tel Aviv after the Entebbe raid. To his left is a map of Entebbe Airport.

dodge the Russian-built radar pickets on sea and land, then had to climb fast to get over the mountains."

The Hippos did not land at Nairobi, but continued on over Lake Victoria; the command 707 was already circling overhead at thirteen thousand feet. Inside the old terminal at Entebbe, the hostages—many of them ill from the contaminated food they had eaten—uneasily awaited the Sunday deadline. Back from Mauritius, Amin came by late in the afternoon (about the same time the Hippos were taking off) to announce that he was doing everything to save their lives, but he could not answer for the obstinacy of the Israeli Government. He then returned to his home in Kampala. "Your government," he warned, "is gambling with your fate." To the American hostages who also had Israeli passports, Sunday, July 4, the bicentennial, promised little cause for celebration.

In the lead Hippo, the pilot, known only as David, "hit Entebbe on the nose." He could hardly believe his eyes; the airport's runways were beautifully lighted. Cutting their plane's speed, he and his copilot guided the aircraft onto the runway. The turboprops enabled the plane to come in with the least degree of sound. No brakes were applied as the Hippo moved toward the old terminal building. He pulled up to it and turned the plane so that its nose faced the building. The cargo door in the rear fuselage opened; the ramp dropped and released the Mercedes limousine and its contingent of commandos (among them sharpshooters), plus two Land-Rovers (not the customary jeeps used by the Israeli Defense Forces). The black limousine aroused no suspicion among the Ugandan guards, who assumed that it was Idi Amin making one of his surprise visits; the Land-Rovers would be carrying his trusted bodyguards. It was close to midnight in Uganda.

"It didn't seem possible," the pilot of the lead Hippo recalled. "The stillness was more frightening than a burst of gunfire. It was a real silence of death, and I sat there, feeling horribly exposed, one hand on the throttles, waiting and wondering when the trap would be sprung."

In Tel Aviv, members of the Israeli Government, the military, and others who had been involved in the planning also waited and wondered. It was 11 P.M. Saturday evening, July 3. Gathered in the Defense Minister's office were many who had been in on Thunderbolt from its inception, including Prime Minister Rabin and Minister of Transport Gad Yaakobi, who had arranged all of the flight plans and the refueling stops in Nairobi. The men had gathered nervously around a radio tuned in to the sets carried by the commandos.

"At 11:30," Yaakobi remembered vividly, "there was the noise of gunfire." It was three minutes after midnight, July 4, in Entebbe.

The last Hippo landed just as the airport lights were extinguished. Something was happening at Entebbe, for the pilot of the plane reported that "as my Hercules rolled to a stop, all hell broke loose." Shomron was first out of the lead Hippo, his men following and then fanning out; the Mercedes, with Netanyahu and his men inside, rolled down the ramp and headed for the old control tower, where the security guards were stationed. The Ugandans came to attention to salute their leader; as they did, they were shot by silenced guns. The limousine swung around the perimeter of the airport and returned to the old terminal building, where, indeed, hell had broken loose. While teams of commandos dispersed to interfere with communications and to blow up the MiGs, the main force rushed the building housing the hostages.

One of Netanyahu's men almost immediately confronted a surprised Bose, whom he shot before the German could raise his Kalashnikov. He then came upon Brigitte Kohlmann; with gun in one hand and grenade in another, she, like Bose, could not believe her eyes. The Israeli cut her down with his submachine gun. He and other commandos burst into the hostage area shouting *"Tiska-vu!"* ("Lie down!"), to take cover on the floor. Two of the Palestinians guarding the hostages began shooting and fell in a concentrated hail of fire. Screams and shouts came from the hostages as the shots rang out. Mothers sheltered their children with their bodies. The son of Ida Borochovitch saw his mother shot by Fayes Abdul-Rahim Jaber just before the Israelis killed him. Two other hostages died in the exchange of gunfire: Jean-Jacques Maimoni, a nineteen-year-old recent immigrant who had served as a nurse to the hostages who had become ill, and a man Maimoni called his "father," fifty-year-old Pasko Cohen, who had survived the Nazi death camps. In the cross fire, other hostages were wounded, but only three died. Another would die but not in the terminal fighting.

As soon as the hijackers were "neutralized," seven of the reported ten hijackers died in the attack, along with at least twenty hapless Ugandan soldiers (the toll may have been as high as forty-five). In the melee, the wily Dr. Haddad and his lieutenant, Bouvier, slipped away. Haddad's meticulous plans could not have gone more spectacularly amiss. The Entebbe rout was his last hijacking; he died of cancer in East Berlin in April 1978. His function in the Popular Front for the Liberation of Palestine was assumed by Dr. George Habash.

As the more than one hundred hostages boarded the waiting Hippos for evacuation, explosions and fireballs rose in several places as buildings (especially the control tower with its radar equipment) and MiG after MiG detonated. The wounded were treated aboard the Hippos even before the big planes lumbered off the runway and headed for Nairobi. Netanyahu's troops, deployed to search for the missing hijackers, found a couple hiding under a bed and another still inside the building. The fighting spread out onto the field, where the Israelis were fired on from the control tower. As he led his men, the young colonel was shot in the back.

"Yonni's hit!" shouted one of his men, but the wound was fatal and nothing could be done. He died before he was carried aboard the first Hercules to leave Entebbe. (Later, Operation Thunderbolt was renamed "Operation Jonathan" in his honor; this soldier-poet-philosopher was one of the most esteemed of the young officers in the Israeli Defense Forces.) Netanyahu was the sole military casualty of the Entebbe raid.

There was one other fatality at Entebbe. Seventy-five-year-old Dora Bloch, with a British passport, had been on her way to the United States to attend her son's wedding, accompanied by another son; both ended up instead in Entebbe. On Friday, July 2, after food had become lodged in her throat and Dr. Yitzak Hirsch found he was unable to remove the obstruction, she was sent to the hospital in Kampala. The piece of meat was removed and she was recovering when the Israelis struck.

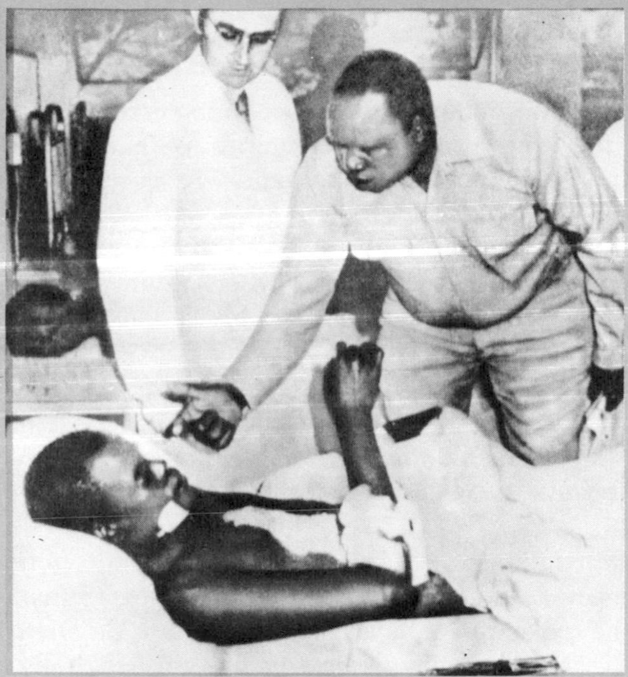

Wide World Photos

On July 5, 1976, Amin visited his wounded soldiers after the Entebbe Raid.

Jubilation in Israel: relatives of the returning hijack victims celebrate at Tel Aviv Airport. The Entebbe drama is over.

United Press International

Within fifty-three minutes after the raid began, the first Hippo carrying the hostages and the bodies of the dead lifted off the runway. Within ninety minutes, the last Israeli, except Dora Bloch, had left Uganda. After refueling in Nairobi, all aircraft returned to Israel.

The entire operation had taken place practically under Amin's nose and he was completely unaware of it. The first inkling came when, around 2 A.M. (after the raid was over), he received a cryptic call from his "good friend" Colonel Baruch Bar-Lev thanking him "very much for your cooperation."

"You know I did not succeed," the still uninformed Amin told him. (That virtually confirmed that plans for executing the hostages were already set.) Bar-Lev persuaded, "I just want to thank you, sir, for the cooperation."

"Have I done anything?" the mystified Amin asked, and later, "What happened?"

He soon learned, and about two hours later (it was barely dawn in Israel) he was on the phone to Bar-Lev demanding in an emotional voice, "What have you done to me?" Later he spoke with an Israeli newspaperman, Uri Dan, saying in undisguised anguish, "I am carrying in my arms the corpses of my soldiers who were killed by the bullets of your men; I think you have repaid me with evil for good."

Amin, after burying his soldiers as well as the seven dead hijackers with full military honors, had his revenge. Mrs. Dora Bloch, fully recovered from her choking episode, was never seen again.

When the Entebbe raid was debated, in July 1979, at the United Nations, the Ugandan Minister of Foreign Affairs, Lieutenant Colonel Juma Oris Abdallah, accused Israel of an act of aggression and condemned the government of Kenya for having assisted the Israelis. He also insisted that Mrs. Bloch had been released from the hospital before the raid and had returned to Israel. His long-winded, convoluted diatribe consisted of several other distortions of fact. After Amin was driven into exile, later in the year, taking refuge in Libya and then in Saudi Arabia, a request from the Bloch family to the new Ugandan Government brought the hijacking story to a bitter end: Dora Bloch's cane, slippers, and other items were returned to Israel with her remains.

Nurses and the director of the Kampala hospital had hidden away Mrs. Bloch's possessions and, after her murder by Ugandan soldiers, had secretly marked her grave.

Entebbe has since stood for an amazing feat of arms, virtually bloodless and stunning in its impact on international terrorism. It certainly helped to bring down the vicious Idi Amin and closed the murderous career of Dr. Wadi Haddad on a note of humiliating failure.

For the Israelis, it was a momentous victory. Danny Bloch, Israeli writer and son of the murdered Dora Bloch, put the comparatively modest exploit in the Israeli experience into perspective when he said, "After the Yom Kippur War, in 1973, people felt we had lost our secret weapon, the special spirit of Israel. Entebbe gave it back."

5

The Arab-Israeli Wars

Prelude to War

LONG BEFORE the last British soldier withdrew from Palestine when the mandate ended officially, on May 14, 1948, and the first of the Arab-Israeli wars erupted, the two factions had engaged in a savage sequence of skirmishes, hit-and-run raids, terrorist attacks, and reprisals.

The beleaguered British were forced to contend with both sides as early as 1945. Zionist guerrillas, many of whom had fought alongside the British against the Nazis, were especially aggressive, aroused by the turning away of Jewish refugees by the British. The British, headquartered in the King David Hotel, in Jerusalem, not only prevented European Jews' entry into Palestine, but had, on June 29, 1946, sent some twenty-five thousand troops into Jewish settlements in Palestine, smashed doors, arrested twenty-five hundred Jewish leaders, and confiscated weapons.

The Irgun Zvai Leumi (National Military Organization), an underground extremist group led by Menachem Begin, retaliated in July by planting bombs in the King David Hotel. Despite warnings phoned from a pharmacy across the street from the hotel by a teenage girl, Adina Hay-Nissan, the British did not evacuate. She also phoned the French Consulate and *The Palestine Post*. As she walked up the Jaffa Road and passed a police station, Hay-Nissan "heard the big explosion." She was appalled to learn that all her phone calls had been in vain. Ninety-one people—British, Arabs, and Jews—died in the explosion. In April 1947, the beset, frustrated British referred the problem of Palestine to the United Nations.

The bombing of the King David Hotel marked the climax of Jewish guerrilla operations against the British; during the previous decade, the Palestinians had been most active. The 1936 Arab rebellion, fueled by the formation of an Arab Higher Committee, incited guerrilla raids against Jewish settlements in rural areas, the boycott of larger Jewish communities, and a call for a general strike against the British. Soon dominated by the ambitious Grand Mufti (the civil-political leader of the Muslims) of Jerusalem, Haj Amin el-Husseini, the committee demanded that Jewish immigration stop, that no Palestinian land be available for purchase by Jews, and that a Palestinian national state be established.

The guerrilla operations resulted in the destruction of more than a dozen Jewish-owned factories and random killings in the countryside in 1936. The British moved to suppress the rebellion, which lasted for six months, and jailed its leaders. Husseini fled to Lebanon and exile. A short period of deceptive calm ensued, while the Arab forces were augmented by sympathizers from neighboring Arab countries. By October 1938 these Mujahedeen (Holy Warriors) controlled most of the roads in southern Palestine, cutting off communications between Gaza, Jaffa, and the Old City of Jerusalem. The British were forced to crack down again, and the fighting resulted in the deaths of more than 1,000 guerrillas, more than 450 Arabs, nearly 300 Jews, and 93 British.

The Jewish response to this setback was to prepare their own defenses. The Jewish Agency, which officially and legally represented the Palestinian Jewish

The King David Hotel after the Irgun bombing, Jerusalem, July 1946. Eighty British, Arab, and Jewish lives were lost, and seventy people were wounded. Warnings to evacuate the British offices in the hotel were not taken seriously.

National Archives

Photos courtesy of Consulate General of Israel

In 1909, this site, a barren sand dune, was chosen to become a Jewish settlement in Palestine. By the mid-1920s, it had become a busy town, with dirt streets. By 1969, Tel Aviv had become a major city in Israel, stretching from the original sand dune to the Mediterranean. Arab leaders viewed such expansion and population growth as a threat to their hegemony in the Middle East.

Photos courtesy of Consulate General of Israel/Zionist Archives and Library

After the end of World War II, many of the surviving European Jews wished to go to Palestine. Still under British control and stringent immigration regulations, Palestine was practically off limits to the immigrants. The famous ship Exodus *brought a great number of illegal immigrants, who saw their promised land only from the deck of the ship. They were seized by the British military and deported. Returnees, wired into their train, arrive in Hamburg after their round trip to Palestine. They will return to a displaced-persons camp until the British withdraw from Palestine, in 1948.*

National Archives

Arabs examine the mutilated body of a Jew in Palestine. It is the eve of the Arab-Israeli wars.

community in its day-to-day dealings with the mandate government, impressed on the British the importance of forming a kind of civil defense unit that would defend the Jews from Arab attacks. While not precisely legal, since it was organized as a civil defense unit and not a small army, the Haganah ("defense"), a paramilitary force, was formed in 1920. During the early period of Arab attacks, the Haganah, fearing British repression and negative world opinion, did not engage in offensive operations. Around the same time, Jews joined the regular police force of Palestine. By 1936, the Haganah numbered some ten thousand members; an additional two thousand belonged to the Palmach (Spearhead Detachment), an elite fighting unit.

Not all of the Palestinian Jews agreed with the Jewish Agency's self-restraint, and underground splinter groups began to form, among them the Irgun, which was a direct response to the Arab guerrilla operations in the late 1930s. The outbreak of World War II brought a lull in the Irgun attacks, but led to a splintering within its ranks with the formation of the dissident Stern Gang, which broke with their comrades to continue terrorist attacks on the British.

During World War II, members of the Haganah were given guerrilla training by the British; Jewish Rural Special Police were specially trained in case the Nazis succeeded in taking the Middle East. Palestinian Jews were trained by, and served in, the British armed forces. By 1943, there were more than forty thousand British-trained Jews in British uniform—a disciplined, tough fighting force familiar with modern warfare and its sophisticated technology. By the next year, when it appeared that the Allies would crush the Axis, the

Jewish leaders in Palestine began to consider the consequences of the 1939 white paper. Even the generally conservative Jewish Agency became more critical and openly hostile to the British. Its military arm, the Haganah, began cooperating with the Irgun in raids on government buildings, with especial attention given to immigration offices.

The Haganah's underground radio, "The Voice of Israel," resumed broadcasting in English, Hebrew, and Arabic after a period of silence during most of the war. These began again in March 1945. Eventually this plus guerrilla attacks by Jewish underground units on Arab and British targets moved the British to discipline the Jewish Agency in June 1946; a month later, a bomb exploded in the King David Hotel.

Such acts of violence did not express the mood of all of the Jewish community. The Agency's head, and later first president of the state of Israel, Chaim Weizmann, condemned the "resort to terrorism" as "tragic, futile" and "un-Jewish . . .," "a perversion of the purely defensive function of Haganah."

The Arabs, sensing the inevitable expansion of Zionism in Palestine, met in Cairo in March 1945 to form an Arab League (with encouragement from the British, who believed that this would help to block the threat of a Soviet presence in the Middle East). There were seven original member states: Egypt, Syria, Lebanon, Iraq, Transjordan (all sharing frontiers with Palestine), Saudi Arabia, and Yemen. Although Palestine was not officially a member state, a representative of the Palestinian Arabs was also present. (The Palestine Liberation Organization, the PLO, was granted full membership in 1976.)

Although the Arab League was a rather loose confederation, because of

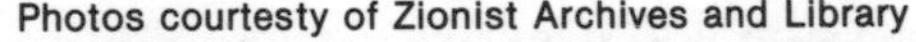
Photos courtesty of Zionist Archives and Library

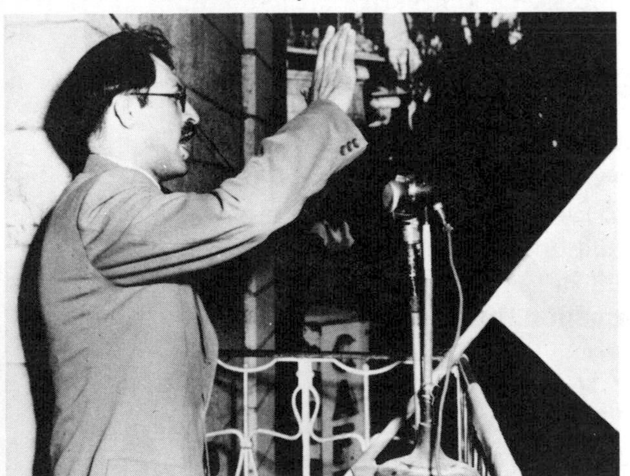

Menachem Begin, militant leader of the underground Jewish military force Irgun Zvai Leumi. Besides contending with the Arab threat, the Irgun also fought the British with terrorist attacks.

Begin and his followers in Jerusalem, 1948.

Zionist Archives and Library

Soldiers of the Irgun harrying the British in Jaffa, 1947.

internal jealousies and divided interests, not to mention the jockeying for leadership, its major unifying force was its opposition to Zionism and to the formation of a Jewish national state in Palestine.

American pressure for an increase in the numbers of Jewish immigrants, British waffling, and "The Voice of Israel" broadcasts stiffened the Arab position and obduracy. They rejected outside recommendations (e.g., the 1946 report of an Anglo-American Committee of Inquiry). A series of conferences held in London ended without agreement in February 1947, when Britain recommended that the Palestine question be referred to the United Nations. At the end of August, a majority report was issued recommending that Palestine be divided into two separate states, one Arab and one Jewish, with an international zone, which would include Jerusalem, under UN trusteeship.

Zionist leaders approved this plan, but the Arab Higher Committee (which reported to the Arab League) renounced it and threatened military action. The Arab League ordered its members to station troops along the borders of Palestine, in readiness for the eventual British evacuation. On November 29, 1947, the UN voted to accept the majority's partitioning of Palestine. The Arab members of the United Nations again denounced the plan and walked out of the meeting. In December, the Arab League pledged to aid Palestinian Arabs in resisting the partition.

Acts of violence that followed the announcement of the UN decision led to a United States embargo on the shipment of arms to the Middle East. This was a vain gesture, for the region was cluttered with arms, some that had been abandoned during the war by both the Axis and the British; some were simply stolen from Allied stores. Other supplies were smuggled into Palestine, with Zionists as the major purchasers.

Those Arab states that had standing armies—Egypt, Syria, Iraq, Lebanon, and Transjordan—were supplied with French and British equipment. Between

December 1947 and the end of the British mandate, in May 1948—a period of supposed lull before the first Arab-Israeli war broke out—hundreds of "incidents" were reported throughout Palestine: trains were blown up, mobs clashed with police or rival mobs, banks were looted, various government offices were attacked; there were at least five thousand casualties reported in this five-month period.

An Arab Liberation Army, under the command of Lebanese guerrilla leader Fawzi al-Kawukji, was formed and trained in Syria and began infiltrating into Palestine. By March 1948 there were five thousand Arab troops inside Palestine, broken up into four commands (Kawukji headed the northern command, with headquarters at Tubas; the eastern command, under Abdul Kader, was based in Jerusalem).

As early as January, Kawukji's troops began hit-and-run forays out of Syria, without much success; one attack on the Jewish settlement Tirat Zvi in February was beaten off. Kawukji's Arab Liberation Army's incursions proved to be ineffective, and by July, after he initiated a howitzer siege on another settlement, Mishmar Ha Emek, in the Plain of Esdraelon, he was counterattacked by the Haganah, which drove his unit south to Megiddo. His competence and that of his Arab Liberation Army were sorely questioned. Another blow came with the death of Kader, on April 9, in the battle for Kastel, west of Jerusalem. Kader had been popular with his men; his death disheartened them, and his unit withdrew from the battle.

The fighting around Kastel, on the way to Ramleh on the highway connecting Jerusalem with Tel Aviv, was part of the Haganah plan to keep that supply route in Israeli hands. Engaged in this operation were three Irgun platoons and many Stern Gang fighters. On the same day that Kader was killed, Jewish troops took the Arab settlement of Deir Yassin. After the Haganah withdrew, the remaining Irgun and Stern troops then proceeded to kill the Arabs of Deir Yassin: 254 men, women, and children (according to figures released by the British).

This massacre so shocked the Jewish community that the Jewish Agency sent a message of condolence to King Abdullah of Transjordan. The Arab guerrilla response was to ambush a convoy en route to the Hadassah Hospital on Mount Scopus, north of Jerusalem, killing seventy-seven Jews, many of them medical personnel.

By mid-April 1948, the Haganah began counterattacking Kawukji's main army, broke down resistance, and pushed the Arabs away from the strategic Tel Aviv-Haifa road. The settlement of Haifa was an important port and a prize for the victor. The British commander, General Stockwell, caught in between, informed the two contenders that he would withdraw his troops into Haifa's port area. The Haganah, in four columns, swept down from Mount Carmel, crumbling the Arab defenses. The area's Arab commander, Amin Aziddin, with his staff, surreptitiously abandoned Haifa, and Arab resistance shriveled. The hapless British military commander attempted to negotiate a cease-fire and truce. Rather than submit to disarmament, the Arab population chose

Wide World Photos

Ben Yehuda Street, in the heart of Jerusalem's Jewish quarter, February 1948. A planted bomb exploded, scattering debris over a large area.

National Archives

A British tanker burns off the coast of Tel Aviv after being blown up by the Irgun in February 1948.

National Archives

British soldiers searching for Irgun guerrillas in Palestine, 1948. (The identity of the dead person is not given.)

to evacuate Haifa—men, women, and children (the specter of Deir Yassin and rumor contributed to this, the beginnings of the Palestinian refugee exodus). Jaffa, to the south, came under Haganah control and was declared an open city. On May 14, Jewish troops engulfed Acre, north of Haifa, on the Mediterranean. The highway from Acre (also known as 'Akko) to Jaffa-Tel Aviv was clear, as was the bloodied road from Tel Aviv to Jerusalem.

These highways soon filled with Palestinian Arabs fleeing to the neighboring Arab states.

On May 14, the Jerusalem *Post* published accounts of sporadic fighting on the Tel Aviv-Jerusalem road, the Arab evacuation of Kfar Etzion, and the full surrender of Jaffa (most of its seven hundred thousand Arab inhabitants had already left). There was also notice of British tanks firing on Haganah troops at Latrun and that the United States still sought to postpone the partitioning of Palestine. On the same front page a headline read: "Sir Alan Takes Leave of Palestine." The British High Commissioner, Sir Alan G. Cunningham, broadcast a farewell message to the peoples of Palestine, hoping for peace between them, and stating that "Tomorrow, at midnight, the final page in the history of Palestine and the British Mandate in Palestine is turned. On the morrow a new chapter opens and Palestine's history goes on."

Although the mandate was not to end officially until midnight, the Jewish Agency's executive chairman, David Ben-Gurion, proclaimed the existence of

On May 14, 1948, the State of Israel is officially born and declares its independence. Chaim Weizmann (center, with upraised arm) was elected Israel's first President by the Knesset, Israel's parliament. He served until his death, in 1952.

Zionist Archives and Library

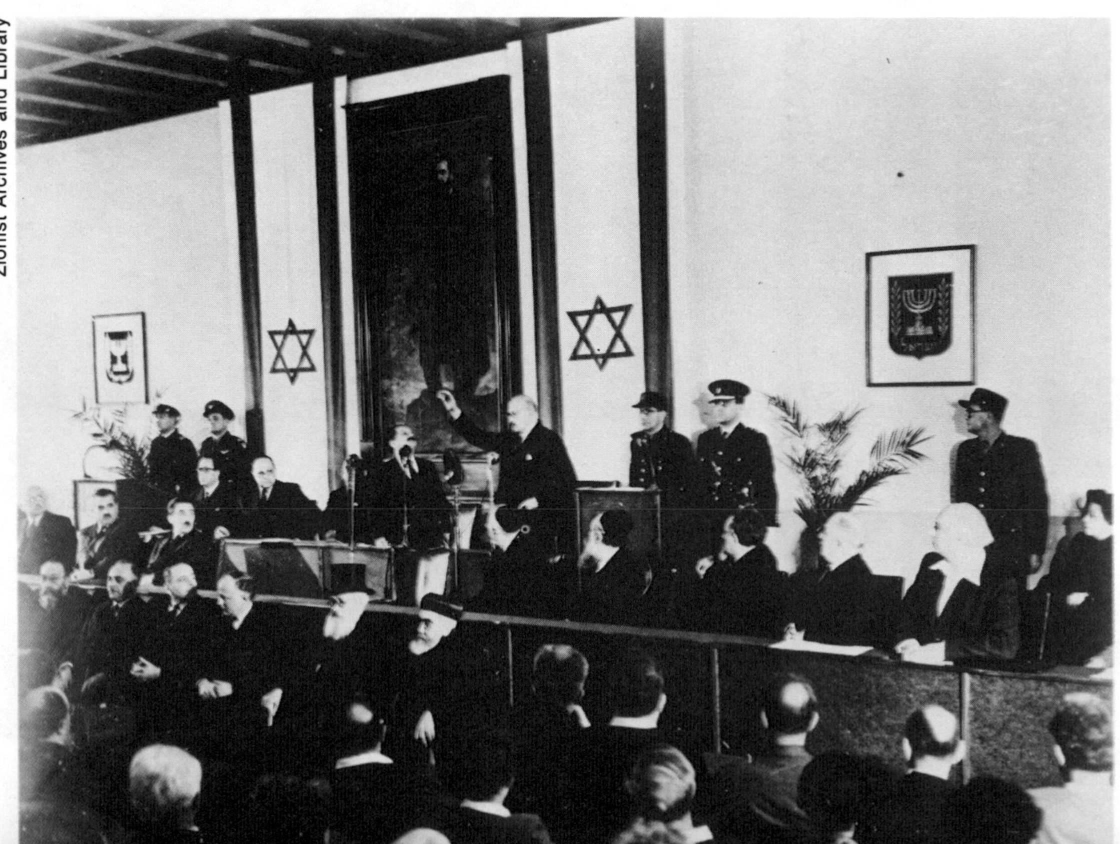

British soldiers on the docks at Haifa, in preparations for leaving Israel, 1948.

Photos courtesy of National Archives

The day after Israel became a state, five neighboring Arab states attacked the new nation. The British, not yet fully evacuated, were caught in the middle; the Royal Artillery moves in its 25-pound tanks to fight off both the Arabs and the Israelis, if necessary.

A British automatic-weapon position; the hope was to keep the belligerents apart long enough for the United Nations to negotiate a peace treaty.

Medinat Yisrael (the State of Israel) that afternoon. Eleven minutes after midnight on May 14, President Harry Truman (in what many considered a hasty political move to gain American Jewish support in his approaching bid for reelection) announced the U.S. recognition of Israel as a legitimate state. Two days later, the Soviet Union recognized the new state. Almost simultaneously with Truman's statement, the armies of five Arab League states—Egypt, Syria, Transjordan, Lebanon, and Iraq—invaded Israel.

1948–49 The War of Independence

The Arabs would call it "The War of Conquest" and the Israelis, "The War of Independence," and while the official beginning of the war is generally considered to be May 15, 1948, there had been intense fighting at least since March. But now there were defined armies, rather than groups of skirmishing irregulars and bands. The bitterness and hatred that generated the war was expressed by Abdul Raman Azzam, secretary-general of the Arab League, who said, as the war intensified, that it would be "a war of extermination and a momentous massacre which will be spoken of as [are] the Mongolian massacres and the Crusades."

Military operations got underway when the Arab Legion, under British Brigadier General John Bagot Glubb (who had formed and trained it), crossed the Allenby Bridge over the Jordan River from Jordan and occupied Bethlehem, south of Jerusalem, Ramallah to the north, and Latrun, on the Tel Aviv-Jerusalem road, in the west. At the same time, Glubb sent detachments to the outskirts of Jerusalem. Glubb's operations were the most effective and disciplined of the Arab forces. The majority of his troops had been drawn from Bedouin tribesmen, whose rough country ways were not always welcomed by city-centered Palestinians—but they were tough fighting men.

The news agency Reuters reported that King Abdullah of Transjordan rode at the head of the column of lorry-borne troops, trailed by artillery and armored cars. Symbolically, the King fired a pistol in the general direction of Palestine and wished them success in the coming battle.

Although it was hoped that a UN cease-fire agreement would spare Jerusalem, by May 14 the Holy City reverberated to the sounds of small arms and came under artillery attack. The destruction of power lines cut off the city's electricity, by which time the water supply had dried up. The Israelis moved into the section of Jerusalem known as the Old City and for about two weeks fought the Arab Legion in house-to-house skirmishing.

The Palestine Post reported: "On Friday morning [May 14, 1948], Jewish forces entered the Russian Compound and Zone C to reoccupy the buildings requisitioned from Jews last year. This operation was almost bloodless, but beyond the western edge of Zone C, Arabs engaged the Jews in Jaffa Road. The Arabs were forced back and the Barclays Bank area was taken."

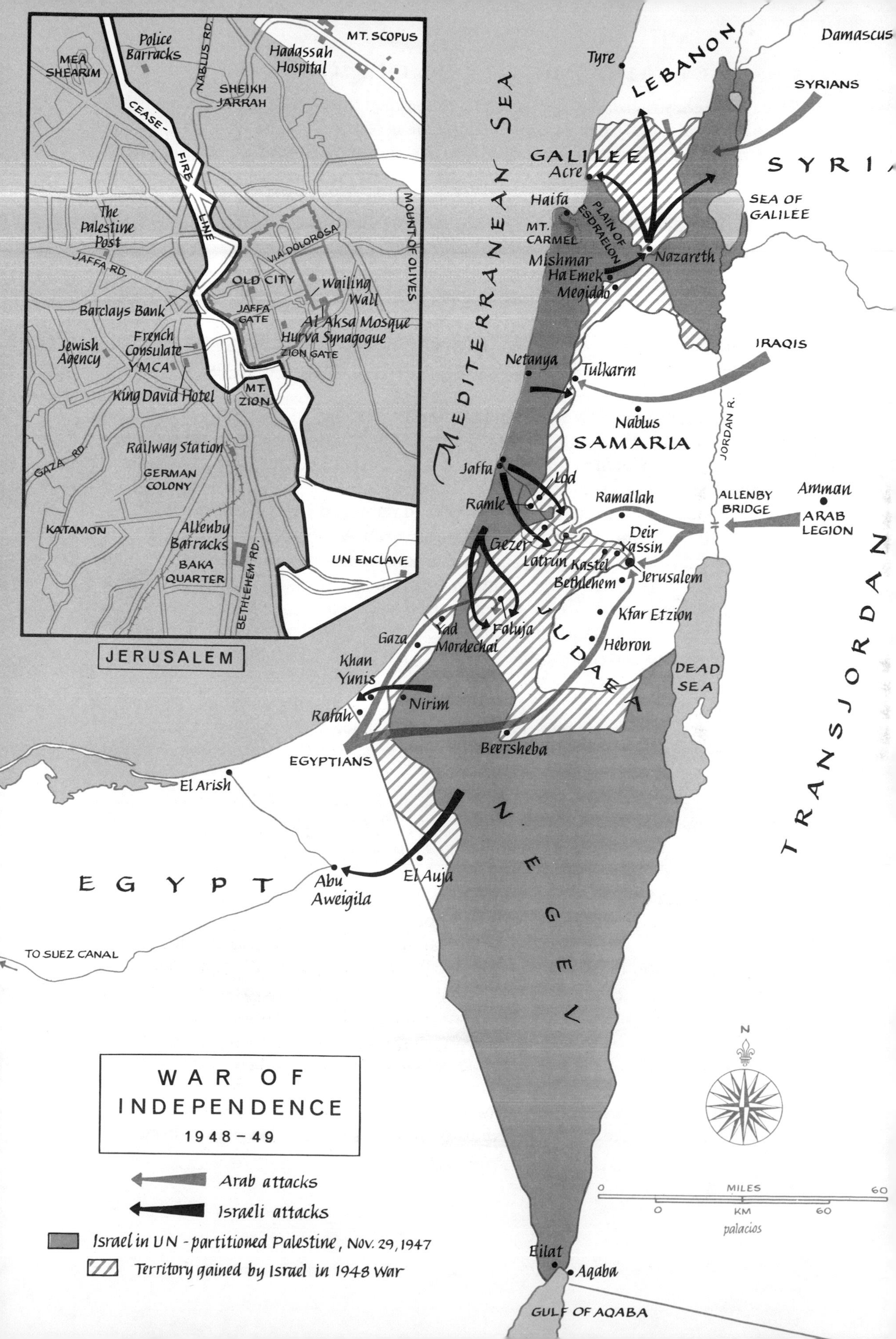
WAR OF INDEPENDENCE 1948–49
Arab attacks
Israeli attacks
Israel in UN-partitioned Palestine, Nov. 29, 1947
Territory gained by Israel in 1948 War
JERUSALEM
MEA SHEARIM
Police Barracks
NABLUS RD.
Hadassah Hospital
MT. SCOPUS
SHEIKH JARRAH
CEASE-FIRE LINE
MOUNT OF OLIVES
The Palestine Post
JAFFA RD.
VIA DOLOROSA
OLD CITY
Wailing Wall
Barclays Bank
JAFFA GATE
Al Aksa Mosque
Hurva Synagogue
ZION GATE
French Consulate
Jewish Agency
YMCA
King David Hotel
MT. ZION
Railway Station
GAZA RD.
GERMAN COLONY
KATAMON
Allenby Barracks
BAKA QUARTER
BETHLEHEM RD.
UN ENCLAVE
MEDITERRANEAN SEA
Tyre
LEBANON
Damascus
SYRIANS
SYRIA
GALILEE
Acre
Haifa
PLAIN OF ESDRAELON
MT. CARMEL
SEA OF GALILEE
Nazareth
Mishmar Ha Emek
Megiddo
IRAQIS
Netanya
Tulkarm
Nablus
SAMARIA
JORDAN R.
Jaffa
Lod
Ramle
Ramallah
ALLENBY BRIDGE
Amman
ARAB LEGION
Gezer
Deir Yassin
Latrun
Kastel
Jerusalem
Bethlehem
Kfar Etzion
Faluja
Yad Mordechai
Gaza
Hebron
JUDAEA
Khan Yunis
Nirim
Rafah
DEAD SEA
TRANSJORDAN
Beersheba
EGYPTIANS
El Arish
NEGEV
EGYPT
Abu Aweigila
El Auja
TO SUEZ CANAL
N
MILES
0
60
KM
0
60
palacios
Eilat
Aqaba
GULF OF AQABA

This constricted, street-to-street fighting flared throughout the eastern portion of Jerusalem as Israelis penetrated the areas of the Old City evacuated by the British. The Haganah soon occupied the Germany Colony, a portion of the Baka Quarter, the section known as Sheikh Jarrah, where, the Jerusalem *Post* reported, ". . . the Jewish flag was flown from the Mufti's house," as well as the Mea Shearim Barracks and the Allenby Barracks, on Bethlehem Road, while the Irgun moved into the Scopus Police Billet.

The Israeli forces were equipped primarily with small arms (pistols, rifles, Sten guns, some light machine guns) and mortars. Field artillery consisted of two 65-mm. field guns—and very little ammunition. When the War of Independence began, some twenty antiaircraft guns had been smuggled into Palestine to counter the Arab air attacks, most of them carried out in British-made aircraft.

The Jerusalem *Post* reported that, on the first day of the war, Tel Aviv was bombed and strafed by Egyptian Spitfires three times. The attacks caused some damage, hit a French airliner at the airport, and caused "some casualties" and fires in the vicinity of the Yarkum River.

The attack on nearby Sde Dov Airfield damaged half of the entire Sherut Avir, Israel's minute air force. Even the Arab Air Forces, by World War II standards, was diminutive. The total among the Egyptian, Iraqi, and Syrian air forces was 131 aircraft, the most formidable being the former RAF Spitfires, with several Italian-made Fiat and Macchi fighters. The Israelis mustered only twenty-eight planes, including nineteen Auster light monoplanes, the British version of the American Taylorcraft. The Austers had been used for artillery spotting in the Western Desert beginning in July 1941, during the North African war. The Sherut Avir had no fighters or bombers. While the motley collection of light planes served as reconnaissance and supply aircraft, the Israelis converted them into makeshift bombers. But these planes were not in the class with Egypt's Spitfires.

This attack on Sde Dov airdrome, north of Tel Aviv, by these Spitfires shot up about a half dozen Israeli planes, but all were eventually patched up and made flyable. Further attacks did no more damage. The Arab Spitfires had control of the skies but were not always in command of the situation. On May 22, Egyptian Spitfires carried out a raid on an airfield near Ramat David, southeast of Haifa, sweeping in to bomb and strafe.

This surprise attack stirred up a great deal of British resentment, for Ramat David was the base of the Royal Air Force's No. 32 and No. 38 squadrons, which were also equipped with Spitfires. They had remained to cover the evacuation of British troops from Palestine. When a second wave of Egyptian fighter planes came overhead, the British Spitfires met them in the air. In the aerial skirmish that resulted, the Egyptians left, minus three Spitfires. Nine of the RAF's planes were left in varying degrees of damage from the strafings, and one C-47 was destroyed by a bomb.

Meanwhile, the Sherut Avir had been organized into three squadrons and

Israeli gun position; the Israeli Army had very few heavy guns to fight the 1948 war.

Consulate General of Israel

An Israeli column moves out, led by an American-made jeep. The objective is the Israeli-Egyptian border.

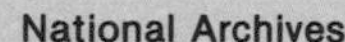

National Archives

An Egyptian Spitfire brought down by the Israelis over the Mediterranean.

Consulate General of Israel

dispersed to various airfields. The Tel Aviv Squadron, based at Sde Dov, began operating its Austers as bombers and ground-attack planes. With a crew of two, the pilot and a "bombardier," the small, thirty-six-foot-wingspan planes took off to seek the enemy. The bombardier carried the plane's bomb load in his lap—a box of hand grenades or some handmade bombs. The homemade 125-pound bombs were called "pushkins," after their method of delivery. If a concentration of Arab troops was sighted, the pilot would swoop down on them and the bombardier would toss his "bomb load" out the window. "The effect fell short of precision," historians Murray Rubenstein and Richard Goldman have written in their book *Shield of David*, "but seemed satisfactorily demoralizing to the Arabs."

By the end of May, the official Israeli Defense Forces Air Force was formed, although it was still a shoestring operation dependent upon light sport planes serving as bombers. Soon after, despite a U.S. embargo, twenty Piper Cubs were slipped into Israel to augment the new Air Force.

Some of these were assigned to the Negev Squadron, which operated from bases in southern Israel. A volunteer, Long Islander Hyman Goldstein, who was second-in-command of the squadron, describes their employment: "We flew bombing raids in the Piper Cubs; we flew reconnaissance; we flew mercy missions; we flew wounded back from the Negev and we flew ammunition into the kibbutzim that were under siege.

"All kibbutzim had an airstrip—not airstrips really; we used to fly down there and land in the desert. We used to fly in supplies, orders, ammunition, food, reconnaissance, the army.

"We worked with the army—the army was responsible for us. In other words, anytime the army wanted to take a town, they'd give us a map that said tonight we're going to take this town. We'd bomb it for them. We used 20-kilo—40-pound—bombs. When we started flying, we carried them in our laps and then they put bomb racks on the planes.

"There were seven planes in my outfit . . . The Egyptians claimed we had thirty or forty planes at times down there. They were trying to find us in the worst way, but never could. We pushed the planes into the brush at the different places where we stayed.

"We ran into Spits pretty often," Goldstein recalled. "One day I was coming back from a reconnaissance. I had an army officer with me in the back seat. The sun gets awfully hot in the desert. I got careless. I looked up and there was a Spitfire diving down on me. I took evasive action, put the stick forward and dived. He never pulled out of his dive. He went right into the desert near El Arish."

Flying missions in the unarmed Cubs and Austers was carried out close to the ground, at an altitude of ten feet. This was the single means of defense from the heavily gunned Spitfires, whose guns (two 20-mm cannons and two .50-caliber machine guns) could disintegrate these aircraft. Dodging trees, buildings, and hills, the little planes of the small Israeli Air Force performed remarkably well in the hands of their dedicated pilots.

The Israeli Army began operations with as many or more handicaps than the Air Force. The ill-equipped, under-supplied Israeli troops were overwhelmed by Glubb's Arab Legion. Cut off from reinforcements, supplies, and even communications (the sole contact with other Israeli units was via one of the little Austers operating from makeshift air strips), Jewish resistance in the Old City ceased around noon on May 28. A surrender was arranged, initiated by two rabbis: seventy-year-old Reuven Hazen and Isarel Mintzberg, who waved an improvised flag (a white tablecloth tacked to a stick).

According to the terms of surrender, all men between the ages of fifteen and fifty were taken prisoner—a total of 294, of whom more than fifty were wounded. They were taken to a prisoner-of-war camp in Transjordan. The Old City of Jerusalem was then evacuated of all its Jewish population; for over six hours, some twelve hundred people—older men, women (some of whom had been armed), and children, carrying small bundles of possessions—streamed through the Zion Gate into Haganah-held Jerusalem.

Rumors spread among the captives and the evacuees that, once they were in Arab hands, they would be massacred. This did not occur; the entire operation was protected by Glubb's disciplined Arab Legion (which employed more than two hundred British officers) under Red Cross observation.

The two weeks of fighting, most of it with small arms and Arab artillery, damaged the historic Old City. A Reuters correspondent evoked images of "stumps of walls that had once been homes and piles of rubble that were once a synagogue." (The Israelis accused the Arabs of deliberately destroying the Hurva Synagogue in the final battling.)

Although they had taken the Old City, the Arab Legion's attempts to fan out into the north and west were stopped by the Haganah.

While the Arab Legion had been fighting around Jerusalem, their brothers-in-arms, the Egyptian Army, set out in two columns from El-Arish, in the Sinai—one column moving along the coastal road toward Gaza and Tel Aviv and the other column northeastward toward Beersheba and Bethlehem to join with the Arab Legion in the Jerusalem battle area. Small Jewish farming settlements, *kibbutzim*, blocked their paths.

One of these was Yad Mordechai, at the Gaza end of the main coastal highway. The kibbutz was named for a twenty-two-year-old hero killed in the Warsaw Ghetto uprising in 1943, Mordechai Anilevicz. Yad Mordechai was founded by Zionists, among the last who had fled Poland before the Nazi invasion. It lay just a bit more than halfway from the Egyptian border to Tel Aviv. In the weeks before there was all-out war, Yad Mordechai's residents had been assured that an Egyptian invasion was unlikely, but that they should be prepared for attack by Arab bands of irregulars or local armed Arab villagers. Rudimentary defenses were prepared: barbed wire barriers, concrete dugouts, and trenches.

The "army" of Yad Mordechai numbered less than one hundred men and boys, armed with rifles, two machine guns, four hundred hand grenades, and two 2-inch mortars complete with fifty shells. This was all that stood between Tel Aviv and perhaps five thousand Egyptians in armored vehicles, tanks, artillery, infantry, and aircraft.

By May 15 the Egyptian column had passed through Gaza, and on May 18 it reached Yad Mordechai. For six days the few defenders of the kibbutz checked the advance of an entire Egyptian brigade. The settlement was surrounded and attacked from the air and by artillery. On the second day, the water tower was destroyed. The younger fighters attacked Egyptian tanks with home-made Molotov cocktails (bottles filled with a flammable liquid). The outcome was inevitable, especially when it became obvious that it would be impossible to get reinforcements and supplies. Casualties were high and morale was low by the fourth day of the attack. Even so, although it was decided to evacuate, many of the Israeli defenders argued in favor of fighting to the last man, as had their countrymen at Warsaw.

The town was aflame and the last machine gun burned out on May 23, when the final decision was made. Twenty-three men and boys were dead; another thirty were wounded. The survivors, including women, carrying the wounded, slipped out of Yad Mordechai during the night and infiltrated through Egyptian lines to a neighboring settlement. Although the kibbutz was destroyed, the militarily minor battle for Yad Mordechai inspirited the Israelis. Yigael Yadin, chief operations officer of the Haganah (who later became a professor of archeology), admitted that the forces they were facing were formidable and Arab arms superiority was "considerable." There was no true Israeli Air Force, he noted; the Israeli tank "corps" consisted of three tanks (one British, two American) that had been acquired under a system that American soldiers called "midnight requisition."

But, Yadin observed, "Evaluation of the possibilities cannot merely be a military consideration . . . the problem is to what extent our men will be able to overcome enemy forces by virtue of their fighting spirit . . . It has been found that it is not the numbers and the formation that determine the outcome of battle, but something else." That "something else" had been affirmed in the battles for the Old City and minuscule Yad Mordechai.

Egyptian forces continued their push northward along the coastal road; the eastern column moved more rapidly and had already linked up with the Transjordanians (i.e., the Arab Legion) in the vicinity of besieged Jerusalem. The western column was stopped by the Haganah at Isdud, about thirty-five miles west of the Holy City.

An important element contributing to the Israelis' defense was the lack of a unified, cooperative effort among the Arabs. The major participants were

Photos courtesy of National Archives

Arab artillery shelling Israeli troops at Bab el Wad, on the road to Jerusalem.

British soldiers taking refuge behind an armored vehicle; they have come under Arab fire.

An Israeli village burns after Arab bombardment.

the Transjordanian Arab League and the Egyptian Army; movements by the other Arab armies were quite tentative: the Lebanese forces moved up to Palestine's frontier in the north; a small Iraqi unit claimed that it had occupied the Arab towns of Nablus and Tulkarm and was positioned about fifteen miles north of Tel Aviv. A Syrian army moved cautiously across the Palestinian frontier from the northeast. These forces shared one quality with the Israelis: they were ill-equipped. They were not, except for the Jordanians, well trained, either, and their commanders were timorous and mutually suspicious. After the war, Musa Alami, one of the founders of the Arab League, observed bitterly that "In the face of the enemy the Arabs were not a state, but petty states; groups, not a nation; each fearing and anxiously watching the other and intriguing against it."

This was particularly obvious in the rivalry between the Egyptians and the Transjordanians. King Farouk suspected that King Abdullah, with his efficient Arab Legion, had plans for taking all of Palestine for Transjordan. Egyptian troops went so far as to intercept military supplies intended for Transjordanian units, thus undermining their fighting capability. When Abdullah began calling himself the Supreme Arab Commander, the suspicions and jealousies intensified.

Not that all was serene among the Israelis, either. With the coming of war, an attempt was made to organize a legal National Army whose members swore allegiance to the State of Israel and prohibited all other armed groups—specifically the difficult-to-control Irgun and Stern Gang. The Irgun clearly objected to this treatment. (The "control of manpower" decree authorized the conscription of all adults between the ages of seventeen and fifty-five; those who did not serve in the Israeli Defense Forces were pressed into agricultural service.) The fact that the new government meant business was dramatically demonstrated at Tel Aviv on June 22, when the Haganah sank the *Altelena*, carrying arms and ammunition destined for Irgun groups. This occurred during a period of truce between the Arabs and the Israelis.

The truce had been brought about through the efforts of the Swedish UN mediator, Count Folke Bernadotte, who had arrived in Palestine on May 20. A British resolution proposing a four-week truce was undoubtedly welcomed by both sides, for the Arab forces were generally demoralized and short of supplies, and the Israelis, also ill-equipped, needed time.

Among the prime stipulations of the truce was that the belligerents were not to move more troops or military equipment and supplies into those sectors they held at the time of the truce. The truce, when finally agreed upon, was to run from June 11 until July 9; during this period neither side complied with its conditions.

There were curious fluctuations in Arab manpower. The Egyptians increased their numbers by about eight thousand, bringing their force in Palestine up to eighteen thousand troops; Iraqi forces could call upon some fifteen thousand men, some of them local Palestinian irregulars. Kawukji's Arab Liberation Army had shrunk to some two thousand men. Even the Transjordanian Army

Soldiers of the Syrian Army, west of Jerusalem.

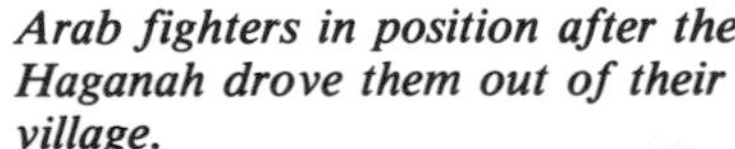

Arab fighters in position after the Haganah drove them out of their village.

Photos courtesy of National Archives

Fawzi al-Kawukji, Lebanese leader of the Arab Liberation Army, inspects his troops.

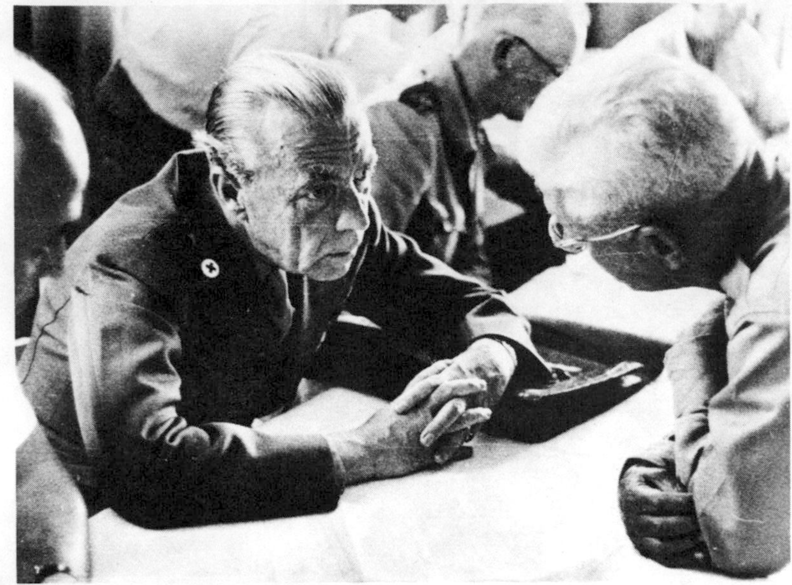

United Nations mediator Count Folke Bernadotte (left) in conference with Colonel Wendell McCoy, the U.S. Army's senior UN military observer. Bernadotte was assassinated by the Stern Gang in Jerusalem, September 1948.

United Nations/Department of Public Information

dwindled from five thousand to four thousand, partly because of internal problems in Transjordan; an additional shock resulted when, under American pressure, Britain ordered all British Army officers serving with the Arab Legion to withdraw. (This did not include Glubb, however.)

The Israelis took full advantage of the truce by organizing their Army into four "fronts" (equivalent to the standard European corps) and could draw upon some sixty thousand to one hundred thousand troops to man them. (The Arab numbers lessened during the truce to about forty-five thousand; precise troop numbers from either side are hard to come by.)

As for the fronts, the First and Second, in the North, faced the borders of Lebanon, Syria, and Transjordan; the Third, in central Palestine, ran from Tel Aviv to Jerusalem, where Palestine jutted into Transjordan; the Fourth Front lay in the South, in the Negev, facing Egypt on the west and Transjordan to the east.

Besides reorganizing its forces, the Haganah restocked its weapons, ammunition, and supplies, acquiring goodly supplies of weapons and ammunition via Czechoslovakia. Aircraft, ranging from British Bristol Beaufighters to three American Boeing Flying Fortresses, were smuggled into Israel by volunteer pilots. When the truce ended, on July 9, the Israelis were better prepared and organized than when the fighting began, and the Arabs, thanks to their internal disarray and despite some troop increases in the Egyptian and Iraqi forces, were not.

On July 9, 1948, the Israelis mounted what has come to be called the Ten Days' Offensive, concentrating their forces in the first three fronts: on the Tel Aviv-Jerusalem sector, on the Syrian-held section in the North, and on Kawukji's Arab Liberation Army in Galilee. Colonel Yigal Allon's Palmach brigade was

National Archives

Haganah soldiers with a light mortar and an automatic rifle.

Colonel Yigal Allon, commander of the Palmach Brigade on the Southern Front.

Consulate General of Israel

An Israeli patrol in the Katamon quarter, Jerusalem.

National Archives

divided into three battle groups, about two thousand troops each. Their infantry was transported in jeeps, and they were also equipped with artillery, half-tracks, and armored cars. During the period of the Ten Days, the Palmach depended a good deal on night attacks, which proved to be most effective. To buttress the defense of Tel Aviv, one of the Palmach battle groups set out under cover of night on July 9; another moved out of Gezer, southeast of Tel Aviv. These groups formed a pincer movement on Ramleh and Lod in an effort to begin clearing the road to Jerusalem. They faced some four thousand troops of Glubb's Arab Legion as well as Arab Liberation Army units in Lod and Ramleh.

The third Palmach group was deployed to counter Egyptian forces moving northwestward from Bethlehem toward Latrun on the Tel Aviv-Jerusalem highway. This group pushed the Egyptians out of several small towns—Sara, Suba, Deir Rafat—and then retook the Jewish settlement of Hartuv. To the north, the other two Palmach groups concentrated on Glubb's Arab Legion, which was spread rather thin along its defense line, and converged on Hadita; on July 11, the Israeli troops attacked Lod. The Arabs held firm, but an attempt to relieve them with armored cars was driven off and Lod fell into Israeli hands the next day. The Arab populations of Lod and Ramleh, which was abandoned by its military defenders, were driven out of the towns (often under mortar fire) eastward into Samaria, behind the Arab-held lines.

Latrun, where the Arab Legion occupied the police station and on whose roof a single artillery piece was positioned, held out for four days. This one gun disabled the five Israeli tanks in the Palmach vanguard. Over the four days of conflict in Latrun, the gun crews were regularly replaced as men were killed or wounded. The fighting continued without conclusion until another truce was declared, on July 18.

Farther north, on the Syrian front, the Israelis' attempt to recover the Jewish settlement of Mishmar Hayarden failed, although when the truce was called on July 11, they did occupy Dardara, on the eastern shore of Lake Huleh, inside Syria. The fighting in Galilee was more successful, and by July 18, the Haganah smashed Kawukji's Arab Liberation Army, took Nazareth (from which Kawukji fled with his staff), and occupied several small Arab villages northeast and west of Nazareth, reinforcing their hold on Haifa and Acre, on the Mediterranean, and expanding their area of occupation.

Except for the unsuccessful thrust into Syria, the Ten Days' Offensive was an Israeli victory; what followed was a curious lull that would hardly qualify as a truce. This lasted longer than the first—from July 18 until October 15, a period in which men, arms, and other weaponry arrived in Israel from assorted sympathetic sources. The Arabs were not so resourceful and their cause continued to suffer from internal rivalries. During the truce, an Arab Government

The "Palestinian question": What is to become of these people? This family has found refuge in the sand dunes near Gaza; the tent has been constructed of blankets provided by the United Nations. Homeless Palestinians are forced into a homeless, nomadic life by war.

Palestinian refugees who have fled from the war in what was once their traditional homeland to sanctuary in Lebanon and Syria.

Photos courtesy of
United Nations/Department of Public Information

An Israeli woman mourns over her son's grave, Tel Aviv, July 1948.

of All Palestine was proclaimed and was recognized by all Arab governments except Transjordan, which, in turn, proclaimed a National Congress.

Transjordan's King Abdullah further antagonized his brothers-in-arms by publicly disparaging the other Arab armies as compared with his (or more precisely Glubb's) Arab Legion.

During the period of truce, the Israelis suffered in the eyes of the world when an apparent ambush by the Stern Gang resulted in the assassination of United Nations peacemaker Count Bernadotte and a French observer, Colonel André Serot, in Jerusalem on September 17, 1948. Bernadotte's party was being driven from Jerusalem's neutral zone into Jewish-occupied territory in the New City. Their cars flew the United Nations flag; a third car flew a Red Cross flag.

In the Katamon quarter of Jerusalem, their convoy stopped at what was believed to be a checkpoint. An Israeli jeep blocked the roadway. Men in Israeli Army uniform, with guns, approached the convoy; one ran toward the UN cars, passed by the first one, and when he came to the second car (containing Bernadotte and Serot), he put the muzzle of a machine gun into the open window and opened fire on the back-seat passengers. Serot died instantly and Bernadotte soon after, before their car reached Hadassah Hospital.

Why the Stern Gang or the "Fatherland Front," as they called themselves when they claimed responsibility for the murders (the Irgun denied any connection), wanted the UN mediator out of the way is not clear. Both the Israelis and the Arabs rejected the UN plan for the partitioning of Palestine. The Israelis, by the time of the second truce, were quite certain that they would win the war and all of Palestine; the Arabs believed that Transjordan's King Abdullah would benefit most from such a solution and that he would, if there were an Islamic victory, get the lion's share of the spoils. There were rumors that Bernadotte had been a Nazi sympathizer during World War II. Further, he was believed to be pro-British, and his plan for an Arab-Israeli peace was thought to call for turning Jerusalem over to the Arabs.

The Israeli Government immediately denounced the assassination. "This murder," the official statement read in part, "is an attack on the authority of the U.N. and a calculated assault on the sovereignty of the State of Israel. It is an act of treachery against the Israel Defence Army. It is a desecration of the Holy City of Jerusalem." *The Palestine Post* announced that the Israeli Army was taking "swift action to wipe out [the] dissident murderers of Bernadotte." Known bases of illegal guerrillas were raided by the Army and hundreds of suspects were arrested, but the man with a machine gun was never identified, nor was anyone charged with the killings.

Bernadotte was succeeded almost immediately by an American, Dr. Ralph Bunche, who fully intended to carry on where Bernadotte left off and to maintain the truce. Meanwhile, the Israelis grew stronger and the problems of the disuniting Arabs were compounded by the refugees expelled or fleeing from Israeli-held territory. By October 1948, after some five months of fighting, it was estimated that more than four hundred fifty thousand Palestinians had fled to Transjordan, Syria, and Lebanon (placing a burden on their war-strained, often corrupt economies and governments) or crowded into those sections still held by Arabs in Palestine. This was the beginning of an anguish that has beset the Middle East ever since.

The long, strife-ridden truce ended in mid-October, although skirmishes and artillery exchanges had continued through September, making the peace-keeping efforts by UN observers quite difficult. The Israelis mounted two major

Israeli refugees and casualties await evacuation from the war zones by United Nations representatives.

United Nations/Department of Public Information

operations: "Hiram," in the North, against the remnants of Kawukji's Arab Liberation Army; and "Ten Plagues," in the South, against the Egyptian Army, headquartered in Gaza.

The objective of Ten Plagues was to drive the Egyptians out of the Negev and back into Egypt. The Egyptian forces were spread rather thin, holding several towns on the Hebron-to-El-Auja road in the east. Along the Mediterranean coast to the West, they were positioned from Isdud in the north, to Rafah in the south. The Haganah was concentrated primarily in between and to the north. Both contenders had roughly the same number of troops, fifteen thousand each.

Fighting began in the evening of October 15, when the Israeli Air Force attacked the enemy airfields in the Negev as the main Israeli thrust came from the north, where the Arabs held several positions, west to east, from Isdud to Beit Jibrin.

Colonel Yigal Allon was assigned to lead the Haganah, which also included a Palmach division, in the Ten Plagues offensive. The battle, lasting from October 15 to October 21, consisted of feints, probes, and the taking of important road positions to cut off Egyptian supplies and to open up a supply line to the Israelis in the Negev, ringed by Egyptian-held towns. On October 19, Allon mounted a night attack on Huleiqat and secured the town by the next day; this successful operation broke the Egyptian ring and provided the Israelis with surface communications with the Negev troops. Pushing southward, Allon captured Beersheba on October 21, cutting off the Egyptians holding Hebron.

Beit Hannon, to the north of Gaza, was soon taken by the Israelis. The Egyptians on the northern section of the Mediterranean coast were virtually isolated, as were others who held fast to a five-mile strip along the west-east road between Al-Majdal and Beit Jibrin, which was called the Faluja Pocket.

Egyptian forces began falling back toward their homeland, leaving the men in the Faluja Pocket and those in the Hebron area to hold out as best they could, with some aid from the Arab League.

The focus of the fighting then shifted away from Ten Plagues to Galilee and Operation Hiram, where Kawukji, with some two thousand men, harassed the Israelis from bases in the mountains south of Lebanon. Operation Hiram was assigned to Colonel Moshe Carmel, who planned the operation in two phases: The first, opening with bombing attacks on the Arab Liberation Army, began with diversionary attacks from the south, while the main assaults thrust into the Arab-held area farther north, toward Tarshia from the west and Sa'sa' from the east. Kawukji, suspecting an attack, moved his forces away from the south, thus strengthening them where the main Israeli attacks were supposed to strike. The attacks opened on October 28 against Tarshiha, but were turned back; the eastern assault was more successful and the Israeli infantry and armored troops took Safsaf and Sa'sa'. Tarshia was softened by bombing and strafing by the Israeli Air Force, and by October 30 it fell to the Israelis.

In turn, they began driving the Arabs into Lebanon from the south and the east. On October 31, Carmel's forces had retaken Arab-controlled territory

Incited by exaggerated atrocity rumors, Arabs pack up their belongings and flee before the Israeli Army; some find refuge in a Quaker camp supplied by the United Nations.

Photos courtesy of United Nations/Department of Public Information

in Palestine and crossed the Lebanese frontier. When he stopped, Carmel occupied a section of Lebanon fifteen miles long and five miles deep.

Meanwhile, a new cease-fire, which had been announced by the UN on October 22, was blatantly disregarded by all. With the Egyptians still dug in in the southern sector, attempts to break out of their pockets led to Egyptian-Israeli patrol clashes. The UN observer Henri Vigier noted that after the cease-fire the Israelis continued to move troops to the southern sector. *The Palestine Post* reported on November 4 that the Iraqis violated the truce by firing upon Israeli positions for an hour with mortars, and that Egyptian troops had attempted to break out of the Faluja Pocket at Iraq Suweidan and failed, setting off a skirmish of patrols and an artillery duel.

On November 16, 1948, the UN Security Council approved a resolution calling for an armistice in Palestine; three days later, the fighting reignited. The Egyptians moved first, pushing eastward from their positions in the Gaza area, and occupied two high points in the Negev. The objective was to head northward toward the troops trapped inside the Faluja Pocket. On December 7, with sixteen tanks and a combined infantry-armored assault, they struck at Israeli positions. The Egyptians were driven back with a loss of five tanks. Another Egyptian push was made on December 10, this time from Rafah toward an Israeli concentration near Nirim; not only was the attack repulsed, the Israelis counterattacked and took back the ground the Egyptians had seized in their November push.

Colonel Allon then planned "Operation Ayin" to end all Egyptian offensive capabilities. For this he had approximately the same number of troops as for the Ten Plagues offensive, in October. With the other fronts virtually dormant, the Israelis could concentrate on breaking the Egyptian Army. "Ayin" began on December 22 with diversionary skirmishing in the west, with air strikes and artillery barrages against Gaza, Khan Yunis, and Rafah (on the Egyptian-Israeli frontier). The main assault then was unleashed in the east on Asluj, moved southward across the frontier, then swung eastward towards El-Arish. Some of these movements were accomplished by using an old, abandoned Roman road that ran between Beersheba and El Auja (the Egyptians habitually took positions along modern highways).

United Nations/Department of Public Information

The dimensions of the 1948 war are illustrated by this photograph taken from the Mandelbaum Gate, Jerusalem. Israelis occupy the buildings on the left, and the Arabs hold the buildings on the right.

By December 28, Israeli columns had penetrated inside the borders of Egypt itself on the way to El-Arish, capturing an Egyptian air base at Bir Lahma and supplies at Abu Aweigila. But Allon did not capture El-Arish. International pressure was applied to get the Israelis out of Egypt. The Egyptians' pleas for help from their Arab brothers were not heeded. Inside Egypt itself, the Israeli invasion produced questions and recriminations. The Egyptian Army had set out believing in certain victory over the Israelis. On December 28, Egyptian Premier Nokrashy Pasha was assassinated and the new Premier, Abdul Hadi, took over, stating that Egypt did not require proffered British intervention to save the situation.

By January 3, 1949, Israeli troops had begun to withdraw from Egypt and Egyptian troops were hopelessly enclosed in the Negev. On January 7, the Egyptians asked for an armistice, just in time to cancel an Israeli assault on Rafah, in the Gaza Strip. By January 10 the last Israeli soldier had left Egypt.

Formal armistice agreements were signed with Egypt in February, with other Arab states (except Iraq, which refused) joining in: Lebanon in March, Jordan (as it came to be known) and Syria in July. When the war ended, Israel had more than a third more territory than had been originally assigned by the UN plan, some twenty-five hundred square miles. Egypt retained the Gaza Strip; Jordan annexed the West Bank of the Jordan River (gaining some twenty-two hundred square miles); and the Holy City was divided up between the new Hashimite Kingdom of Jordan and the internationally recognized State of Israel. Some seven hundred thousand Palestinians had no state at all.

The fighting had stopped, but there was no official peace. The impact of the war's outcome stunned the Arabs. With their long and honorable tradition of *jihad*, they had been beaten by a tiny nation wedged into the Arab world and enclosed by Arab nations and the sea.

Arab disunity and corruption had contributed greatly to the Israeli victory. The defeat embittered junior officers in the various Arab armies. One officer, who had been a major during the war and was wounded in battle, spoke for his Egyptian brothers-in-arms when he said, "We are fighting in Palestine, but all our thoughts were concentrated on Egypt . . . left an easy prey to hungry wolves [he was referring to the Farouk government] . . . We have been duped—

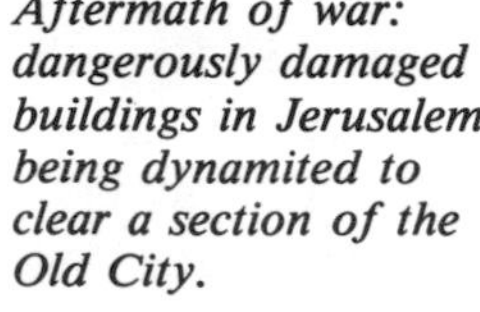
Aftermath of war: dangerously damaged buildings in Jerusalem being dynamited to clear a section of the Old City.

United Nations/Department of Public Information

United Nations/Department of Public Information

Peace talks after the 1948 war involve how the nomadic Bedouins will be affected by altered territorial boundaries after Israel's victory over the Arabs. In the right foreground is Major Radi Hindawi, of the Arab Legion. Israeli Colonel Moshe Dayan converses with a Bedouin chief.

"Operation Magic Carpet," in which Jews from all over the world were brought to Israel. These are Yemenites, from southern Arabia.

Consulate General of Israel

pushed into a battle for which we were unprepared. Vile ambitions. . . insidious intrigues. . . are toying with our destinies, and we are left under fire unarmed."

The major, Gamal Abdel Nasser, once a law student, a graduate of the Royal Military Academy, had been militantly anti-British since his student years. In 1942 he founded the clandestine Society of Free Officers, with which he planned, in company with other dissident young officers, to root out the corruption and inefficiency of Egyptian politics and any foreign interference in Egypt's affairs. So it was that when the 1948 Arab-Israeli war ended so ignominiously for Egypt, he had the instrument with which to deal with Farouk's government (which had provided the Egyptian Army with worthless ammunition and arms from Italian sources) and with the victorious "Zionists."

The victims of war: Palestinian children and the aged—neither understanding what the war was about—depend on United Nations care for housing, food, and education. Some of these children knew no other home but the austere camps; some will grow up to be ruthless guerrillas.

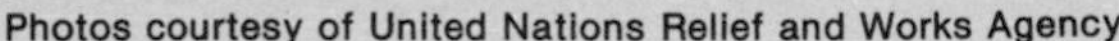

Photos courtesy of United Nations Relief and Works Agency

United Nations/Department of Public Information

In the aftermath of the 1948–49 Arab-Israeli war, Arab farmers return to plowing their fields as their ancestors had for centuries, with a camel and oxen.

Encompassed by barbed wire, Arab children play in a United Nations camp in Haifa.

United Nations/Department of Public Information

United Nations Relief and Works Agency

A Palestinian refugee camp in Gaza, maintained by the United Nations. By 1950, one third of the 1,850,000 Palestinian refugees lived in such camps.

Abdul Rahman Azzam, the first secretary-general of the Arab League, voiced the consensus opinion of Arabs at the time when he said, "We have a secret weapon which we can use better than guns and machine guns, and that is time. As long as we do not make peace with the Zionists, the war is not over; and as long as the war is not over there is neither victor nor vanquished. As soon as we recognize the state of Israel, we admit by this act that we are vanquished."

There was no peace in the Middle East. Arab commando raids into Israeli territory and Israeli retaliatory raids kept the frontiers flickering until Nasser was ready for the next round.

1956–57 Sinai-Suez War

The second major flare-up in the Arab-Israeli wars would come in 1956, after a period of stresses, accusations, political assassinations, and cross-frontier raids. Events between the uncertain armistice of 1949 and the Suez War of 1956 pointed toward the inevitable climax of war.

In 1950, when the United States was preoccupied with war in Korea, the Israeli parliament, the Knesset, passed the Law of Return, which specified that any Jew, anywhere in the world, had the right to come to Israel. Contemporaneously, the Swedish Government closed the issue of the assassination of Count Bernadotte, recognizing "with satisfaction that the Government of Israel admits without circumlocution and expresses its regrets of the shortcomings of the original Israel police inquiry in the case which have been pointed out by the Swedish authorities." It also expressed the importance of the continuing inquiry by the Israeli Army, which meant that the government of Israel did not consider the case closed. The Swedish Government, in the same diplomatic note, indicated that "conditions in Israel have been stabilized." To the Israelis, the note had a deeper meaning: an early recognition of the State of Israel, which had been deferred by the murder of Bernadotte.

Peace, too, would be deferred. In March 1950, Turkey became the first Muslim state to recognize Israel; Iran followed suit. Neither belonged to the Arab brotherhood. On April 1, the Arab League voted to expel any member making a separate peace with Israel. On April 24, King Abdullah of Jordan, the new Hashimite Kingdom (named for Beni Hashim, a family affiliation of the King that associated him with Hashim, a great-grandfather of the Prophet Mohammed), formally annexed Jordan-occupied eastern Palestine, including the Old City of Jerusalem with its treasury of religious shrines.

It was in the Old City that, on July 20, 1951, King Abdullah was shot in the head inside the El Aksa Mosque by a twenty-one-year-old dissident, who was killed on the scene by the king's guards. Ironically Abdullah had come to Jerusalem to eulogize the Lebanese Premier, Riad es-Solh, who had been assassinated in Jordan's capital, Amman, the week before. Martial law was immediately declared in the Old City of Jerusalem and Amman. Abdullah's

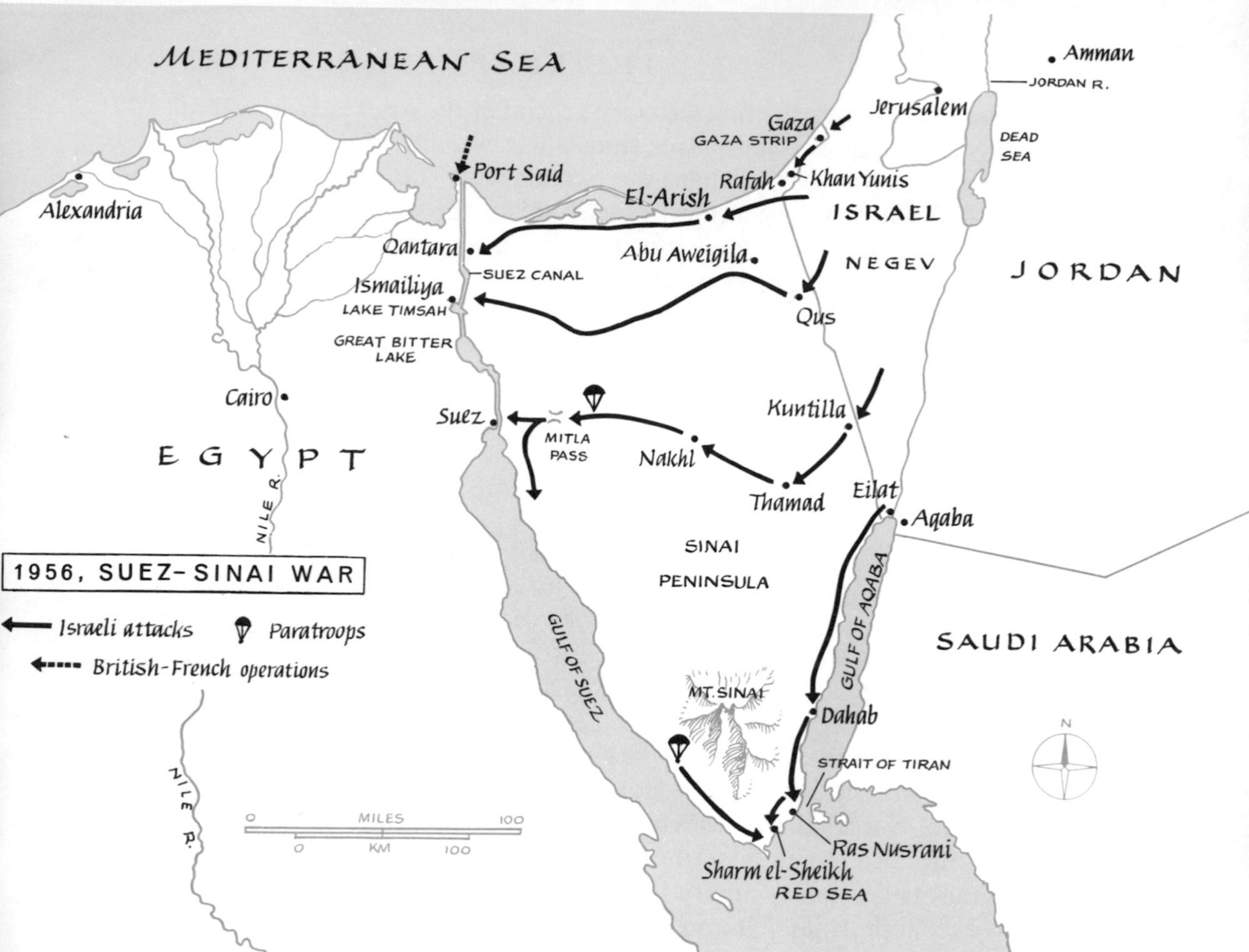

younger son, thirty-eight-year-old Naif ibn Abdullah, was appointed regent by the Jordanian Council of Ministers. Later in the year, the older son, Tallal, was crowned King of Jordan. (His peculiar behavior eventually led the Parliament to declare him mentally ill and depose him the next year. He was succeeded by his son, Hussein ibn Tallal, then only eighteen, who was crowned on May 2, 1953.)

Meanwhile trouble was brewing for King Farouk in Egypt; violent anti-British and antiroyalist riots led to the declaration of martial law in Cairo late in January 1952. Rioters ranged through the streets, attacking and often killing foreigners; special targets of their outrage were the commander-in-chief of the Army, Field Marshal Mohammed Hadar, and King Farouk. When security forces brought the disturbances under control, more than twenty people were dead, and damages to property—mostly American, British, and French—amounted to more than $10 million. The British were naturally anxious to continue their hold on the Suez Canal, and the more nationalistic Egyptians were just as eager to take back their property. By May 1952 the British had agreed to an eventual evacuation of British troops from the canal zone, provided that

Farouk gave up claims to Sudan (which had been under joint English-Egyptian control since the beginning of the twentieth century).

Soon after, a new bombshell landed in the political labyrinth of the Middle East. Certain patriotic-nationalistic members of the Egyptian Army had formed a Revolutionary Command Council, whose nominal leader was Field Marshal Mohammed Naguib but whose motivating personality was Colonel Gamal Abdel Nasser. Still bitter over the corruption displayed by the army high command during the 1948–49 war with Israel, and with Farouk's blatantly luxurious way of life in a poverty-stricken land, the Revolutionary Command Council made a sudden move on July 22, 1952. Nasser's secret Society of Free Officers swept down on army headquarters and the national radio station at midnight. Naguib's troops surrounded Farouk's summer residence in Alexandria, the Ras el Tin Palace. For Farouk, the situation was hopeless and his palace guard capitulated without a struggle, after firing a few shots into the air. Naguib obtained two demands from the king: that he sign an abdication paper and that he leave Egypt by noon July 26. Farouk's other palaces—one in Alexandria, two in Cairo—were also surrounded and cordoned off, virtually without resistance from the guards.

As demanded, Farouk abdicated and boarded the royal yacht in Alexandria's harbor; he was accompanied by the American ambassador, Jefferson Caffery, which led to rumors that Farouk would seek asylum in the United States (actually he fled to Italy, where he died, at the age of forty-five, in 1965). His six-month-old son, Ahmed Fuad II, was proclaimed King of Egypt by the Cabinet.

Having deposed a most unpopular king, the Revolutionary Command Council was faced with the formation of a new, functioning government; in this they were confronted with the established civilian government, the powerful landlords, and a people not especially enamored of revolutionary change. A power struggle soon became evident within the council; there was agreement on ending the monarchy, and in 1953, Naguib dropped his military titles and became President of Egypt. But he and the more powerful, revolutionary Gamal Abdel Nasser clashed. Nasser's public statements about land reform smacked

Culver Pictures

Gamal Abdel Nasser, soldier-politician, President of Egypt (1956–70), and instigator of the second Arab-Israeli war, in 1956.

David Ben-Gurion, organizer of the Haganah and Prime Minister and Minister of Defense after the founding of Israel, retired to his farm, circa 1953.

Because of Arab shellings of Israeli settlements along the borders, farm settlers prepared trenches as well as their fields for agriculture. An armed "peace" ensued.

Fact of life: a bomb shelter near an Israeli village.

Photos courtesy of Consulate General of Israe

During the false peace of the war of attrition, Israelis keep their weapons in trim in case of attack.

of socialism and offended the Muslim Brotherhood, which attempted to assassinate him on October 26, 1954. Consequently, Naguib was placed under house arrest six days later and Nasser became Premier. In 1956, unopposed, he was elected President.

While still Premier, Nasser negotiated a pact calling for the withdrawal of British troops from Suez (this was concluded by April 1956). Eventually his stand against an Arab monarchy, his introduction of economic and political reforms, and his break with the West (he even turned to Soviet Russia in a disagreement with the United States over the financing of the Aswan High Dam) won him the admiration of Arabs throughout the Middle East. To the consternation of other ambitious Arab leaders, Nasser was emerging as the strong man of the Middle East.

Having deposed the monarchy, having become powerful in his own land, having taken care of the British, and having stood up to the mighty United States, Nasser was ready to attend to Israel.

Egyptian-backed raids on Jewish settlements in the Sinai Peninsula and across from the Gaza Strip (with its large population of Palestinian refugees) escalated during the 1950s. The Israelis were certain that the Palestinian commandos were supplied with arms and munitions by Nasser. As early as 1954, Israel announced a policy of "massive retaliations" to such incursions. While the raids were persistent, they were not truly organized and were random, making them difficult to predict and intercept. The "massive retaliations" plan, it was presumed, might force the host countries—Egypt and Jordan—to exert some control over the marauding infiltrators.

An act of Arab terrorism that provoked a strong retaliatory action by the Israeli Army occurred in March 1954. Gunmen attacked a bus in the eastern Negev, killing eleven passengers, most of them tourists returning from an outing; only three passengers escaped unharmed. Among them was a Hollander, Miriam Lesser, who, bloodied by those who had been shot around her, was considered dead. She heard the killers speak Arabic and watched them methodically pull the wounded and dead passengers out of the bus, executing those that appeared to be alive. Lesser was dragged by the hair from the bus, searched for arms, shot at, and missed again.

The cartridges found at the scene were of a type used in German machine guns and rifles. A cap used by the Jordanians was also found. (Jordan disclaimed any knowledge of the massacre but ordered an investigation.)

Among the dead were the driver and his wife; their five-year-old daughter escaped unharmed, but their eleven-year-old son was shot in the head. A nurse, Esther Levy, who was shot in the abdomen, administered first aid to the boy. Emergency surgery failed to save his life.

The murderous, merciless attack brought an immediate response. The Israeli Government stated that it considered the bus ambush "a clear warlike act" and retaliated with regular army units attacking Nahhalin, Jordan.

Zionist Archives and Library

Industrial expansion in Israel. Children play near the village of Beit Shemesh, in the Judaean Hills, southern Israel. A new cement factory spouts smoke in the background.

Tensions on the Mediterranean coast were even more incendiary. Anger flared over the hanging of a young Jewish schoolmaster and a Jewish doctor in Cairo in February 1955; both had been accused of espionage and sentenced by an Egyptian military court. The Israeli Prime Minister, Moshe Sharett, denounced the execution and termed it an act of "criminal war." Within two weeks Israel entered into a more offensive stance with the resignation of Minister of Defense Pinhas Lavon and the appointment of his successor, the organizer of the Haganah and former Minister of Defense, David Ben-Gurion. On the day Ben-Gurion's appointment was announced (February 18, 1955), the Jerusalem *Post* also reported that Nasser had denied the use of the Suez Canal to the Israeli ship *Bat Galim,* en route to Haifa.

At the end of February 1955, to discourage Palestinian raids into Israeli settlements in the Negev from the Gaza Strip, the Israeli Defense Forces had staged a heavy reprisal raid on the Egyptian Army headquarters in the Strip, which resulted in thirty-eight dead and more than thirty wounded Egyptians. This raid had a strong impact on the Egyptians. Nasser later said that the Gaza operation caused him to turn for arms to the Communist countries, notably Czechoslovakia and Soviet Russia. He blamed Ben-Gurion for the intensity of the Israeli reprisal raids and insisted that the border incidents had been fewer until the Gaza raid. "Israel," Nasser said to American newsmen, "is dangerous on our border."

There is a curious historical footnote to this statement by Nasser. Late in 1982 it was revealed by a key figure in a sequence of secret talks, Quaker representative to the United Nations Elmore Jackson, that around the same time he made this comment, Nasser had initiated secret negotiations that might have brought a political settlement between Israel and Egypt. With the backing of the United States, Jackson met with Nasser, Moshe Sharett (Prime

Consulate General of Israel

A vigilant Israeli guard from the Kibbutz Nevin on patrol near the Gaza Strip, where Arab guerrillas raid Israeli settlements in lightning attacks.

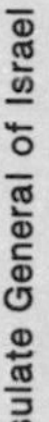

Victorious Israeli soldiers pose with a captured Egyptian vehicle. They have taken the Gaza Strip and the coastal town of El-Arish and are about to move toward Suez.

Avions Marcel Dassault

The French-manufactured Dassault Mystère IV (in French markings), which was effectively employed in the Sinai-Suez campaign.

Minister of Israel), Ben-Gurion, and other Israeli and Egyptian officials. These meetings occurred between April and August 1955. Agreement seemed possible, and at moments, the meetings were amiable. Ben-Gurion assured Jackson that "Nasser is a decent fellow who has the interest of his people genuinely at heart." He even offered to meet with the Egyptian leader in Cairo.

Of all the Arab leaders, Nasser might have succeeded. As Jackson wrote in his summary: "He was a symbol of Arab nationalism, and the Egyptian revolution had stirred deep emotions throughout the Arab world. The fact that Nasser explored seriously the possibilities of a peace settlement with Israel—before he turned to Eastern Europe for arms supply—should be of major interest to those who seek an end to the cycles of violence which periodically convulse the Middle East."

But the talks ended with no peace. Under pressure from his military leaders for a new source of military supplies (the United States had begun to look doubtful), Nasser turned to Czechoslovakia. This underscored the belief in Tel Aviv that Egypt was dedicated to the policy of destroying Israel.

The guerrilla incursions from both sides soon became commonplace: sniping across the frontier, an Arab attack on a Jewish wedding party, skirmishing border patrols. The United Nations Mixed Armistice Commission had a full agenda. Their cease-fires were literally impossible to enforce. A flurry of raids at the end of August and early September in the Gaza area left about ten dead on each side before the harassed chief of staff of the UN Truce Supervision Organization, Canadian Major General E. L. M. Burns, called for a truce. Egypt agreed, but a military spokesman warned that Egyptian troops were stationed along the line of demarcation, "poised for battle."

There was neither war nor peace, but in October 1955 the caldron began to heat up. On October 12 it was disclosed that the Soviet Union might consider selling arms to both Israel and Egypt; on October 20, Syria and Egypt signed a mutual defense pact, which placed Israel between these two Arab states, on its northeastern and southwestern borders. Concerned, Ben-Gurion ordered his chief of staff, Moshe Dayan, to make plans for a preemptive strike on Egyptian forces when the right time came: as soon as Egypt's belligerent stance made it impossible not to lash out in Israel's defense.

While the Egyptians traded cotton and rice for Czech arms, the Israelis began negotiating for modern jet fighters with the French (who were eager to embarrass Nasser for aiding the revolt against them in Algeria). The British remained aloof but were concerned about how Nasser's policies and actions might affect the Suez Canal. In December, Nasser blamed the Israelis for clashes with the Syrian Army. On the day after Christmas, it was announced that Egypt, Saudi Arabia, and Syria would combine their armies and place them under a single command, that of the Egyptian Minister of War.

In March 1956, after two years of relative quiet, Jordan began commando raids into Israel from the east; two days later, on March 12, the Egypt-Saudi Arabia-Syria pact became more specific: they would unite their defenses against Israel.

In May, Jordan and Egypt unified their armies. Israel's pleas for arms from the United States and Britain were ignored. Secretary of State John Foster Dulles admitted that the United States was selling arms to Saudi Arabia but would not sell them to Israel because he wished to avoid a U.S.-Soviet confrontation in the Middle East. The United States, however, gave tacit approval to the shipment of French jets to Israel.

To this shifting, seemingly irreversible sequence of events, Nasser finally contributed the element that gave it form. On June 18, 1956, after more than eighty years of occupation, the British relinquished their control of the Suez Canal. On June 24, with 99 percent of the vote, Nasser became Egypt's first elected President. On July 20, both the British and the Americans withdrew their financial backing of the Aswan Dam in a dispute with the new President. On July 27, Nasser declared, at the end of a three-hour speech, that he would nationalize the Suez Canal (shares in the Suez Canal Company could be owned only by Egyptians). Income from the canal would be used to finance the dam project. At the same time, Nasser imposed martial law in the Suez. In his speech he also attacked Israel as a "puppet of imperialism."

Nasser's move, a dozen years before the original Suez agreement was to expire, stunned those "imperialists" to whom the fiery colonel alluded. On August 16, more than twenty nations met in London to discuss the future of the Suez Canal and how to keep it open to international traffic (Britain had already frozen Egyptian and canal assets in Britain); Nasser countered by taking over the canal completely on September 14. On October 1, fifteen nations—including the United States, Britain, and France—established a Canal Users' Association.

By this time sub-rosa meetings among British, French, and Israeli leaders were underway. The precise arrangements are unclear. (Any suggestion of collusion among these governments was denied.) However, an Israeli preemptive strike against Egypt and push toward the Suez Canal would have been reason enough for British and French intervention.

Israel had reasons for concern; Egypt not only denied them use of the Suez Canal, but Nasser also blocked Israeli access to the Red Sea and the Indian Ocean by placing heavy guns in the southern tip of the Sinai, at Ras Nusrani, northeast of Sharm el-Sheikh. On October 25, an announcement of great import was made: that the Egyptian, Syrian, and Jordanian armies would be placed under the command of an Egyptian general.

On October 29, 1956, the Israelis struck with Operation Kadesh (a biblical place-name associated with Moses and also with Joshua, who had conquered the southern section of Palestine from Kadesh to Gaza). It would be a curious war with a curious outcome and a remarkable sequel. It engendered a strange, covert alliance among Israel, Britain, and France (as well as an even stranger one between the United States and the Soviet Union); when a truce was finally established, it was rather difficult to determine the victor, and in time the Sinai-Suez war proved to be a prelude for the more spectacular "Six Day War," to come.

The British and the French hoped to topple Nasser, who was emerging as

Egyptian prisoners, taken in great numbers after Israeli victories in the Gaza Strip.

Photos courtesy of Consulate General of Israel

Consulate General of Israel

United Nations observers in the Sinai; their peacemaking efforts were frequently frustrated.

the nominal leader of the Arab world; the Israelis shared that view; the Suez Canal was secondary. With Nasser out of office, the aggressions of the Fedayeen (the raiders from the Gaza Strip) might be curtailed and the Strait of Tiran reopened to Israeli shipping.

The threats and movements of Nasser and other Arab leaders prompted Dayan to set his plan for the preemptive strike in motion. Even as the Israeli Air Force's Dassault Ouragans cleared the air over the battlefields, an airborne battalion was dropped in the vicinity of Mitla Pass, some thirty miles east of Suez, in the midafternoon of October 29, 1956. The rest of the brigade, under its commander, Colonel Ariel Sharon, moved westward out of the Negev by armored car and jeep into the Sinai Peninsula to take the garrisons at Kuntilla and Thamad, and continued west to join up with their airborne battalion. To the north, on October 30, an armored infantry force moved into Egypt, secured the road junction at Qusseima, and began pushing toward Suez.

Also on October 29, a mechanized infantry brigade moved out of the southern tip of the Negev, took Ras el-Naqb, and continued south toward Sharm el-Sheikh, near the contested and strategically situated Strait of Tiran. An Egyptian air base was in the same area.

Although the Egyptian Army had been preparing for its own invasion, as well as possible Anglo-French activity in Suez, the fast-moving Kadesh opera-

Captured Stalin tank taken near Bir Gifgafa during "Operation Kadesh" (October 29 – November 5, 1956).

Zionist Archives and Library

Captured Russian-manufactured Egyptian MiG-15; although the aerial strength of the Arab air forces was greater than that of the Israeli Air Force, Egyptian air activity proved to be minimal, and Israeli aircraft roamed over the Sinai virtually unopposed.

Captured Egyptian Army tank; this is an American-made Sherman tank of World War II vintage.

When the Israelis overran Egyptian installations, they took military vehicles—such as these Russian tanks and personnel carriers—intact.

Photos courtesy of Consulate General of Israel

tion came as a surprise. Within hours, Israeli troops enveloped several Egyptian positions, took over important road junctions, captured air bases, and cut off some Egyptian troops in the Gaza Strip (one of the major objectives, with its nest of Fedayeen bases). None of Egypt's Arab allies sent help of any kind.

By October 30, Sharon's Israeli airborne brigade (although traveling by surface vehicle) moved onward from Thamad and captured Nakhl before proceeding to the area of the Mitla Pass, to regroup with its advance battalion, which had arrived there the day before. On that same day, the British and the French issued a joint ultimatum threatening to send troops to Egypt unless both belligerents withdrew ten miles from the Suez Canal and ceased fighting. Nasser rejected the ultimatum; Israel accepted it, provided that Egypt accept it (the ultimatum was, of course, no surprise to the Israelis).

What followed was what one military historian, Otto von Pivka, has termed the "final show of colonialist, gunboat diplomacy." Despite UN Security Council resolutions calling for no use of force, the French and the English began bombing Egyptian airfields (the Anglo-French forces were staged out of Cyprus) and other targets in the canal area. From the sidelines, both the United States and the Soviet Union voiced alarm and ominous objections. Egypt broke off diplomatic relations with Britain and France, following up with its seizure of British and French holdings in Egypt. In a supportive action, Jordan also broke off with the two nations and denied the British the use of Jordanian military bases.

Israeli forces, despite the sand that bogged down the civilian buses that transported troops, continued to push back or encircle the demoralized Egyptians. The Egyptians had neglected to establish a defense of the Dayqa Pass, and an Israeli armored brigade slipped by to attack positions around the Rawafa Dam and tiny Abu Agueila. This sudden stab isolated an Egyptian brigade to the northeast; this unit, estimated to have numbered nearly three thousand men, was doomed, but not as it eventuated, by Israeli action.

During the night of November 1, while the troops of Colonel Uri Ben-Ari, the Israeli commander, waited for supplies and reinforcements, the Egyptian troops slipped away into the desert under cover of darkness. Their commander, Brigadier Gaafer el Abd, who had arrived at Abu Agueila the day before, saw that the situation was hopeless, especially since the water supply was virtually exhausted, and gave the order to abandon the town.

Hundreds of men, without water, set out over the fifty or so miles of desert characterized by loose, shifting sands and no vegetation. Their commander had doomed them. This lost brigade hoped to reach El-Arish—but no one had informed them that it was already in enemy hands. But that would not have mattered. The Israelis became aware of their retreat the next day, when they took the position and found that guns had been abandoned, along with other military equipment, with no attempt to destroy them. The powdery sand showed that it would be pointless to pursue the Egyptians on foot, and vehicles would have been impractical.

Israeli half-tracks transporting infantrymen in the Sinai Peninsula.

David Ben-Gurion, who came out of retirement to serve as Defense Minister during the Sinai-Suez war, tours the front with an aide.

Photos courtesy of Zionist Archives and Library

With the coming of light, the Piper Cubs of the Israeli Air Force spotted the Egyptians. "They saw masses of men staggering, crawling, and reeling around crazily as if drunk or stone-blind," historian S. L. A. Marshall has written.

"They saw many of these men fall face forward in the sands, lie still, and not rise again. They saw bodies already partly buried by the drift and could not tell whether they were alive or dead.

"They saw desert Bedouins stalking the fringes of this pitiful host to prey on those who fell or were too exhausted to resist. Some of the Egyptians had tried to carry along their rifles, which are much prized by the tribesmen. Those who were murdered for their arms, trinkets and clothing were at least spared a worse death from thirst, shock and madness."

The only survivors of the battle around Abu Agueila were seven hundred Egyptians who were taken prisoner.

General Dayan assigned the taking of the city of Gaza to a reserve brigade commanded by Colonel Aaron Doron. Moving his infantry in buses and half-tracks, accompanied by a few tanks, Doron reached the outskirts of the strongly held city by November 1, 1956. Except for Fedayeen raiders that slipped into the Israeli-held positions and were captured, there was little Egyptian response to the Israeli threat. In the morning of November 2, when Doron ordered his brigade to move toward Gaza, there was some token firing from two Egyptian-held hills that dominated the road into the city. One of the hills was overrun within twenty minutes. According to historian S. L. A. Marshall, "The Egyptians manning the bunkers fired just long enough to satisfy honor and then ran for Gaza."

Inside the town, a United Nations Armistice Commission hoped to arrange for a cease-fire; all members had given up except one, an American, Colonel R. S. Bayard, who urged the Egyptian commander in Gaza, Fuad Al General Dijany, to surrender. He refused, stating that his troops would murder any officer suggesting such a thing.

Having cleared the two hills of the enemy, Doron's eager troops pushed into Gaza. Although he succeeded in stopping the infantry buses from entering the town, some of his tanks did push their way into the main square. Soon there was a tangle of tanks—a virtual military traffic jam. But the Egyptians made no attempt to take advantage of the Israelis' vulnerability.

Doron managed to free several tanks and half-tracks and dispatch them to patrol in the vicinity of the main government building in Gaza. Machine-gun fire from a rooftop killed the leader of the patrol, so Doron recalled it. Fighting inside Gaza was not part of his plan.

Meanwhile, Colonel Bayard had pressed General Dijany further on the idea of surrender, threatening to abandon Gaza and join the UN commissioners aboard a ship anchored offshore. The Egyptian general did not want to face the Israelis alone—perhaps he had heard of the fall of Rafah and El-Arish. Around noon, white flags began to appear in Gaza. Soon Egyptian soldiers were tearing off their uniforms and burying the evidence in the sand. Some lit fires, burning camel dung and bales of hay, explaining that they did not want these to fall into enemy hands. No one thought to burn the military equipment, which was taken over by the Israelis.

Once Gaza was secure, Doron led his brigade southward to Khan Yunis to clear more of the Gaza Strip of the Palestine Eighth Division and the marauding Fedayeen. The position did not fall as easily as Gaza, but sharp fighting took it, and Doron had to argue the Egyptian commander, Major General Agroudi, into surrendering. His reasoning was the same as at Gaza: his troops would kill him at the suggestion of capitulation. Doron persisted, and Khan Yunis fell to the Israelis. At the cost of ten men, two tanks, and a half-track, Doron's brigade had taken most of the Gaza Strip.

Aaron Doron, whose troops took the town of Gaza with few casualties on either side; he moved on to take Khan Yunis, which virtually cleared the Gaza Strip of the Egyptian threat there.

Consulate General of Israel

Israeli seamen, aboard one of the two World War II British destroyers in their navy, patrol the waters of the Gulf of Aqaba.

Agroudi, all spit-and-polish and militarily proper, found it difficult to believe that he "was dealing with an army. They looked exactly like a band of robbers."

A similar informal but tough brigade would bring the Sinai war to an end. With Israeli forces poised on the banks of the Suez Canal, as well as holding other positions in northern and eastern Sinai, only the securing of Sharm el-Sheikh was needed to open up the Tiran Strait and the Gulf of Aqaba.

This task was assigned to the 9th Brigade, under the venerable (over forty years old) Colonel Avraham Yoffe. The bulk of Yoffe's command was made

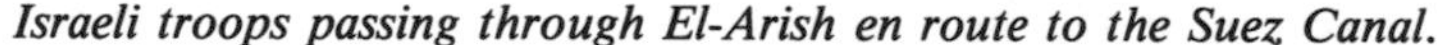

Israeli troops passing through El-Arish en route to the Suez Canal.

Consulate General of Israel

Zionist Archives and Library

Dug in on the front, these Israelis take time out for a few restful moments.

Morning on the Sinai-Suez front; the Orthodox Jew wears his shawl for a moment of prayer.

Consulate General of Israel

Zionist Archives and Library

Having taken an Egyptian town on the way to Suez, this Israeli soldier reads the local paper.

Israeli infantry in the Gaza Strip; they are shelled as they move toward an Arab camp.

Photos courtesy of Zionist Archives and Library

Israeli tanks moving through a town in the Gaza Strip.

up of farmers from the North, from the Haifa area. They had been together since the 1948–49 War of Independence. Yoffe, nicknamed "Gideon," was a trusted commander (the biblical Gideon was a warrior-judge who defeated a large Midianite army with a handful of men).

Yoffe was ordered to traverse some two hundred fifty miles of unmapped desert; there were no roads, either, just tracks and faint trails. The Sinai Desert, facing the brigade, was a waterless, vegetation-less wasteland, virtually unchanged since the time of Moses. Stripping down his brigade to the essential personnel who could be transported in about one hundred eighty vehicles of various types (trucks, command cars, half-tracks, jeeps, etc.), Yoffe set out on his mission with seventeen hundred fighting men and women. It was estimated that some fifteen hundred Egyptian troops defended Yoffe's major objective, Sharm el-Sheikh.

Each vehicle carried about half of its usual number, for it was necessary to carry also the required water and fuel for the journey into the unknown desert beyond Eilat, at the southern tip of Israel's Negev. The rule was that no one would shave or wash until the mission was completed.

The caravan was divided into four widely spaced units. The vanguard consisted of a dozen jeeps, carrying engineers for clearing the way of obstructions and minefields and medics; a company of infantry with half-tracks; four mobile mortars; and an air liaison team. Yoffe set out from the southern tip of the Negev. A preview of what was to come was demonstrated in his advance on Kuntilla through the eastern Sinai desert: it took eighteen hours to cover seventy miles. From Kuntilla, Israeli troops moved over a thirty-mile stretch of good road and took the Egyptian position at Ras el Nagb. After a day's rest, on November 2 the brigade set out from Ras el Nagb for Sharm el-Sheikh, two hundred miles to the south. Yoffe hoped to be there by November 5.

To avoid detection, the Israeli columns moved forward along trackless wadis (dried-out, boulder-strewn watercourses, active only during a rainy spell). Since Yoffe's line of march skirted the Gulf of Aqaba, across which lay the Arab lands of Jordan and Saudi Arabia, keeping inland was necessary. Stretching out his motorcade also lessened the degree of telltale dust clouds.

Initially the Israeli brigade made good time in the graveled wadi beds; by night of the first day, they had covered about a third of the distance to Sharm el-Sheikh. Then they were confronted with a sea of sand that stretched for eight miles before them. "There were no dunes," Yoffe recalled. "Save for great ripples, the face of this sea was fairly smooth. How deep the sand was piled, there was no telling."

Truck tires were deflated; the men dismounted to help by pushing, at the cost of much fuel and many breakdowns; the brigade struggled for ten hours to get through the eight miles of sand. To replenish the gasoline, Yoffe radioed to Eilat, where landing craft were stationed for such an emergency. Two of them with cargoes of fuel set out for a rendezvous with the brigade at Dahab, farther down the Sinai coast.

Sharm el-Sheikh, where Egyptian guns dominated the Strait of Tiran, Israel's outlet to the Red Sea. Yoffe's brigade has taken the post.

Photos courtesy of Consulate General of Israel

A spiked Egyptian gun in Sharm el-Sheikh; with its muzzle and interior barrel blown, the gun will no longer be a threat to Israeli shipping in the Gulf of Aqaba.

An Israeli ship passes through the Strait of Tiran.

As the brigade continued to push through the sand, the advance guard drove carelessly into what they believed to be an abandoned settlement, which was occupied by a small force of Egyptians. Before this squad was eliminated, three Israeli soldiers were killed and several were wounded. Dahab was now secure for the arrival of the LCMs, landing craft with supplies from Eilat.

Searching for a shortcut to Sharm el-Sheikh, the Israeli brigade faced another obstacle: a mile of boulders covered their pathway. It was past midnight; after more than five hours of hard labor by engineers and infantry clearing the way, the advance guard finally moved ahead. As they approached a narrowing of the wadi, Yoffe proceeded with caution. He was right, for as the vanguard approached the funnel-like mouth of the dry watercourse, it came under fire from the Egyptian ambush awaiting them. The firing was wild and ineffectual. Yoffe pulled back to rest his troops and wait for dawn.

By daylight, as the Israeli brigade pressed ahead, the Egyptians pulled back into the fortified village of Ras Nasrani, which dominated the Tiran Strait and lay in the path of the approach to Sharm el-Sheikh, their objective. Ras Nasrani, with its concrete bunkers, minefields, and wire mazes was a formidable barrier.

But again there was no one to challenge the Israeli advance; the Egyptians had fallen back to the last stronghold, Sharm el-Sheikh. On Sunday, November 4, on schedule, Yoffe's brigade reached the approaches to the Egyptian positions and dug in along a ridge. Yoffe asked for the Israeli Air Force to soften up the position by strafing and dropping napalm bombs. Then his infantry rushed the trenches.

In the fierce, tumultuous fighting, ten Israelis were killed and thirty-three wounded; Egyptian losses may have exceeded two hundred. A thousand Egyptians surrendered to the small Israeli unit (about five hundred).

On Monday, November 5, 1956, Yoffe informed Dayan, "It is finished. Praised be God, the Creator of the earth."

With the fall of Sharm el-Sheikh, the Israelis dominated all of the Sinai Peninsula. The Air Force controlled the air, and Israeli troops were stationed on the banks of the Suez Canal. Technically the war was over. However, Anglo-French forces under General Sir Charles Keightley occupied Port Said, at the northern entrance to the canal, while sputterings and threats emanated from Washington and Moscow.

Even as its own army was crushing the Hungarian revolution in Europe, the Soviet Union called for a cease-fire in the Middle East and made it clear that it would use force—"including rockets"—to restore peace in the area. Moscow also suggested "joint action" with the United States against the aggressors. The proposal was rejected by the United States. (Eisenhower's landslide reelection was attributed greatly to his promise not to become involved in the Middle East war.) Diplomatic pressures, via the UN General Assembly, were applied to force Britain and France out of Egypt and the Israelis out of the Sinai. President Eisenhower, also, with a wary eye on the Soviets, put U.S. armed forces on a global alert.

Photos courtesy of Consulate General of Israel

With Sharm el-Sheikh secure and the Sinai-Suez war over, captured weapons are studied by Israeli civilians and soldiers. The women peer at an Egyptian (i.e., Soviet) self-propelled cannon; army technicians inspect antiaircraft guns.

Victims of War: Arab refugees in the Gaza Strip.

Consulate General of Israel

Clearing the Suez Canal. Nasser had the canal blocked by sinking ships in the passage. The United Nations began its salvage and clearing operations as soon as possible after the truce.

United Nations

United Nations

Consulate General of Israel

Architect of victory in the Sinai-Suez campaign, chief of staff General Moshe Dayan (right); with him is Canadian Major General E. L. M. Burns, commander of the UN Emergency Force.

Dayan receives the Haganah Medal from Minister of Defense Ben-Gurion.

Zionist Archives and Library

Helicopter from the Canadian carrier Magnificent *brings the United Nations' General Burns to oversee the withdrawal of troops from El-Arish, following the truce.*

On November 7, 1956, the United Nations announced a cease-fire; demands were made for the withdrawal of all British, French, and Israeli troops from Egyptian territory. By the middle of November, a United Nations Emergency Force began arriving in the Suez Canal zone to enforce the cease-fire. (The Soviet Union promised Soviet "volunteers" who would join the Egyptian Army if the withdrawal did not occur; the United States stated that it would oppose any such move.)

The British and the French were decidedly under diplomatic siege by their chief allies to withdraw from the Suez (consequently, the British pound began to drop alarmingly). However, Israel, whose army had overrun the Sinai Peninsula and was in command of all its strategic ports, as well as the Gaza Strip (after only a week of fighting), was understandably reluctant.

Soviet threats and American pressures initiated some withdrawal from Egypt by all three forces on November 21. By December 22, no French or British troops remained, but the Israelis, although they evacuated the Sinai, held on to the Gaza Strip and Sharm el-Sheikh, to secure the passage through the Straits of Tiran and the Gulf of Aqaba to Israel's port Eilat. The military campaign was over, but the infighting continued, with more and more alarmed attention concentrating on the movements of the Soviets in the Middle East.

It was not until March 1, 1957, that the Israelis agreed to relinquish the Gaza Strip and Sharm el-Sheikh, provided that the United Nations would oversee the Gaza situation and assure free navigation in the Gulf of Aqaba. What followed was some ten years of bellicose peace.

The Suez-Sinai war, in which the Israeli Army was the overwhelming victor, led to unexpected consequences: the loss of Anglo-French prestige in the world community, and the rise of American and Soviet influence in the Middle East.

In the week-long war (from October 30 to November 6), the Israelis had defeated the Egyptian Army, with the loss of 171 dead and 800 wounded. At this cost, the entire Sinai Peninsula was taken, and Egyptian casualties (unconfirmed) numbered in the thousands. The Israelis also captured thousands of tanks, guns, other equipment, and ammunition. Prisoners were eventually released, but the equipment and ammunition remained in Israeli hands.

Perhaps the most surprising denouement of the 1956 war was the rise in Nasser's prestige, among the Arabs as well as worldwide. He had stood alone against two great Western powers along with an aggressive Israel; he had not toppled despite defeat. In the meantime, to replace the equipment lost to Israel in the Sinai, the Soviet Union began shipping arms to Egypt—and sending a small army of advisers to train the Egyptians in the use of sophisticated weaponry.

June 5–11, 1967 Six Day War

Nasser's status, internationally and among the Arab nations, did not please some of his fellow Arabs, who were suspicious of his leftish reforms, his Soviet friends, and his popularity throughout the Middle East. His chief rival was Saudi Arabia's King Faisal; he was watched with apprehension by Jordan's King Hussein. As a step toward Arab unity, at Syria's request, Nasser formed what was called the United Arab Republic in February 1958, with himself as President. Consisting of only two nations (three when Yemen became a member), it was in fact hardly united. In a countermove, Jordan and Iraq formed an Arab League, but it was no match for the ambitious Nasser, whose agents and broadcasts from Cairo—a program called "The Voice of the Arabs"—kept Arab rival countries in ferment and promised a united Arab effort to eliminate Israel from the face of the earth.

There was no true peace after the last Israeli troops withdrew from Gaza and the Sinai on March 7, 1957. The United Nations Emergency Force was dispatched to patrol the frontiers of Israel touching Lebanon, Syria, and Jordan. The next decade was one of an uneasy armed truce, punctuated by guerrilla raids by Arabs and retaliatory assaults by the Israelis. In the background, the Soviets and the countries of the West maneuvered for favored positions in the Middle East and poured arms into the area.

The powder keg had its own internal flarings. Civil war broke out along traditional lines: Christians against Muslims in Lebanon in May 1958. The conflict was about whether the nation should align itself with the West or with Nasser's United Arab Republic. Finally President Eisenhower sent in the U.S. Marines, at the Lebanese Government's request, to put down the rebellion. Nasser's agents were ordered to leave the country under the charge that they had incited the revolt and contributed money for the purchase of arms used by the Muslim soldiers.

In July a military coup led by Brigadier General Abdul Karim Kassim overthrew the Hashimite monarchy of Iraq. The King, Crown Prince, and Prime Minister were slaughtered, and a new, left-wing government took over, which

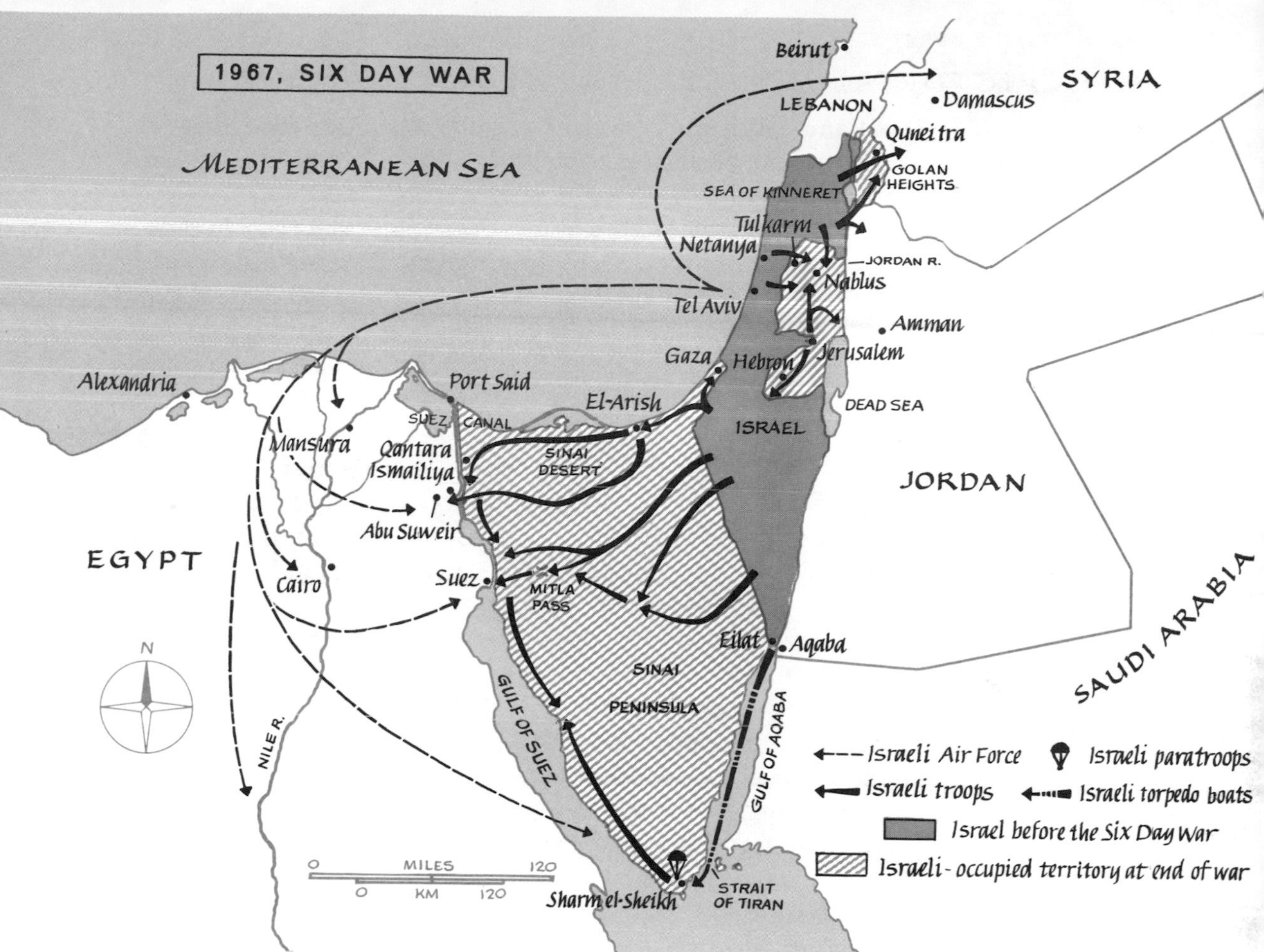

renounced the Baghdad Pact (a mutual defense treaty signed by Great Britain, Iran, Pakistan, and Turkey), established relations with Communist-bloc countries, and began acquiring military equipment from the Soviets. The unstable government of Kassim (who was assassinated in February 1963) suffered coup and countercoup as the military split into factions and maneuvered for power. The internal disarray encouraged a Kurdish uprising in Kurdistan, in northeastern Iraq, a perpetually troubled area. The new, Ba'ath party was led by Major General Hassan al-Bakr; his vice-president, Saddam Hussein, eventually succeeded the ailing Bakr. The Ba'ath regime maintained close relations with Moscow.

Meanwhile, Nasser watched new military leaders emerge on the Middle Eastern scene. His United Arab Republic splintered from within. Claiming that it was becoming too Egyptian and its leaders were overshadowed by the charismatic Nasser, Syria broke away from the United Arab Republic in 1961. Two years later, a military coup placed the clandestine, radical Ba'ath party in power. Pro-Nasser, the new regime nationalized the petroleum and other major industries and accepted Soviet aid. The new government joined Egypt in assailing Israel and called for "a war of popular liberation." Meanwhile Syria was harboring and financing a predominantly Palestinian military organization.

Fatah raids out of Syria into northern Israel, beginning in September 1966, brought severe warnings from the Israeli Government. By the spring of the next year, Prime Minister Levi Eshkol threatened Syria with retaliatory action if the guerrilla raids persisted.

Soviet and Syrian intelligence agents let it be known in all the Arab states that Israel was amassing an army to attack one of them and that the United States was plotting with Israel to topple Syria's government.

As the nominal leader of the Arabs, Nasser began attacking the United States and Israel in fiery, warlike speeches, despite the fact that part of the Egyptian Army was mired in a civil war in Yemen, on the southern end of the Arabian Peninsula. The presence of Egyptian troops in Saudi Arabia did not amuse King Saud or his ally King Hussein of Jordan.

Meanwhile the United Nations Emergency Force in the Sinai and the UN Truce Supervision Organization were caught in the middle. Secretary General U Thant alerted the Norwegian commander of the Truce Supervision Organization, General Odd Bull, of the situation along the Israeli-Syrian border, describing it as "extremely tense and unstable." That was on May 8; on May 13, Egyptian sources announced that they had "received accurate information that Israel was concentrating huge armed forces of about 11 to 13 brigades on the Syrian border." Nasser even claimed to know the day that the Israelis would strike. The "accurate information," disseminated by Soviet Intelligence in Cairo and Damascus, inflamed an already angered Nasser. On May 14 he ordered his troops into the Sinai.

Pockmarked by Arab artillery, this dwelling in an Israeli border town was one of the basic reasons for what became known as the Six Day War. Such random shellings and Arab infiltrations resulted in retaliation by the Israel Defense Forces.

Consulate General of Israel

Zionist Archives and Library

Israeli Air Force Dassault Mirage III-Cs, the harbingers of the Six Day War; their preemptive attack on Egyptian air bases decided the outcome of the war in its first three hours.

Egyptian Air Force aircraft burn on the ground; a Soviet Tupolev bomber, in protective revetment, awaits destruction.

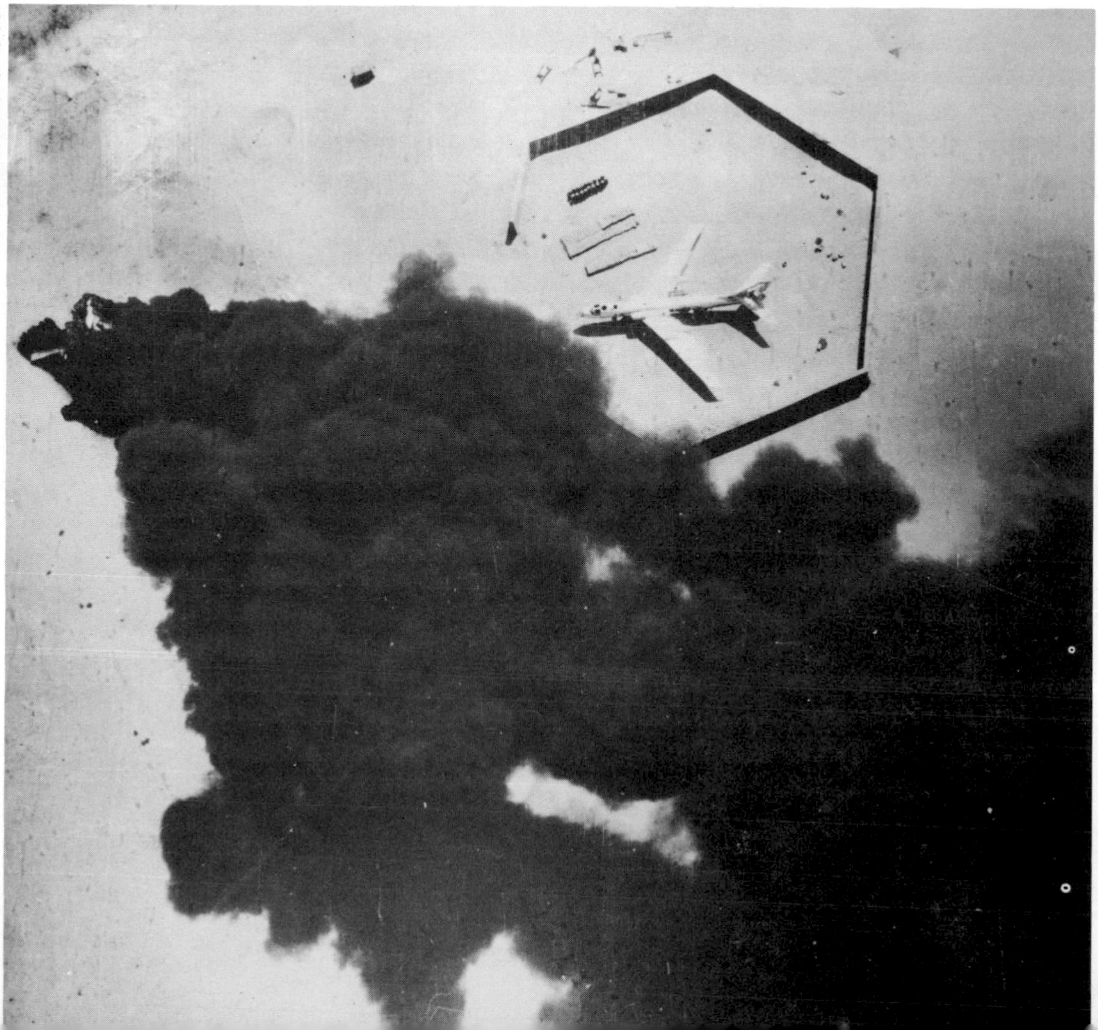

Consulate General of Israel

In the wake of Israeli Air Force attacks, Israeli infantry move through the Sinai in comparative safety from Egyptian air strikes.

Israeli tanks (British Centurions), armed with 105-mm. guns, in the Negev approaching the border of the Sinai Peninsula.

Photos courtesy of Consulate General of Israel

Desert scene: Israeli Army supplies were carried by trucks; helicopters were used to transport personnel and to deliver messages during periods of radio silence.

The next day, his chief of staff, General Muhammed Fawzi, flew to Damascus to confer with Syrian military leaders. On May 16, he took a step that almost assured a military encounter between Israel and the United Arab Republic. Fawzi wrote a letter to the commander of the UN Emergency Force in Gaza, General Indar Jit Rikhye, ordering the peace-keeping United Nations units out of the Sinai Peninsula, explaining that he had given "my instructions to all U. A. R. armed forces to be ready for action against Israel the moment it might carry out any aggressive action against any Arab country."

U Thant tried to dissuade the Egyptians from this threatening position. By May 18, Egyptian troops began pushing the UN forces from their positions along the Egyptian-Israeli border. The UN force—made up of units from seven nations—was small (fewer than thirty-five hundred men) and unarmed. Once the UN began leaving, Egypt requested that all UN forces be withdrawn "as soon as possible." U Thant complied reluctantly and under severe criticism.

On May 23, all of the UN peace-keeping troops had left Egypt. The time came for Nasser to throw down the gauntlet. (He had himself been criticized by fellow Arabs for hiding behind the United Nations.) There was no turning back, and he contributed one more element that would determine the course of action in the Middle East. "Under no circumstances will we allow the Israeli flag to pass through the Gulf of Aqaba," he said over Radio Cairo. "The Jews threaten war. We tell them you are welcome. We are ready for war, but under no circumstances will we abandon any of our rights. This water is ours."

With no UN troops at Sharm el-Sheikh, Nasser could once again block the Strait of Tiran and deny Israel access to the Red Sea from Eilat. This was tantamount to a defiance of Israel as well as the rest of the world, who considered the Gulf of Aqaba an international waterway.

A week later, Jordan's King Hussein flew to Cairo and signed a mutual defense pact with Nasser. (Hussein had not been popular for a long time in Cairo and was even publicly branded there as "a traitor to the Arab cause.") Iraq soon after joined the alliance, and Egyptian and Iraqi troops began moving into Jordan. Thus, Israel was confronted by the Fatah incursions from Syria in the north, and the threat of Arab troops moving in from Jordan from the east, and the Egyptians in the Sinai from the southwest.

There was a curious complication among the Arab nations. Because of a bomb explosion on the Jordanian-Syrian border on May 23, Jordan ordered the closing of the Syrian Embassy and dismissed the Syrian ambassador.

Behind the scenes, the United States tried to avert a military clash, primarily by putting pressure on Israel. In the meantime, events and tempers had pretty much gotten out of hand. Ahmed Shukairy, leader of yet another Palestinian guerrilla army, the Palestine Liberation Organization (PLO), said, on June 5, 1967, "We will wipe Israel off the face of the map and no Jew will remain alive."

What occurred the very next morning shook the Arab world. During the decade of the armed truce, 1957–67, Israel had evolved a remarkable army, armored units, and air force. While Israel had no large standing army, it had a well-disciplined, trained population. When war threatened, professors, archaeologists, farmers, pianists, and flutists were transformed into fighting men and women. Just as the Soviets supplied arms to the Arabs—some quite sophisticated, such as surface-to-air missiles (SAMs), jet fighters, and bombers—so did Britain, the United States, and France supply Israel with weaponry. Of especial significance to Israel at this time was the acquisition of French Dassault jet aircraft for the Israeli Air Force.

On June 1, Major General Moshe Dayan was appointed Israel's Minister of Defense by Premier Levi Eshkol. With Eshkol's permission, he had spent several weeks touring Israel's border defenses. Dayan had been appointed rather reluctantly because of his reputation as an outspoken, undiplomatic "hawk." Eshkol's first choice for the post was Yigal Allon, then Minister of Labor and a hero of the 1948–49 War of Independence. Since he was more diplomatic than the impulsive Dayan, it was hoped that Allon's "dovish" tendencies might deflect the threatened Israeli-Arab clash, but the party secretariat demanded that Dayan be Defense Minister.

Before Dayan took over, Israel's plan of action was modest: drive the Egyptians and Palestinians out of Gaza and then trade it back to them for the Strait of Tiran. Dayan's plan was more ambitious: take all of the Sinai Peninsula.

The Arab world literally seethed and achieved a remarkable unity under Nasser's exhortations. King Faisal of Saudi Arabia, long estranged from Nasser and considered a good friend of the West, sent some twenty thousand soldiers into Jordan to be stationed near Aqaba, almost directly opposite the Israeli

Water scene: the Six Day War covered a wide range of settings. An Israeli Navy boat is being salvaged from the waters of the Sea of Galilee, near Syria.

Consulate General of Israel

The swiftness of the 1967 war brought quick dividends in captured war materials. Dozens of 105-mm. howitzers are lined up in the front row; in the back, larger artillery pieces and tanks. A Soviet SAM missile is transported to Israel for study.

Israeli paratroopers prepare to board a helicopter for transportation to trouble spots in the Sinai.

Photos courtesy of Consulate General of Israel

port of Eilat. Iraqi soldiers joined the Egyptian troops at Sharm el-Sheikh; more Iraqis moved into Syria. Kuwaiti aircraft lifted troops (an infantry brigade) into Egypt; other Middle Eastern nations promised aid. Nasser boasted in a Cairo radio broadcast, "Behind us there is the Iraqi Army and the armies of Algeria, Kuwait, Sudan . . . the whole Arab nation."

Dayan's 45,000 soldiers faced about 250,000 Arab troops in the Sinai; the tank count was about even: 2,000 Egyptian, to 1,700 Israeli. Israel had some 350 aircraft at its disposal, of which 196 were fighters. Nasser could count on about 950 aircraft of all types; of these, about 650 were jet fighter planes, the bulk of them Soviet-made MiG (from Mikoyan and Gurevich, the designers) 15/17s, 19s, and 21s. On paper, the Chel Ha'Avir (the Israeli Air Force) was quite seriously outnumbered.

In the final days of May and in early June of 1967, while the United States attempted to resolve the impending conflict diplomatically, Israel appealed, fruitlessly, to the Soviet Union for help in maintaining peace in the Middle East. For some hours, on June 4, matters took a hopeful turn when Nasser accepted President Lyndon Johnson's invitation to send a representative to Washington for talks and perhaps to resolve the crisis. (Johnson was ready to send his vice-president, Hubert Humphrey, to Cairo to talk with Nasser, but this was considered too great a concession to Nasser's prestige.) On Sunday, June 4, Nasser promised to send his vice-president, Zakarya Mohieddin, to Washington, D.C., on Wednesday.

Fearing that this meeting might result in an arrangement inimical to Israel, the Israeli Cabinet gave Dayan unconditional military power. He, in turn and as planned, unleashed the Chel Ha'Avir.

A modest preview of events to come had been demonstrated as early as April 7, in response to morning Syrian shellings of Israeli settlements from a hillside overlooking Lake Kinneret (the biblical Sea of Galilee). The incident began when an unarmored Israeli tractor, tilling Plot No. 52 of Kibbutz Ha'on, came under artillery fire. This did not stop the plowing; an armored tractor was substituted. The Syrians escalated the shelling, bringing heavy artillery and tank guns to bear on the settlement. (Ha'on was one of four kibbutzim shelled that day; the most seriously damaged was Gadot, struck by some two hundred heavy mortar shells; as reported in the Jerusalem *Post*, ". . . not a single house escaped damage."

United Nations

A Palestine Liberation Army ammunition dump near Gaza burns after an attack by Israeli tanks.

When the Syrians ignored a United Nations cease-fire, the Israeli Air Force swept in, at 1:35 P.M. While some of the Mirages flew top cover to fend off Syrian jets, other Israeli fighters and fighter-bombers attended to a dozen Syrian artillery positions. Except for weak ground fire, the strafing and bombing Mirages encountered no resistance. The heavy guns were silenced.

Ten minutes after the Israeli Air Force had joined the border battle, Syrian Air Force MiG-21s challenged them. Even as the attack on the artillery positions continued, the Israeli top-cover Mirages went to their defense. Within minutes, three of the MiGs were knocked out of the battle and fell into Syria. Later, three more MiGs fell over Jordan, and their pilots were seen floating down in their parachutes. The rest of the Syrian jet fighters were chased to the outskirts of Damascus. Not one Israeli Mirage was lost. (Syria claimed that five had been shot down, but Israeli Air Force officers denied it.)

The prelude to the Six Day War was over, a clear-cut triumph for the Chel Ha'Avir. On June 5, 1967, it would perform with such daring and decisiveness that it would stun the world.

In the early-morning hours of June 5, 1967, about one hundred eighty Israeli Dassault Ouragans, Mystères, Mirages, and other jets took off from their bases, climbed westward over the Mediterranean, and vanished. The formations flew to the north of Cairo until they were well to the west of the city. Reconnaissance flights over the past weeks had revealed that the Egyptians were rather careless with the employment of their radar and, even if alerted, took from ten to twenty-

Zionist Archives and Library

David Ben-Gurion, a private citizen again since his retirement as Prime Minister, greeting Lieutenant General Yitzhak Rabin, chief of staff during the Six Day War.

French-manufactured Nord Noratlas, a medium-range tactical transport, was used to carry supplies as well as paratroopers.

Photos courtesy of Zionist Archives and Library

The war is over for these Egyptian soldiers in the Sinai.

five minutes to become airborne. Major General Mordechai Hod's youthful pilots—the average age was about twenty-five—approached their targets with assurance of surprise, and mastery of their complex jet fighters.

It was not yet 8 A.M. when the Israeli jets, at low level, turned over the Mediterranean Sea to strike at the Arab air bases, thirteen in Egypt itself; the four bases in the Sinai were attacked directly from the east, after the initial strikes had staggered the Arabs.

The low-level approach assured extraordinary accuracy, as well as vulnerability to ground fire. Some of the Israeli jets achieved that precision by lowering flaps and landing gears to lessen their speed. They pounded the Egyptian bases, catching virtually the entire air force on the ground, from Mansura, in the north, to Luxor, in the south, leaving a trail of black clouds and destroyed MiGs in their protective revetments. At Luxor, where the Egyptians had based their prized heavy bombers, the Tupolev Tu-16s, all thirty of the twin-engine Soviet bombers were left blazing on the ground in the wake of the Israeli jets. The none too skillfully constructed dummy aircraft scattered about the Egyptian fields were simply passed by.

Some Egyptian planes got into the air. In the vicinity of the base at Abu Sueir, near the west bank of the Suez Canal (west of Ismailia), twenty MiG-21s engaged sixteen Israeli Mirages in a brief dogfight. After four of the MiGs has been destroyed, the Egyptian planes left the combat.

For nearly three hours, the Chel Ha'Avir ravaged the Egyptian air strength, attacking in waves. Pilots flew as many as five missions a day, shooting up their targets, bombing, and returning for more. Within eight minutes after landing, the Israeli planes were refueled, rearmed, and racing back to Egypt. In the first day's attacks, more than three hundred Arab aircraft of all types were destroyed, most of them on the ground. Within this brief, devastating time, the Arab Air Forces ceased to exist. Control of the air over the Middle East belonged to Israel; once Egypt and the Sinai were neutralized, attention was turned to five bases in Syria, one in Iraq, and two in Jordan (estimated aircraft destroyed: sixty, fifteen, and thirty-five, respectively).

The outcome of the 1967 war was determined in the first three hours of the morning of June 5. The overwhelming attacks were so sweeping, the havoc so definitive, that Nasser (as he had argued after the Suez War) attributed the victory to outside aid from Britain and the United States, whose jets, he claimed, had operated from carriers. (The American Sixth Fleet was, in fact, in the Mediterranean.) This was not, of course, true.

Even as the Chel Ha'Avir slashed through Egyptian air defenses, other curious nontruths emanated from Egypt's command center. Nasser's commander-in-chief, Field Marshall Abdul Hakim Amer, informed the commander on the Jordanian front, General Abdul Moneim Riad, that the "Israeli planes have started to bomb air bases in the U.A.R. and approximately 75 percent of the enemy's aircraft have been destroyed or put out of action."

He also assured Riad, chosen to command the attack on Israel from Jor

War damage in an Israeli kibbutz, Tel Ḳatziv.

dan, that the counterattack by the Egyptian Air Force was underway over Israel. In Sinai, U.A.R. troops "have engaged the enemy and taken offensive on the ground." Amer ordered Riad to open a new front and launch the offensive. This would cost Jordan dearly.

There were no Egyptian planes over Israel. If there had been, they would no doubt have crushed the mere dozen fighters that had remained in Israel while the bulk of the Air Force nailed the Egyptian fighters and bombers to the ground. Some Iraqi planes raided Netanya (on the Mediterranean, north of Tel Aviv), with little effect except to prompt an Israeli Air Force strike against an Iraqi air base (requiring a flight across Jordan). Six Iraqi jets were destroyed *in situ.* By the end of the day, the Arabs claimed that eighty-six Israeli aircraft had been destroyed; in fact, Israel lost twenty fighters during all of the Six Day War, most of them to ground fire.

Minutes after the aerial assault on Egyptian air bases had begun, Israeli armor and infantry began to move into Gaza. Without air support—they needed no top cover—Israeli forces cut through the Gaza Strip, isolating some pockets of enemy troops, and breached the line held by the Palestinian 20th Division. Brigadier General Israel Tal's "S" Brigade, after the drive to the west, swung south toward Suez and attacked the Egyptian 7th Division. Another of Tal's brigades turned northward to secure the Gaza Strip. This first blow sealed off thousands of Egyptian regulars and Palestine Liberation Army troops. (Estimates range from five thousand to ten thousand.)

Although Egyptian snipers and Palestinian snipers held out in the city of

Consulate General of Israel

June 7, 1967: Israeli troops have reached the Suez Canal. Egyptian resistance has been broken.

David Harris

Israeli soldier on guard in the Sinai; by this time, there was practically no Egyptian Army to guard against.

Zionist Archives and Library

An Egyptian truck burns, and its dead drivers lie beside it as Israeli forces move through the Sinai.

Gaza until the second day, Tuesday, June 6, the Gaza Strip was under control and full attention could be given to the Sinai. Stubborn pockets of resistance were grouped around Soviet-made tanks, the T-54s, which were dug into the sand, with only their turrets aboveground.

Tal's forces moved quickly along the Mediterranean coast to the south and west, through El-Arish, and sped toward the Suez Canal. At El-Arish, the Israelis met with stiff tank opposition but did not lose momentum in their drive to the west.

The Egyptians had some nine hundred tanks positioned in the Sinai, most of them along the frontier. Besides the T-54s, the Egyptian Army had the more modern T-55s. (Seven hundred T-55s would fall, intact, into Israeli hands before the week was over.) Because the Egyptians had concentrated the bulk of their tank strength along the Negev border, they found themselves in a hopeless situation as soon as Israeli armor and infantry had punched through their line. Once through the Egyptian positions, Israeli forces deployed behind the Egyptian lines and cut them off from retreat and supplies.

To the south of Tal's soldiers and armor, moving almost parallel with his thrust, were the divisions led by Brigadier Generals Abraham Yoffe and Ariel Sharon. Their tanks and mechanized infantry moved quickly through the Arab strongholds, encircling them and then pushing on toward Suez. On Wednesday, June 7, units from Yoffe's force smashed into Egyptian tanks at Mitla Pass, thirty miles east of Suez.

The most intense battle of the Six Day War, the one for Mitla Pass (which is about fourteen miles long and hemmed in by shifting hills of sand), lasted twenty-four hours and involved a thousand tanks, and the fighters and fighter-bombers of the Israeli Air Force.

At the close of that fateful twenty-four hours, Mitla Pass had become a graveyard for men and machines. Israeli tanks and aircraft knocked out six hundred Egyptian tanks and captured another one hundred intact, incorporating them into their own armored brigades. The "spectacular" scene of "vehicular carnage" was described by Los Angeles *Times* reporter Robert J. Donovan: "In one winding two-mile stretch, the highway was virtually paved with blackened metal—tanks, trucks, jeeps, guns—pounded into scrap by Israeli fighter planes. In some cases, vehicles lay atop one another, as if crazed drivers had tried to barrel through the huge, burning traffic jam.

"The Sinai approaches were littered with still other Egyptian equipment, some blasted by gunfire, some charred by napalm, some still intact. Israelis found tanks abandoned with shells still in the guns, as if the Arabs could not take the instant needed to fire a final round already loaded before joining the general retreat on foot."

A pilot's-eye view of Mitla Pass was one of abandoned litter, with blackened tank hulls and scorched sand, where—in the phrase of military writers—the tanks had "brewed up" (burned). Egyptian soldiers had not only died in the "brewing up," they also died in the strafings, and of thirst, dehydration, and infection.

Israeli Prime Minister Levi Eshkol in the southern extremity of the Six Day War battle area: the Tiran Strait. Israeli Navy chief Shlomo Erel stands behind Eshkol's left shoulder.

"The full horror of war was really borne in on me when I saw mounds of Egyptian dead," recalled an Israeli officer identified only as Asher, in a posthostilities collection of interviews published under the title *The Seventh Day.* "Enormous great mounds of them. Young and old mixed together. And then, I don't know how to explain it, there was some sort of inner compulsion to go along and see if perhaps there wasn't a picture to be found on one of them, a child, a wife, something of that sort. But if you had found it, you would have left it immediately, you didn't want to touch, to have anything to do with it at all, as if you personally weren't to blame, as if to say, 'I didn't do it.'"

And so the Israelis slashed through the Sinai desert. By Thursday, June 8, when the Israelis pressed against the east bank of the Suez Canal and moved northward and southward along the coastal road of the Gulf of Suez, the desert war was over. Elements of Yoffe's force, after taking Ras Sudar and Abu Zenima, on the the gulf, pushed to the south, where they met with units of an airborne battalion that had come up from Sharm el-Sheikh.

Taking that position on the southern tip of the peninsula was the major variation from the tactics of the 1956 war. Instead of making the long, wasteful trek over sand and rock—as Yoffe had done in 1956—to secure the Strait of Tiran, Israeli torpedo boats were dispatched from Eilat, and airborne troops were flown in. When they converged on Wednesday, June 7, the patrol boats arriving first, they found that the Egyptians had abandoned the garrison.

On June 8, the most controversial incident of the Six Day War occurred: it cost thirty-four American lives. For reasons not yet fully explained, the USS *Liberty*, an "electronic surveillance vessel" (a spy ship) was operating in the Mediterranean Sea a mere fifteen miles off the Sinai coast, slightly northwest of El-Arish. The runways at El-Arish had been spared in the attacks on June 5, and two days later the Israeli Air Force was using them as a base of operations.

The *Liberty* was equipped with sophisticated radios, computers, and cryptographic devices; its crews could intercept and decode messages from all battlefronts in the Sinai. While the United States informed all nations of the presence of the Sixth Fleet, some four hundred miles away from the Sinai, no one was informed of the *Liberty*, which had been converted into a spy vessel from a merchant ship.

When Israeli jet pilots came upon the ship, so near the coast, they claimed, they thought it was an Egyptian supply vessel. Officers aboard the *Liberty* said that the American flag was flying, that their ship should have been easily identified, and that it was cruising in "international waters."

Conjecture aside, three Israeli jets spotted the ship and, just after 2 P.M., began an eighty-minute attack, strafing with gunfire, rockets, even napalm. The *Liberty* also took a torpedo from a torpedo boat in the side and developed a ten-degree list to starboard. As soon as the *Liberty* sounded the distress signal, American jet aircraft took off from the carriers *America* and *Saratoga* and raced to the scene. Word was immediately sent to the White House, where President Lyndon Johnson, aware of the fact that the Soviets were keeping the Sixth

Wounded American seamen are evacuated from the USS Liberty *after it was hit by Israeli aircraft. Thirty-four Americans were killed in the attack.*

U.S. Navy/Department of Defense

Zionist Archives and Library

On the northern front: Eshkol in the Golan Heights. To his right are Minister of Defense Moshe Dayan and the front commander, Major General David Elazar, who would serve as Commander-in-Chief of the Israeli Defense Forces in the 1973 war.

Fleet under radar surveillance and would be disquieted by formations of American jets dashing toward Sinai, picked up the hot-line phone to Moscow. He quickly explained the situation and assured the Kremlin that the United States was not becoming involved in the war.

By this time, too, the Israelis realized that the *Liberty* had been attacked by mistake and sent an apology to Washington. The American jets were recalled and returned to their carriers before reaching the stricken ship. Tilting to the right and down in the bow, the *Liberty*—with thirty-four dead, seventy-five wounded, and its electronics a shambles—headed northward for a rendezvous with two destroyers speeding medical aid to the ship. The incident, although never sufficiently explained, was officially closed in 1980 after a U.S. Navy court of inquiry admitted it could make no judgment as to the reason for the attack, owing to "insufficient information" and a payment amounting to about $13 million by Israel. This decision was challenged by James M. Ennes, one of the cryptanalysts aboard the *Liberty* that day and one of the wounded who survived. In his book *Assault on the Liberty,* Ennes claimed that the incident was covered up and that the Pentagon had failed to protect the ship by not ordering it out of what was in reality a war zone. He also questioned the veracity of Israel's reason for attacking the ship. The mystery of the *Liberty* remains.

Even as the jets of the Israeli Air Force were wiping out the air forces of Egypt, Jordan, and Syria, the Israeli Government sent a message to Jordan's King Hussein, via the United Nations' General Odd Bull, of the Truce Super vision Organization, informing the King that Israel would not launch a ground attack on Jordan unless attacked first. Hussein's response was to open a heavy artillery barrage on Israeli-held Jerusalem. This began around 11 A.M. on June 5. Israeli machine guns, positioned on Mount Zion, opened fire over the Old City on Jordanian concentrations on the Mount of Olives. The fight over divided Jerusalem had begun. The streets reverberated to the sounds of machine guns, mortars, and artillery, further pulverizing buildings that had been abandoned since the War of Independence.

Hussein's decision to open up a second front may have been predicated on the false information he was receiving from Cairo that all was well on the Egyptian Front. Marshal Amer informed the Jordanian Front commander, General Riad, hours after the Israeli Air Force had finished with the Egyptian air bases in the Sinai and Egypt (as well as Jordan and Syria) that the Egyptians had knocked out three quarters of the Israeli planes, Arab bombers had "destroyed the Israeli bases in a counterattack, and that the ground forces of the Egyptian Army had penetrated into Israel by way of the Negev!"

Since only two Jordanian bases had been attacked, Hussein felt safe in attacking Israel. But no one had informed him of the fate of the other twenty bases in Syria, Egypt, and the Sinai.

Nasser corroborated Amer's assertions by phone on the first day of the hostilities and again on the second day, when he knew the tide had turned heavily against the Arabs, Nasser suggested that both he and Hussein issue statements accusing the British and the Americans of cooperating with the Israelis in carrier-plane attacks on Egypt. According to Hussein, Nasser called him on the morning of June 6 and declared, "We will fight with everything we have. We fought on all fronts, all night. If we had a few problems at the beginning, so what? We'll come out of it all right. God is on our side . . . We dispatched our planes against Israel today. Our planes have been bombing the Israeli airports since early morning."

However, by noon that day, Hussein was ready to inform Nasser that his troops in Jerusalem were in serious trouble.

Jerusalem war damage, 1967. Consulate General of Israel

On the Jordanian front, fighting was personal, street by street, house by house, soldier against soldier—and civilians.

"We went into the Old City and from then on it was hand-to-hand and house-to-house," a young Israeli experiencing war for the first time recalled. "That's the worst thing in the world. In the desert, you know, it's different. There are tanks and planes and the whole thing is at a longer range. Hand-to-hand fighting is different, it's terrible. I killed my first man there . . .

"All of a sudden I saw this man coming out of a doorway . . . We looked at each other for half a second and I knew that it was up to me, personally, to kill him, there was no one else there. The whole thing must have lasted less than a second, but it's printed in my mind like a slow-motion movie. I fired from the hip and I can still see how the bullets splashed against the wall about a meter to his left. I moved my Uzzi [submachine gun] slowly, slowly, it seemed, until I hit him in the body. He slipped to his knees, then raised his head, with his face terrible, twisted in pain and hate, yes, such hate. I fired again and somehow got him in the head. There was so much blood . . . I vomited until the rest of the boys came up . . ."

This brutal, personal fighting continued until the next day, Wednesday, when paratroopers and armor began moving into Jerusalem under artillery fire. Israeli troops were transported to the battle in buses that were still in their civilian bright blue finish. An armored column pushed into the Old City and moved swiftly along Via Dolorosa toward the Wailing Wall. There was little Arab resistance; most of it was from snipers. Soon the Star of David flew over the Mosque of Omar, the Muslim mosque in the Christian quarter.

An emotional but brief ceremony took place at the Wailing Wall, led by the Israeli Army's senior chaplain, Rabbi Shlomo Goren. Also present were Prime Minister Levi Eshkol, Defense Minister Dayan, and former Premier David Ben-Gurion. Rabbi Goren caught the fervency of the moment when he spoke: "We have taken the City of God. We are entering the Messianic era for the Jewish people. And I promise to the Christian world that we are responsible for, we will take care of the holy places of all religions here. For all people, I promise them, we will take care."

Dayan made a more soldierly promise, saying, laconically, "We have returned to the holiest of our holy places. We will not give up this place."

The joy that swept through Jerusalem among the Jews was marred by snipers, who killed two of the celebrants; even more tragic were the deaths of three children, who had stepped on land mines.

With the Old City secure, armored forces moved east toward Jericho while an infantry brigade advanced northward toward Nablus. Simultaneously the Jerusalem Brigade prepared to drive the Arab Legion out of Bethlehem and Hebron.

Major Raanan Lurie, a portrait painter from Montreal, had traveled some six thousand miles to join his infantry company in the taking of Nablus, on the West Bank. Nablus was a strategic outpost on the left flank of any thrust

Consulate General of Israel

Triumphant entry into the Old City, Jerusalem. Major General Uzi Narkiss, in charge of the Israeli Central Command (whose troops encircled and took Jerusalem), Defense Minister Moshe Dayan, and army chief of staff General Yitzhak Rabin.

Zionist Archives and Library

An Israeli soldier praying at the Western ("Wailing") Wall of the Temple destroyed in A.D. 70.

Minister of Labor Golda Meir at the Western Wall, Jerusalem.

Zionist Archives and Library

into Jordan. Taking it would also block any attempt by the Jordanian and Iraqi troops to cut Israel in two at its narrowest point (only eleven miles from the Jordanian border to the Mediterranean).

Lurie led his men practically from the moment his plane touched down in Israel, just a week before the Six Day War erupted. Taking position opposite the Jordanian city of Tulkarm and digging in, the company came under heavy artillery fire on the first day. The next day, they were ordered out to begin the push toward Nablus. It became a personal war of hill after hill, village after village, town after town. (Nablus is the second-largest city on the West Bank.)

The company proceeded, engaging in skirmishes, with Lurie leading in one of two jeeps, occasionally accompanied by tanks. With the tanks in tow, the company passed through the village of Anabta, supposedly in the hands of the Arab Legion, without firing a shot.

By Thursday, June 8, Lurie's company had reached Nablus. "Another unit from the north had already reached the city," he wrote. The Arabs in Nablus had been expecting the Iraqi relief forces to come to their aid. When they first saw the Israeli tanks they were sure that the Iraqi troops had arrived.

Lurie soon learned why his unit had been able to advance on the city with comparative ease: outside the town, they found "a Jordanian column of about 30 American-made tanks [that] had been smashed into bits . . . by our air force. It was a terrible sight to see what had happened to those tanks, but when I thought what would have happened if those tanks had faced my jeeps and my *two* tanks, I wasn't so very sorry."

By the time Israeli troops reached Nablus and controlled virtually all of the West Bank, Hussein accepted the United Nations' call for a cease-fire. On June 7, Jordan officially stopped fighting. Although occupation of the West Bank continued on June 8, Nasser, too, had his troops stop fighting. On June 9 he resigned, only to withdraw his resignation a day later, to general rejoicing in the streets of Cairo. He had lost his war, but not his hold on the Egyptians.

Only Syria remained at war with Israel. Despite the Syrian agreement to comply with the UN cease-fire, its artillery batteries continued sporadic shelling of Israeli border settlements. The Israelis dug in and waited until Gaza, the Sinai, and the battle for Jerusalem were decided. Once these were secure, troops would be free to engage Syria.

On Friday, June 9, armor-supported infantry moved out of the northern tip of Israel into Syria. The Syrians proved to be a tough fighting force.

The advance into Syria was an uphill struggle. Israeli troops attacked the Syrian positions dug into the ridges that dominated the Galilean plain. Israeli infantrymen used British-made Centurion tanks against the Syrian fortifica-

With Sinai and Jerusalem in Israeli hands, the Israel Defense Forces turned their attention to the Golan Heights and to the Syrians. Major General Elazar's armored brigades began the attack on June 9, 1967.

Photos courtesy of Consulate General of Israel

An intact Egyptian MiG taken by the Israelis in the Sinai.

tions and Russian-made tanks. The terrain itself was rugged and under heavy Syrian artillery fire.

In the north the objective was Baniyas; in the center it was Quneitra, twelve miles inside Syria and situated on the highway to Damascus, the capital. The fighting was brutal: in the thirty hours or so that this phase of the war lasted, the Syrians lost two thousand men, more than twice the number the Israelis lost during the entire Six Day War. By nightfall, Israeli troops had penetrated Syria. During the night, bulldozers—their operators ignoring the random artillery shells—cut roads into the Syrian ridges for the next day's attack.

With reinforcements from the Sinai, the Israelis again ignited the Syrian front; the strategic Golan Heights fell to armor and infantry in a sweep around the southern border. Quneitra fell, its crossroads blocked with Israeli vehicles and troops. Forty miles to the northeast lay Damascus. The Israel Defense Forces remained poised, awaiting word from the UN in New York and Dayan in Tel Aviv. At 6:30 P.M., June 10, word came that a new cease-fire had been agreed upon. On Sunday, June 11, 1967, it became official. The Six Day War was over.

In this brief period, Israel had taken and occupied territory four times its own size: the Sinai Peninsula; the West Bank, occupied by Jordan since 1948; and the Syrian Golan Heights. Strategically, these were good, solid defense positions (the gun positions on the heights, from which Israeli villages and farms had been shelled for some twenty years, were removed).

The swift, stunning war had cost the Israelis about 750 lives (the figures vary) and about 2,500 wounded. Arab casualty figures are even less accessible, but a reasonable estimate would place the total Arab number at around 25,000.

One of the two Syrian MiGs that were forced to land in western Galilee; like the Egyptian Air Force, the Syrian Air Force had not proved very effective during the Six Day War.

Consulate General of Israel

Refugees from the fighting in Jerusalem, aided by an Israeli soldier, return to the West Bank over the damaged Allenby Bridge. The West Bank, once controlled by Jordan, is now under Israeli jurisdiction. Like the problem of the Palestinian refugees, the West Bank, and its subsequent proliferation of Jewish settlements, would become a troubling problem in the Middle East.

Consulate General of Israel

(One military historian, Otto von Pivka, has written that "the Arabs lost over 15,000 dead and wounded, with 6,000 prisoners having been taken" . . .)

While the Israeli casualty figures are remarkably low for so ferocious a war, the nation found that it had acquired a burden of human misery along with its awesome conquests. In the territory that Israel held at the time of the cease-fire, and planned to hold on to until Israel's right to exist was recognized, were some one and a half million Arabs; the Gaza Strip was clustered with refugee camps in which three hundred thousand humans, most of them Palestinians, lived in hopeless desperation.

These homeless, virtual noncitizens would generate the cadres—women and men—for future skirmishing, guerrilla action, and terrorist raids.

The smashing Israeli victory presented a severe, humiliating setback for the Arab military leadership. King Hussein of Jordan feared a military coup that never did materialize, despite disruptive activity by the Palestinian guerrillas; Syria blamed Nasser, who, in turn, blamed everybody, even himself.

At first Syrian President Noreddin al-Atasi attributed the defeat to the "aid" given the Israelis by the British and the United States. That could not be substantiated, so he took the responsibility and offered to resign. (His offer was overruled.) Subsequently more than fifty of Egypt's highest military leaders, including Marshal Amer, were arrested. On September 15, 1967, it was announced that Amer had committed suicide.

1973 The Yom Kippur War, and Its Aftermath

The Six Day War was over, and what came to be called the "War of Attrition" began. There was no true peace in the Middle East, despite the tremendous and decisive Israeli victory.

What followed was a time of "no war, no peace." It was a time also of random violence, international skulduggery, exits (some dramatically fatal), and entrances by new dramatis personae on the Middle Eastern—even international—stage.

Despite what can only be termed his ignominious blundering during the Six Day War, Egypt's Nasser continued to dominate the Arab World—and the future course of events in the Middle East. In April of 1968 he stated that Egypt was "fully prepared to support and arm the Palestine resistance movement" in its terrorist activity against Israel. Soon after, Iraq announced that it would form a committee to raise funds for Arab guerrillas. By August, however, Nasser proposed the demilitarization of the Sinai, concessions in regard to demands for the return of Arab refugees to their homeland, the internationalization of the Gaza Strip, and granting Israel cargo access through the Suez Canal in Israeli vessels through the Strait of Tiran. Israel replied with an offer to withdraw from the occupied territories once certain "permanent boundaries" were established between Israel and the Arab states. Such boundaries, if accepted by the Arabs, would imply an Arab recognition of Israel's existence, and the offer was rejected on October 9.

On October 27, Israeli and Egyptian artillery exchanged fire at a point on what was called Israel's Bar Lev Line (named for chief of staff Rav-Aluf Chaim Bar Lev), along the Suez Canal. As a result, Egyptian oil refineries at Port Suez were set ablaze. The Bar Lev Line was an elaborate defensive rampart that ran from Qantara, in the north, to Port Tewfik, on the Gulf of Suez. The line was not intended to contain the Egyptians, in case they decided to move against Israel again, but to check such an attack until Israel could mobilize its defense forces. The artillery duels along the Suez Canal during the War of Attrition left many Egyptian settlements in ruins.

Toward the end of 1968, Israeli and Jordanian troops clashed; Syrian shells were lobbed into Israeli settlements along the border. The Israeli Air Force responded with strafing and bombing attacks. On December 5, 1968, King Hussein of Jordan sent a message to several Arab countries calling for unified action to "Liberate Arab lands." The year closed with the destruction of an Israeli airliner at the Athens air terminal. In retaliation, Israeli helicopters swept down on International Airport, in Beirut, and destroyed thirteen aircraft on the ground. Beirut was selected because Lebanon was known to shelter large numbers of Palestinian guerrillas.

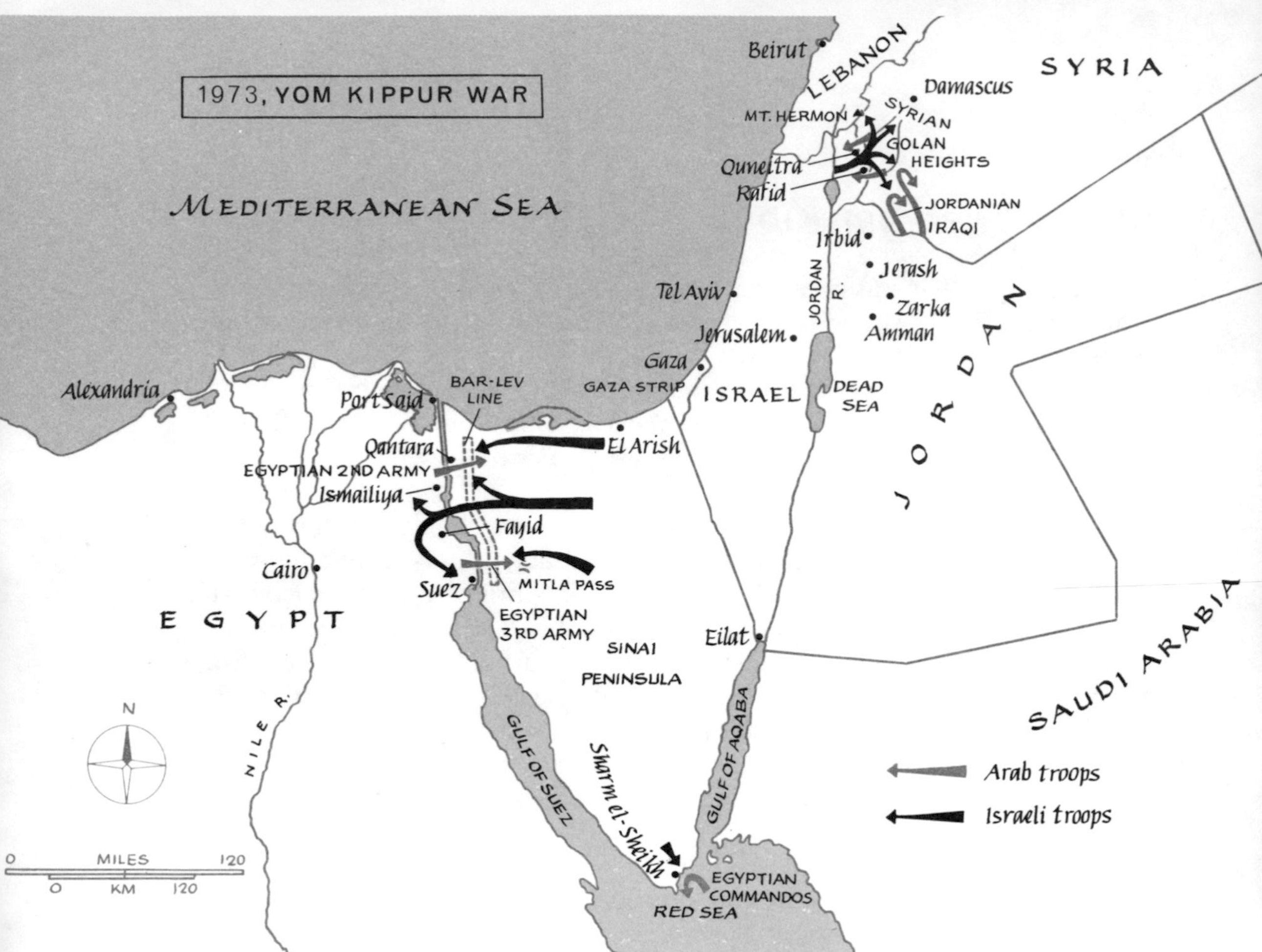

Early in 1969—when the War of Attrition heated up dangerously—Premier Levi Eshkol of Israel died suddenly of a heart attack and was succeeded by Foreign Minister Golda Meir. The Russian-born, U.S.-educated labor activist had immigrated to Palestine in 1921, at the age of 22. A confirmed Zionist, she was active in the establishment of the Jewish state. After the War of Independence, she served in many posts, among them ambassador to the Soviet Union. Her policy vis-à-vis Arab-Israeli relations was quite inflexible: the only acceptable sequel to the cease-fire was "signed peace treaties." On March 7, 1969, Golda Meir, as leader of the Labor Party, became Israel's Premier.

Two days later, when the announcement of Meir's election and appointment appeared in the Jerusalem *Post*, the front page also carried the stories of the destruction of an Egyptian MiG-21 over Sinai in the vicinity of Great Bitter Lake and a five-hour artillery duel along the Bar Lev Line. In the counter-barrage, Israeli artillery set oil installations along the canal ablaze and flamed an Egyptian tanker in the Gulf of Suez.

In April, reports of Soviet missile installations along the Suez Canal chilled the world community. Dismayed, UN Secretary General U Thant admitted that the UN cease-fire had become "totally ineffective in the Suez Canal Sector" and that Israel and Egypt were in "a virtual state of war." Nasser underscored that with a repudiation of the cease-fire, on April 23. In July, U Thant unhappily announced that open warfare had resumed along the Suez Canal, and on July 20 Israeli jets attacked Egyptian ground installations for the first time since the Six Day War. Syria joined in on the last day of the month with heavy artillery and jet attacks.

The bitter stalemate continued, for Israel was determined to hold onto its conquests from the 1967 war to protect its security. On August 23, Nasser called for total war on Israel, because the Al Aksa Mosque, in Jerusalem, had been set afire. (It was learned later that the fire had been set by an Australian, not an Israeli.)

Arab commandos—or guerrillas (often terrorists)—most of them Palestinians, had begun to gain stature in the Middle East with their incursions into Israeli-occupied territory and Israel itself. Random attacks and assassinations outside the Middle East, while they accomplished little toward the eradication of Israel, brought world attention to the Palestinian cause (or so they were rationalized).

They also brought swift and forceful retaliation from the Israeli Defense Forces. Because some of the Palestinian guerrillas were harbored by Jordan, their unrestrained activities made King Hussein uneasy. In July 1970, Egypt and Jordan, and then Israel in August accepted a U.S. proposal for a ninety-day cease-fire. (It was rejected by Yasir Arafat, chairman of the Palestine Liberation Organization.) One of the terms of the proposal was that Jordan would do something to control the guerrillas operating out of Jordan.

An unsuccessful assassination attempt on Hussein's life by Palestinian commandos on September 1, 1970, unleashed a fury of retribution that virtually ended the Palestinian threat from Jordan. For the past year, Hussein had accepted the commando presence and their attacks on the Israelis. (He only asked that they not fire until they crossed the border.) His adviser and uncle, Major General Nasser ben Jamil, was not as complaisant and warned his nephew that the Palestinians, virtually a state within a state, were a threat to the throne. With his own "special branch" of intelligence operatives, Jamil was a serious threat to the guerrillas. When he was dismissed in June, it was an obvious concession to the burgeoning Palestinian popularity in the Arab world.

On September 16, 1970, King Hussein declared martial law in Jordan and formed a new government of an absolute military posture. Anan Safadi reported in the Jerusalem *Post* the effect of this change: "Fierce fighting raged throughout Jordan yesterday [September 17] after the new military government launched a wide-scale assault on terrorist positions. Five cities, including Amman, were hit by heavy artillery and rocket fighting. The new military governor, Field Marshal Habis el-Majali, clamped down a 24-hour curfew in Amman and Zarka, and ordered his troops to shoot to kill any violators. He asserted that he would continue with the government's task to restore law and order to Jordan during the night."

Consulate General of Israel

An Israeli armored unit during a rest stop on the way to the front.

Tension in Amman had been especially acute. The Palestinians seized and occupied two of the capital's major hotels and held sixty occupants, to gain world press attention. Rockets were lobbed at the radio station and even the royal palace. The guerrillas made a point of flaunting their dashing camouflaged jumpsuits and their new Kalashnikov automatic rifles, a gift from the Soviets. (The Jordanian troops wore drab uniforms and carried American surplus rifles of World War II.)

Jordanian soldiers moved into the Palestinian sections of their cities and the known encampments and smashed them, not only with rifles, but with heavy artillery. Within the ten days that Palestinians call "Black September," the Jordanians attacked the refugee camps around the seven hills of Amman, as well as the guerrilla-held towns in the North, including Irbid, Jerash and Ramtha. This cut supply routes from Iraq and Syria. For a few hours, Syria intervened, sending armored units into Jordan bearing the markings of the Palestine Liberation Army. They were turned back by a combined effort of Jordanian armored units and Air Force.

Majali's troops zealously followed orders and, by the time the shooting diminished, toward the end of the month, casualties numbered in the thousands. (The precise number, as is usual in such prairie-fire clashes, is moot. The highest number was twenty-five thousand; the lowest, five thousand. These would have included great numbers of civilians, since the Jordanians destroyed entire camps and sections of various cities and towns housing Palestinians. Whatever the final number, it eradicated the Palestinian resistance movement in Jordan. King Hussein's throne was safe.)

September closed with a stunning sequel to Hussein's solution to his "Palestinian question." On Sunday, September 27, 1970, King Hussein and guerrilla leader Yasir Arafat met in Cairo, as guests of Nasser, to work out a treaty that would end the hostilities in Jordan. Nasser was still the "iron man" among the Arabs, and it was hoped he could bring peace to his fellow Arabs.

On Monday, Nasser suffered a massive heart attack and died. His voice breaking with emotion, Vice-President Anwar el-Sadat announced the death over radio and television from Cairo.

"In Egypt," Sadat wrote in his *Revolt on the Nile*, a memoir about the 1952 revolution that had put Nasser in office, "personalities have always been more important than political programs." But who was Anwar Sadat, this man who had been such an obscure personality during Nasser's turbulent presidency? Virtually unknown abroad, he was regarded as Nasser's "black donkey" (because of his dark skin)—a mere errand boy. Born in 1918 to a poor family in a mud-brick village, Sadat worked his way up in Egyptian political life through the military. A captain during World War II, he was jailed by the British for his contacts with Nazi agents in Cairo. After the war, he became active in Nasser's clandestine Free Officers Organization, which, in 1952, forced the abdication and exile of King Farouk. Nasser then emerged as Egypt's strong man, and Sadat was content to remain in his shadow. When Nasser appointed him vice-president, the attitude in Cairo was that he was being rewarded with a ceremonial role, without power, for his modesty.

After Nasser's sudden death, Sadat became acting President. His appointment to the presidency was assured by his colleagues, who assumed that they could easily manipulate Nasser's "black donkey." They were destined for a few surprises.

In his biography of Sadat in the New York *Times*, Eric Pace noted: "In those first weeks [following his taking over the presidency] many Egyptians, especially students and young intellectuals, found it difficult to take him seriously. With his grin, his fancy suits and his frequent hollow-sounding vows to wage war on Israel, he did not seem to be a strong and purposeful leader." They, too, were destined for some jolts.

Within months after taking office, Sadat dismissed and imprisoned the powerful Vice-President Ali Sabry (who was very close with the Soviets, who were influential in Cairo) and the Minister of the Interior, Sharawy Gomaa (who also controlled the secret police).

On July 18, 1972, Sadat shook up the world when he ordered between fifteen thousand and twenty thousand Soviet military advisers and other "experts" out of Egypt and put all Soviet bases and equipment under Egyptian control. He rationalized this unexpected move on the "excessive caution" of the Russians, who advised him on Israel and held back on the delivery of Soviet weapons to Egypt.

Soon after, in August, Sadat issued a joint declaration with Libya's new radical firebrand Colonel Muammar al-Qaddafi, to establish a "unified political leadership." Qaddafi, who had led a revolt against and deposed Libyan King Idris, proved to be unfriendly toward the West and an enemy of Israel. He was, in fact, regarded by the majority of Arabs as the heir to Nasser's mantle as the leader of the Arab world.

Although not connected with the Egyptian-Libyan pact, a series of inflammatory guerrilla strikes exacerbated Arab-Israeli relations. These forays by Palestinian guerrillas calling themselves the "Black September" organization were designed to dramatize their cause with random assaults mainly in the West. On September 5, 1972, they struck in Munich at the Olympic Games. Three days later, Israel launched reprisal raids on Palestinian guerrilla bases in Syria and Lebanon. Letter bombs, addressed to Israelis, exploded in London and New York.

Assassinations, hijackings, and shootings—all believed to be the work of the Black Septembrists—contributed to the tensions in the Middle East.

The seizure and attack on a Japanese Air Lines jet at Lod Airport was followed in August by another attack at Athens Airport, similar to that at Lod; three people died and more than fifty were wounded. Later that month, Qaddafi and Sadat proclaimed "the birth of a new unified Arab state." Egypt, it might be added, had been under martial law since late March. While world attention was distracted by the Black September assaults, Sadat prepared for his next move. It should not have come as much of a surprise; as early as November 1971, in an address to Egyptian troops on the Suez Canal front, he had said that war with Israel was "inevitable . . . because this is the only way to liberate our occupied land."

Later he would say that "The time has come for a shock." However, no one took Sadat's pronouncements about war with Israel seriously; Egyptian preparations for war were ignored: the stockpiles of ammunition, the large-scale army maneuvers. Few seemed to take seriously a meeting in Cairo, which brought together Jordan's King Hussein, Syria's President Hafez al-Assad, and Sadat. Ostensibly it appeared to be a gathering in which the leaders of the Arab states could discuss diplomatic solutions (i.e., world pressure on Israel through the United Nations), but no one expected anything to come of this. What was not known was that, since June, Sadat and Assad had agreed upon a plan of battle and had already selected a date for a two-pronged invasion of Israel.

Saturday, October 6, 1973, was Yom Kippur ("Day of Atonement"), the most sacred day of the Jewish calendar, a day on which Israeli defenses might be expected to be minimally manned and the thoughts of devout Israelis on more spiritual matters than war. The date was also significant to the Arabs: the tenth day of the Muslim month of Ramadan, commemorating the day on which the Prophet had begun preparing for the conquest of Mecca. It was during this ninth month of the Muslim lunar year that the Koran was revealed to Mohammed. The symbolism to both adversaries, while incongruent, greatly affected the opening phase of the Yom Kippur/Ramadan war of 1973.

At about 2 P.M., Syrian forces in the north attacked Israeli positions in the

Consulate General of Israel

The beginning of the Muslim holy month, Ramadan, is marked twice a day by cannon fire—at sunrise and sunset, at the beginning and end of fasting. The charge consists of small bags of gunpowder and salt. During the month of Ramadan, only the ill and soldiers are exempt from fasting. In October 1973, the Ramadan gunfire coincided with the first shot of a new Arab-Israeli War: the Yom Kippur War.

Golan Heights while Egyptian troops moved against the Bar-Lev Line, in the Sinai. The Israelis were caught off guard—like the Arabs in the Six Day War. The Egyptians, especially, were well prepared and trained (although their mentors, the Soviets, had long since left the scene). King Hussein—who had not been informed at the meeting with Sadat and Assad of their specific plan for war—was also surprised. Qaddafi, his relations strained with an ascendant Sadat, chose to keep the Libyans out.

The Yom Kippur assault began on the night of October 5, when Egyptian frogmen and commandos crossed the Suez Canal to plant explosives and to plug oil pipelines that the Israelis had installed in the east bank. In the event of an Egyptian attack, the canal was to be flooded with oil and set afire to incinerate the attackers. This mission was carried out effectively without detection by the Israelis, who that night manned only a fraction of the posts along the Bar-Lev Line.

The attack opened with air strikes on Israeli positions as the Egyptian Army crossed the canal in the wake of landings by commandos. Three bridgeheads were established to enable the Egyptian tanks (Soviet-built T-54s and 55s predominantly) to cross the canal. The Egyptians moved quickly, for the impact of the Israeli Air Force during the Six Day War had not been forgotten. Although the Egyptian and Syrian air forces were no match for the Israeli Air Force, they were prepared for it on the ground.

The Soviets provided the weapons that would confound the Israeli Air Force, which had performed so brilliantly in the 1967 war. Dense concentrations of antiaircraft missile sites were situated on both the Suez and the Syrian fronts.

Avions Marcel Dassault

Dassault Mirage, a French-designed plane that the Israeli Air Force flew during the Yom Kippur War.

McDonnell F-4C "Phantom," one of the superior fighter-bombers of the 1960s. Originally designed for the U.S. Navy, the Phantom was also used by the U.S. Air Force in Vietnam. The modified "E" version saw action with the Israeli Air Force during the Yom Kippur War.

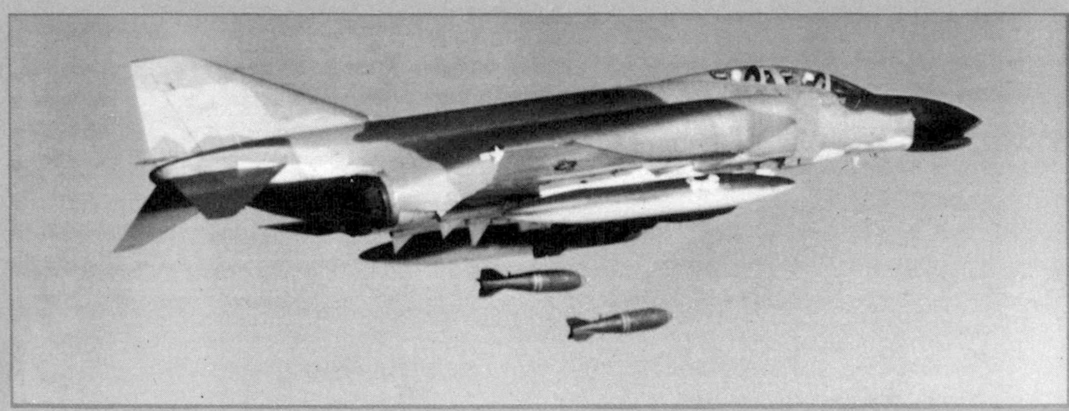

U.S. Air Force

Israeli paratroopers prepare for a jump. The plane is a C-47, the military transport version of the venerable pre-World War II DC-3.

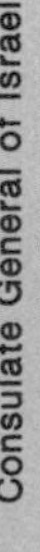

Consulate General of Israel

The Israelis miscalculated the effectiveness of the Soviet surface-to-air missiles (SAMs) and their evolution since the Six Day War. Not only were the Arabs equipped with a new, deadly, self-propelled, radar-controlled, 23-mm, four-barreled ZSU-23s, there were also the more mobile SAM-6 (much improved over the SAM-2 and SAM-3) and the SAM-7, which could be fired from a shoulder tube.

The various effective ranges of these weapons forced the Israeli pilots to fly at lower altitudes than before this outbreak (a pilot only had to fly below the range of the SAM-2, for example; but that put him within range of the SAM-3, and, eventually flying at unaccustomed low altitudes, also within reach of the ZSU-23). The SAM-6, like the SAM-3, was vectored by radar to its objective; it was also guided to the enemy aircraft by an infrared homing device. The Israelis had no means of jamming these systems and paid heavily for it.

Missiles also figured largely in the ground fighting in the tank and armor clashes.

Initially, then, the Yom Kippur War was the Six Day War in reverse, with the Arabs providing all of the surprises and overrunning the battlefield.

The Egyptian breaching of the Bar-Lev Line was especially noteworthy. Under the bristling cover of artillery and several types of missiles, powerful water cannons mounted on pontoons washed away the great sand rampart that Israeli bulldozers had pushed into place. The high-pressure water jets were more effective than dynamite would have been. Through these breaches, Egyptian troops, tanks, and other vehicles poured into the Sinai over several pontoon bridges. The Israeli Air Force, flying American-built Douglas A-4E Skyhawks, McDonnell-Douglas F-4E Phantoms, and a few French-built Mirages, attempted to counter the invasion but encountered an effective wall of missiles. Few Israeli aircraft got through to the pontoons and Egyptian troops pouring over them; sheer courage was no match for the phalanx of fire.

It was the same on the ground. As two armored divisions moved into and through the Bar-Lev Line, the stunned Israelis began rushing reinforcements to the two battlefronts. In the Sinai, their tank crews raced into an unexpected resistance: well-trained Egyptian infantrymen, armed with the Soviet "Sagger" missile launcher, blasted the Israeli Centurions into flaming wreckage. Virtually undetected as they lay flattened in the sand, the Egyptians took a heavy toll of Israeli armor. On the first day of the war, Israel lost about half of the total of tanks lost (about eight hundred) in the Sinai.

Within twenty-four hours, the Egyptians had moved more than five hundred tanks across the three bridgeheads on the Suez Canal, had taken Qantara, in the north, and were moving on Khatmia Pass, in the center, and Mitla Pass, opposite Suez, in the south. Egyptian commandos in helicopters attacked Sharm el-Sheikh, on the southern tip of the peninsula, but with little success. But in the north, the Egyptian Army had pushed across the desert some ten miles east of the canal and halted.

The question was, why did the Egyptians stop? why didn't they exploit the

An Israeli tank crew prepares for action; the tanks are British Centurions.

Although caught relatively unprepared by the sudden outbreak of the Yom Kippur War, the Israelis soon held planning sessions and swept into action.

Photos courtesy of Consulate General of Israel

Consulate General of Israel

Popular Israeli entertainer Aviva Orgad performs for Israeli troops in the desert.

momentum of surprise and success? It would have taken Dayan about forty-eight hours to assemble the holy-day observants of the Israeli Defense Forces and move them to the fronts. Only the Air Force was capable of moving against the enemy, and it suffered severely from the wall of missiles.

Once beyond the Bar-Lev Line, the Egyptians dug into defensive positions—and waited. Military theorists conjectured that once beyond the heavy concentration of their missile umbrella, the Egyptians realized that they would be no match for the aroused Israelis. For Sadat, it was, even in its limited aspects, an international political-diplomatic victory. His prestige rose among the Arabs, and so he waited and hoped for the intervention of the big powers of the West to put pressure on Israel to put an end to the fighting.

It was the same on the Syrian Front: initial surprise and success. Simultaneously with the outbreak in the Sinai, Syrian artillery batteries and aircraft pounded Israeli positions on the Golan Heights. Under this cover, the Syrians began moving on those positions in their Soviet T-54 tanks and a few of the more formidable T-62 tanks. No less than five hundred tanks smashed across the Israeli lines at Quneitra, in the center, and eight hundred pushed through at Rafid, breaching the 1967 cease-fire line and the UN buffer zone. At the northern end of the line, on strategic Mount Hermon, Syrian commandos dropped from helicopters and took an Israeli observation post, killing or taking prisoner the entire garrison.

Despite their meager strength of one hundred fifty tanks, the Israelis on the Golan Heights fought the attackers ferociously, inflicting heavy losses in men and machines (estimates put the figures at eight thousand Syrian infantrymen alone and hundreds of tanks). However, the massed armored formations inexorably broke through. The Israeli Air Force was thrown into the battle but, as in the Sinai, was met by a devastating hail of SAMs.

By 7 P.M., the Syrians had broken through the crack Barak armored brigade and charged toward their objective, the Jordan River. By this time, the Israelis had begun rushing reservists to the front, and by late evening the Syrian thrust had been decelerated. The Sunday issue of the Jerusalem *Post* published a statement by Defense Minister Dayan, who dramatically promised that, while it might take a few days, the Israeli Defense Forces would "smite the Egyptians and Syrians hip and thigh."

The next day, Monday, October 8, the forces threatening Israel appeared to impend more formidably when Tunisia, the Sudan, and Iraq pledged support to the troops fighting the Israelis. Of these, only Iraq honored its pledge, sending three divisions of ground troops (about thirty thousand men), plus tanks and a handful of planes. Then Jordan joined, with about twice as many troops, hundreds of tanks, and fewer than eighty aircraft. Saudi Arabia and Morocco eventually sent token forces (a brigade each, totaling altogether about three thousand men), but no armor or planes. On paper, at least, the Israeli Defense Forces, of fewer than three hundred thousand, stood against a combined force of roughly five hundred thousand.

By the third day, October 8, it was clear that Sadat's plan had worked; the Arabs were solidly positioned on the east bank of the Suez Canal and held a portion of the Golan Heights. Dayan had been right: it would take a few days before the Israeli Defense Forces could fully mobilize. In the south, the Egyptians dug in, waiting for their missile umbrellas to be moved forward. In the north, in the face of counterattacks by Israeli reservists and the Air Force, the Syrians pulled back slightly to consolidate their lines. The aerial attacks were costly: at least fifty first-line combat planes were destroyed, most of them by lethal SAM-6s. It was also noted that not all of the batteries responded to the Israelis' attacks from the air. The Arabs had begun to run out of missiles, and some of the attacks had destroyed some of the SAM sites.

By Thursday the tide began to turn. Syria was the first to receive fulfillment of Dayan's biblical vow of death and destruction; even the capital, Damascus, was a target. In retaliation for the only attack during the war on Israel itself—a dozen or so Frog-7 missiles launched into northern Israel—the Israeli Air Force bombed Damascus, a raid that resulted in the death of about two hundred civilians.

Major General Rafael Eytan's division (consisting of the 7th Armored and the "Golani" Infantry brigades) opened the counteroffensive by pushing through a deep belt of fortifications positioned to provide mutually supporting fields of fire—barbed wire, antitank ditches, minefields, and field guns—

Consulate General of Israel

The Israelis retake Mount Hermon, an observation post in the Golan Heights. During the early fighting in the Yom Kippur War it was taken by Syrian commandos transported by helicopters.

Defense Minister Dayan meets with the maverick hero of the Yom Kippur War: Major General Ariel Sharon.

Wide World Photos

toward Damascus. Heavy Syrian losses in the Golan fighting rendered this bastion less formidable than it might have proved if it had been fully manned.

Other divisions joined in the attack to the north and to the south, so that by October 12, the Israelis had not only pushed the Syrian Army back to the 1967 cease-fire line but continued on toward Damascus. This came after massive tank battles in which, according to the Jerusalem *Post*, the Syrians lost eight hundred tanks, which were destroyed or captured. Dayan felt certain enough of victory that he announced that Syria was "finished for all practical purposes" (a somewhat premature prediction). He also said that "We have to teach the Syrians a lesson—that the road to Damascus to Eretz Yisrael also leads from Eretz Yisrael to Damascus." Dayan's tanks and infantry were on that road, inside Syria, and only thirty miles from Damascus.

Although the battle did not end on the Golan front, the outcome was inevitable. Counterattacks, accomplishing little, were launched against the Israelis, many of the most hapless by troops from other Arab states that had joined Egypt and Syria. Jordanians, Saudi Arabians, and Iraqis were thrown into the battle, with heavy losses. On October 13, the day Jordan made public its decision to join the battle, Israel wiped out nearly an entire Iraqi division.

This static and bloody warfare continued until a series of not-always-effectual cease-fires ended it. The first took effect on October 22, the day Israeli paratroops retook the critical positions, held by a Moroccan infantry brigade, on Mount Hermon.

With the Golan-Syrian Front under sporadic, violent control, the Israeli Defense Forces were ready to turn to the Egyptians, in the Sinai. The most dazzling (some would have called it "rash") breakthrough was carried out by a man often called the "maverick of the Israeli Army," Major General Ariel Sharon. Reconnaissance in the area of Great Bitter Lake had revealed that the western side was not occupied or was poorly defended, and that there was a gap between the Egyptian Second and Third armies. If the Israelis could get through the gap, they might overrun the SAM sites on the west bank of the canal and clear the air for their own air support. Such a thrust would also cut lines of communication between the Egyptian armies, place Israelis behind their lines, and threaten Cairo and Suez.

Sharon led his reserve division, without interference, across the Negev Desert and smashed through Egyptian lines with his tanks. By the afternoon of October 15 his unit faced the sandbank along the eastern shore of the Suez Canal, just north of the Great Bitter Lake, near Deversoir, in the center of the Suez battle line. Sharon was informed by his engineers that it would take hours to dig through the great sandbank to reach the water before they could drive into Egypt. Sharon, who had once commanded this sector, instructed the engineers to search for a section of the bank marked by red bricks. Months before, he had prepared a spot in the bank by deceptively attenuating the sand, allowing the bank to be readily cleared and breached. This was accomplished, and by the morning of October 16, Sharon was poised on the west bank of the canal. Rather than wait for reinforcements, as would have been customary, he plunged across, ferrying both tanks and troops on rafts. Encountering virtually no resistance, he gained a foothold on the west bank, established an incipient beachhead, and fanned out to the north and south. This daring stroke separated the two Egyptian armies and, indeed, put the Israelis (though not yet in great numbers) behind the Arab lines.

As the day went on, despite Egyptian attacks from both sides of his salient, more of Sharon's tanks and armored vehicles (initially one company of each) crossed into Egypt and began eliminating the SAM sites. The bridgehead swelled, and so did Israeli numbers, when Sharon's vanguard was joined by a division commanded by Major General Avraham Adan. With additional pontoons carried by Adan, the crossing was widened; a paratroop brigade joined the troops moving into Egypt.

When the Egyptian Third Army attempted to cut the salient from the south, Adan's unit wiped out the Egyptian 25th Armored Brigade. By October 17 the tide in the Sinai had turned around completely and, though the Arabs found it hard to believe, an Israeli victory was inevitable. Hard fighting continued for two more days, resulting in yet another bridge over the canal. Israeli troops streamed into Egypt. Sharon's division turned northward, toward Ismailia (Egyptian Third Army), as Major General Adan, with reinforcements, turned south toward Suez and the Second Army.

With the threat of the SAMs extirpated, the Israeli Air Force joined in the assault, shackling units of the Egyptian Third Army to the east bank. On October 20, Israeli paratroops took Fayid Airport, on the west bank of Great Bitter Lake, as Adan pushed southward toward Suez. On October 21 Sharon had reached Ismailia, and the Cairo-Suez road belonged to the Israeli Defense Forces.

During these few helter-skelter days, moves in the United Nations, with pressures behind the scenes by the United States and the Soviet Union (in opposition, but working toward the same goal, lest the situation get out of hand) moved in the direction of a cease-fire. It was during this period also that the Arab oil-producing countries—Libya, Saudi Arabia, Kuwait, Bahrain, Qatar, and Dubai—cut off the export of oil to the United States in retaliation for aid to Israel in the form of aircraft and other war materials. (Little was said about Soviet aid to the Arabs.) This was the introduction of the "oil weapon" upon the international scene.

The first cease-fire was declared on October 22, in a joint resolution prepared by the United States and the Soviet Union and proposed to the UN Security Council. It was to have taken effect on the Sinai Front, but neither side complied and the fighting continued. By the following day, Israeli troops were poised on the outskirts of Suez, where Egyptian resistance was tough. The Egyptian Third Army, however, was isolated and surrounded, while to the north, the Second Army remained in limbo.

President Sadat himself had already requested a cease-fire, certain that vic-

Israeli Air Force encounters with Syrian MiGs resulted in the destruction of the Soviet fighter plane. In the background is a war-damaged Muslim mosque in the village of Mazraat bet Jann. The vehicles belong to the UN and to the Israeli Army.

An Israeli-held position in the Mount Hermon range on Pitulim Peak, Syria. The command post flies the Israeli flag (right).

A Syrian woman walks through the ruins of the much-fought-over town of Quneitra, in the Golan Heights.

Photos courtesy of United Nations, Y. Nagata

tory lay within his grasp. What he did not know was that, almost at the same moment, the audacious Sharon was ferrying his troops across the Suez Canal. Sadat appealed to the United States and the Soviet Union to dispatch troops to supervise the cease-fire. Accusations as to who was responsible for the violations of the cease-fire were veiled by the escalation of international tension. The United States maintained that it would not send troops but would continue to lend its "full support" (aircraft, tanks, weapons, missiles). The Soviets, whose mass airlifts could not compete with those of the Americans, began to have qualms, but there was apprehension that they might attempt to send troops to aid the twenty thousand men of the Egyptian III Corps, trapped on the East Bank of the Canal.

President Richard Nixon, whose administration was crumbling in the midst of the Watergate scandal, seized the opportunity. On October 25 he ordered a worldwide U.S. military alert, in case the Soviet Union actively intervened in the Middle East. Meanwhile, Secretary of State Henry A. Kissinger moved among the various capitals—Moscow, Washington, Tel Aviv, Amman, Riyadh, Cairo—in what was termed "shuttle diplomacy," to settle the uneasiness in the Middle East. The UN Security Council responded by establishing an emergency supervisory force, a unit that explicitly excluded troops from the U.S.A. and the U.S.S.R.

Other cease-fires on the Sinai Front were announced, but by the end of the month serious confrontations were over. On October 28 the Israelis permitted the passage of food, water, and medical supplies through their lines to the isolated Egyptian III Corps, thus diminishing the Soviet threat. It was not until November 11, 1973, however, that Kissinger's shuttle diplomacy produced results, when Israel and Egypt signed a cease-fire accord. On the Syrian Front, intermittent fighting dragged on, at times with rising intensity. Finally, on May 31, 1974, Israel and Syria signed an accord in which they agreed to disengage, each pull their troops back from the front, and to establish a United Nations buffer zone in between. To the final moment, however, Syrians continued firing artillery shells into Israeli positions.

The cost of the October 1973 Arab-Israeli war had been shockingly high, especially for Israel, with its comparatively small population. The official figure of the dead was 1,854 (other sources estimate the figure to be closer to 3,000) and 6,000 wounded. This represented about 10 percent of the Israeli Defense Forces. To comprehend the impact of this figure on the Israelis, a proportional comparison with the United States, and its population, with Israel's, would have resulted in 140,000 dead. For Israel, with its population then at less than 3,000,000, this was a chilling blow. The cost in equipment was also high, about a third (102) of the Israeli Air Force's combat aircraft, more than 800 tanks, and about 300 armored vehicles.

The Arab casualties and losses were even greater (accurate figures are hard to come by): 19,000 dead, more than 50,000 wounded, and 9,000 captured or missing. The combined Arab forces lost more than 350 fighter planes, 1,300 tanks, and 11 ships.

Sadat had lost the war but won the political victory; he emerged as the nominal leader of the Arab world. He had achieved a great measure of respect for the Arab fighting man; the humiliation of the Six Day War was palliated.

Even as the war raged, questions were raised in Israel, and Chief of Staff Rav-Aluf David Elazar promised an "unflinching" probe by the Army into "reported shortcomings on the eve of the Yom Kippur War and the conduct of the war itself." An investigation, concluded in early April 1974, did arrive at some unflinching decisions: Elazar was the first to go, along with his intelligence chief, Aluf Eliyahu Zeira, plus four other high military officials. Although Dayan and Meir were exonerated, public opinion forced their resignations soon after. Upon Meir's resignation, a voice was raised in the Knesset calling for elections and for a "government of a different composition" from that of Golda Meir's. The voice, which would become more assertive over the ensuing weeks, belonged to the leader of the militant right-wing Likud Party, Menachem Begin.

Yitzak Rabin—who had represented the Labor Party in Meir's Cabinet, was a former ambassador to the United States, and had won high honors as chief of staff during the Six Day War—was asked to form a new Israeli Government. Rabin was a native-born Israeli, a *sabra* (named for the local cactus fruit: "prickly on the outside and sweet on the inside")—the first Israeli-born Prime Minister. He evinced the *sabra* essence in his firm, but judicious, stand during the search for peace after the final 1973 war cease-fire, in May 1974. He refused to deal with the Palestinian guerrilla organizations. Soon after, the Palestine Liberation Organization was officially recognized by the Arab world in Cairo; by November 1974, its leader, Yasir Arafat, addressed the UN General Assembly in New York.

Even as Rabin was forming the new government and the peace process seemed to be uneasily forming, a trio of terrorists broke into a schoolhouse in the Israeli town of Maalot. Such incidents did not provide a healthy climate for peacemaking, but Rabin persevered.

Late in June 1974, Israeli-occupied territory on the Golan Heights was evacuated; in September, Rabin proposed troop withdrawals from the Sinai. In June 1975, Israel ordered the partial withdrawal of its small force occupying the Sinai, and on June 5, President Sadat led a ceremonial convoy of ships through the Suez Canal. For the first time in eight years, the canal was open to commercial shipping. In September, Israel and Egypt signed a Sinai pact, one of its stipulations being the stationing of United States "technicians" in the Sinai. For his part in the signing, Sadat was branded by the PLO's Zuhayr Muhsin as a "traitor and conspirator." A week later, Sadat closed down the PLO's radio station, "Voice of Palestine," in Cairo.

It was not a true time of peace in the Middle East, but a period of random violence and retaliation: there was unrest on the West Bank; there was the perennial Palestinian question; and there were flare-ups in the area. In 1975, Lebanon was divided by civil war (Christian versus Muslim), and the Syrian Army came in as Arabian "peace-keepers." The PLO presence in southern Lebanon con-

Israeli kibbutz after being shelled by Syrian guns.

A view of Lower Galilee. Kibbutz Tel Katzir is within easy shelling distance of this Syrian stronghold at Tawfik, in the Golan Heights.

Kibbutz Yehi Am, in northern Galilee, viewed through the ruins of a crusader fortress/castle. These agricultural settlements had little protection from random Syrian shellings and air attacks.

Photos courtesy of Consulate General of Israel

United Nations, T. Chen

PLO leader Yasir Arafat appears before the United Nations, in New York, to address the Palestine question. The decision to invite Arafat was made during the Yom Kippur War, in October 1973, during the height of battle on the Golan Heights.

tributed to the rending of the nation and, literally, future disaster. While Sadat's fame was enhanced, Rabin's political career came to a surprising, abrupt end.

In March of 1977 the Israeli newspaper *Ha-Aretz* revealed that Lea Rabin held an illegal bank account in Washington dating from their years there when Rabin was ambassador. Further investigation uncovered that it was a joint account. Their "crime" was that, when they returned to Israel, they had neglected to bring their money with them. Rabin resigned from the Labor Party and relinquished the post of Prime Minister, to spare his party political embarrassment. Both he and his wife were fined and Rabin continued to be active with the Labor Party—although behind the scenes.

A general election was held the next month (May 1977), and to worldwide surprise, not only did the Labor Party suffer an overwhelming defeat, but Menachem Begin's Likud Party was swept into the Knesset with a solid majority. Conservative, militantly Talmudic Begin's shift into the center of power portended a dramatic shift in Israel's political climate. Former Defense Minister Dayan implied just that when, commenting on the Likud victory, he said that it represented "an expression of the public feeling against territorial concessions in Judea and Samaria [i.e., the West Bank]." While he was happy about that, Dayan also added that he was not happy "operationally." He did not expand on that observation, however.

"War is at the gate," declared Shulamit Aloni, whose Citizens Rights Movement did not win a single seat in the Knesset. Begin's victory, she believed, meant that Israel was becoming "less rational, more nationalistic, more mystical, less governed by common sense . . ."

United Nations, Y. Nagata

Israeli reserve troops, whose courage and tenacity brought final, although costly, victory for Israel in the Yom Kippur War. In accordance with the truce negotiated by the UN, these soldiers withdrew from their position in Tel el-Shams, deep inside Syria.

Consulate General of Israel

Prime Minister Yitzhak Rabin and Minister of Defense Shimon Peres are present at the first flight of a new Israeli Air Force fighter, the Kfir *(Lion Cub), in April 1975.*

The Kfir, *Israel's first home-built fighter plane, is an Israeli modification of the Dassault* Mirage *crossed with a General Electric J-79 turbojet engine. The* Kfir *is capable of speeds in excess of Mach 2.*

Consulate General of Israel

Kissinger in Saudi Arabia with King Faisal in the Royal Palace at Riyadh. Although Faisal encouraged ties with the United States, he enforced an oil embargo and oil-price hike, during the Yom Kippur War, against the United States, Western Europe, and Japan. Not long after this photo was taken, Faisal was assassinated by his young nephew, Faisel ibn Musa'id.

Henry Kissinger meeting with Jordan's King Hussein: The King refused to recognize Israel despite Kissinger's efforts.

Photos courtesy of Library of Congress

The fruits of Kissinger's "shuttle diplomacy": Kissinger (left) initials the September 1975 Sinai Accord in Alexandria, Egypt. In twin ceremonies in Egypt and in Jerusalem, representatives of Israel and Egypt signed the accord that set in motion a treaty of peace between Egypt and Israel.

Like Begin, Sadat was deeply religious, and frequently quoted from the sacred texts of his faith. Both were former soldiers and both were tough. Yet these men, so similar and at the same time antithetical, very nearly changed the course of the history of the Middle East. History itself fatally interrupted their sometimes frustrating enterprise, with Sadat's assassination in 1981; what might have been ultimately accomplished is rendered pointless by that shocking interruption.

Of the two, Sadat was the more adept diplomat, and it was he who initiated what might have led to peace in the Middle East. Even as Israeli bombers attacked Palestinian guerrilla positions in war-wracked Lebanon, and American diplomats tried to bring the Arabs and the Israelis together for peace talks in Geneva, Sadat declared, on November 9, 1977, that he "was ready to go to the Israeli parliament itself to discuss [peace]."

On November 15, enlisting American ambassadors as messengers, Begin invited Sadat to Israel; a reply arrived within hours accepting the unprecedented invitation. Although the Israeli chief of staff, Rav-Aluf Mordechai Gur, intimated that Sadat was probably duping Israel and asserted that Egypt was at the peak of war preparations, Gur was rebuked by Defense Minister Ezer Weizman, and the unique interplay continued.

Calling his mission a "holy job," and over the objections of his advisers, Sadat, on November 19, became the first Arab leader to visit Israel since its founding, in 1948. Reactions throughout the Arab world were violently negative to this peace overture. There were also demonstrations in Athens (in which an Arab student died during an attack on the Egyptian Embassy), London,

Library of Congress

U.S. Secretary of State Henry Kissinger and Egyptian President Anwar el-Sadat. Although he technically lost the Yom Kippur War, Sadat won personal and political advantages that would enable him to attempt to bring peace to the Middle East. Kissinger, following the 1973 war, was active in negotiations between Israel and the Arab states.

Consulate General of Israel

In response to an invitation from Israel's Prime Minister Menachem Begin, Egyptian President Anwar el-Sadat made an unprecedented trip to Israel on November 19, 1977. In this photo Sadat is seated between Foreign Minister Dayan and Prime Minister Begin at a working dinner.

Golda Meir, Prime Minister of Israel during the Yom Kippur War; the confusion of its opening battles would cost her her political career. Meir resigned in 1974.

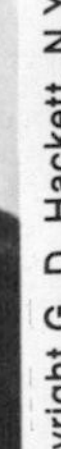

Copyright G. D. Hackett N.Y.

Paris, Madrid, Bucharest, and Stockholm. Damascus denounced November 19, 1977, as "a black day in the history of the Arab nation." Libya cut all ties with Egypt, and in Tripoli a mob set fire to the Egyptian Embassy.

In Israel, Sadat was warmly greeted at Ben-Gurion Airport by a distinguished welcoming committee and a large crowd of cheering, applauding Israelis. Even before leaving the plane, Sadat inquired if Minister of Agriculture Ariel Sharon would be present. Referring to Sharon's daring breakthrough and crossing of the Suez Canal in the Yom Kippur War, Sadat shook Sharon's hand and said, "I wanted to catch you there." "I'm glad to have you here," the former general replied.

To the applause and cheers of the crowd, Sadat moved along the red-carpeted reception line to shake the hands of Moshe Dayan and, when he came to Golda Meir, embraced her, saying that he had been waiting a long time to see her.

"Mr. President," she told him, "I too have been waiting a long time to see you." (Later Sadat told a *Time* reporter that of all the recent Israeli Prime Ministers, the one he would have preferred to negotiate with was "the old lady"—a term of respect and affection. To that he added, "She has guts . . ." In just over a year after their historic meeting, Meir died, in her eightieth year, of lymphoma.)

Sadat conceded, however, that Begin was "strong"—also abrasive, a sharp negotiator not given to compromise. Sadat returned to Cairo certain that their meetings would bring about peace in the Middle East; his dream was not merely for peace between Egypt and Israel, but with the other Arab states. Messages, diatribes, threats out of Syria, Libya, and the PLO in Beirut continued to fulminate.

Negotiations were not the equivalents of historic ceremonials. Both men were firm—and in direct opposition—regarding the Sinai and the West Bank. Begin wanted the territory, and Sadat did not feel that keeping Arab lands

Consulate General of Israel

Sadat at prayer at the El Aqsa Mosque, Jerusalem. He is the first Arab leader to visit Israel since it was established as a nation, in 1948.

contributed anything to Israel's security. When there seemed to be no agreement on these problems, Sadat made a disquieting move, on January 18, 1978, when he broke off talks underway in Jerusalem and recalled the Egyptian delegation. He accused Israel of trying to deadlock the situation by "submitting partial solutions" (to the Sinai and West Bank questions).

This deadlock prevailed, while President Jimmy Carter and Secretary of State Cyrus R. Vance worked behind the scenes to keep the talks going. It was not an easy period in Middle East history: several scattered terrorist attacks (one resulting in the death of a Sadat confidant, Egyptian newspaper editor Youssef el-Sebai, in Cyprus) and a serious incursion by the Israeli Defense Forces into southern Lebanon occurred.

The attack on Lebanese Palestinian camps contributed only further bitterness to the peacemaking initiated by Sadat. Talks between Carter and Begin, held in Washington on March 23, got nowhere, and a week later, Israeli Defense Minister Ezer Weizman flew to Cairo to meet with Sadat, hoping to break the new impasse.

The Middle East and tempers simmered. Clashes continued in Lebanon, despite the United Nations presence. In early June, an exasperated Sadat, in a speech to Egyptian troops, warned that if Israel continued "not to under-

Following a series of meetings at Camp David, Maryland, with President Jimmy Carter, Anwar el-Sadat and Menachem Begin signed the Camp David Accords, outlining the terms for peace between their countries. On March 26, 1979, they returned to Washington, D.C., where they signed an Israeli-Egyptian Peace Treaty at the White House. Sadat, as well as Carter and Begin, were denounced and vilified throughout the Arab world.

Consulate General of Israel

stand" his motives behind the peace initiative, Egypt's armed forces would have "no alternative but to complete the battle of liberation." He was alluding to the withdrawal of Israeli forces from the occupied territories and self-determination for the Arabs in Gaza and the West Bank (which was becoming spattered with Israeli settlements, to Arab dismay).

Despite the almost daily incidents and disturbances, and Israeli tenacity vis-à-vis the Gaza Strip and the West Bank, Sadat's initiative was kept alive through the efforts of President Carter. This culminated in the September 1978 meeting between Sadat and Begin at Camp David, Maryland, with Carter as a welcome participant. On September 17, the two leaders signed two documents popularly known as the Camp David Accords, outlining peace between Egypt and Israel.

One of the agreements, which has since been fulfilled, dealt with the signing of a peace treaty between Egypt and Israel and with the withdrawal of Israeli military personnel from the Sinai Peninsula. This part of the agreement was complicated by the gradual occupation in the interim of more than a dozen settlements in the Sinai by Israeli residents; their removal when the time came for compliance with the agreement (April 1982) led to clashes between Israeli civilians and soldiers.

The second agreement was not as specific; it set up a "framework" which promised to deal with the future of the West Bank and the Gaza Strip (i.e., the Palestinian question). Provision was made for the participation of Egypt, Jordan, Israel, and Palestinian "representatives" over a period of five years. While no true or final solution to the question, it was a beginning. That the solution was not at hand was made clear a week after the accords were signed, when Libya, Syria, Algeria, South Yemen, and the PLO severed all political and economic relations with Egypt.

Fittingly, Sadat and Begin were recipients of the Nobel Peace Prize in December. A note of sorrow subdued the event: the death of Golda Meir. Also, the Egyptian-Israeli peace-treaty talks had broken down, and Secretary of State Vance, continuing in the Kissinger shuttle tradition, flew to Oslo to confer with Sadat and Begin (with, unfortunately, no results).

Early in the next year, 1979, although preoccupied with an eruption of violent events in Iran, President Carter flew to Cairo and Jerusalem for further meetings. Initially, Begin and Sadat remained obdurate on the subject of Gaza and the West Bank. Exuding a biblical Eretz Yisrael mysticism, Begin wanted to hold on to these territories; Sadat, conscious of his precarious standing in the Arab world, wanted these lands returned to the Arabs. However, while passing through Cairo on March 13, Carter dramatically announced that his proposals for compromises had been accepted by Begin and that an Israel-Egypt peace treaty was assured. (Additional inducement included generous U.S. financial aid to both countries.)

Inexorably the historic event approached, while Arab voices were raised in denunciation of all three leaders. Radio Amman called the imminent peace treaty an "illusion" and accused Sadat of selling out "Arab land, Jerusalem, and Egypt's Arab identity." Damascus Radio called the treaty one of "treachery and surrender." The Iraqi Government issued a statement calling Carter's Middle East efforts nothing less than an "aggressive and conspiratorial" attempt "to inflame the situation in the Arab world." In Beirut, PLO leader Arafat underscored that with the vow that the Palestinians would "burn everything" to prevent a separate Egyptian-Israeli peace.

On March 26, 1979, in a meeting with Carter in Washington, Sadat and Begin signed a peace treaty formally ending a state of war that had existed between their two nations for over thirty years. Carter signed as a witness, saying, "Today we celebrate a victory, not of a bloody military campaign, but of an inspiring peace campaign." Outside the White House gates, Palestinian students and their supporters demonstrated and shouted slogans vilifying the ceremonies. On the same day, leaders from several Arab countries met in Baghdad and threatened to take "concrete measures against Sadat on a political, economic, informational, and mass mobilization basis." The treaty was denounced in Moscow. By April 27, no fewer than fifteen Arab states had cut their ties with Egypt, among them the usually moderate Saudi Arabia in an unexpected move.

Peace had come to Egypt and Israel, but the Middle East burned with rancor. From his hideaway in western Beirut, Yasir Arafat not only vowed to chop off Sadat's hands, he also pledged to drive Sadat, Begin, and Carter out of the Middle East. There was irony and tragedy in this braggadocio, in light of events that followed. Carter, in a sense, was driven out of his presidency by the hostage crisis in Iran and its failed rescue; Arafat, of course, had nothing to do with that.

Sadat's extraordinary and courageous initiative in the search for peace would cost him his life. Arafat had nothing to do with that, except to incite and encourage Egyptian dissidents with pronouncements. As for Arafat himself, his position in Arab-Palestinian affairs was jeopardized when the final target of his vow, Begin, virtually drove him out of the Middle East with the Israeli invasion of Lebanon in June 1982.

The signing of the 1979 peace treaty did not lead to immediate smooth relations among Egypt, Israel, and the United States; there was much friction and name-calling. Still, Israeli forces withdrew slowly out of the Sinai; the borders were declared open between Egypt and Israel; and peoples of both nations traveled between their countries by air or sea (but not through the Sinai). The complete pullout from the Sinai was not scheduled until 1982.

Before that occurred, Sadat and Begin met from time to time in generally near-hostile confrontations. Sadat hoped to talk Begin into calling off the Israeli attacks on Palestinian camps in Lebanon. He was embarrassed when, on June 7, 1981, Israeli planes destroyed an Iraqi nuclear reactor shortly after the two men met. Not one word was spoken of this "unlawful, provocative" act, as Egyptian Foreign Minister Kamal Hassan Ali labeled it.

Concurrently, Sadat's troubles at home had multiplied. In June of 1981 a government prosecutor uncovered a plot to overthrow the Sadat regime by Egyptian dissidents in exile, funded by Libya's Qaddafi, at the urging of Syria. By summer, religious rioting led Sadat to crack down on his opponents. For the first time in his eleven years in office, Sadat revealed his toughness against his political adversaries. He ordered the expulsion from Egypt of more than one thousand Soviet citizens, including the Soviet ambassador. The number of uniformed armed guards on college campuses increased.

In a two-hour speech on television, Sadat declared that "Lack of discipline in any way or form, in the streets, in the government, in the university, in the secondary schools, in the factory, in the public sector, in the private sector, this all has ended, it has ended."

He was wrong.

On October 6, 1981, as he watched a parade celebrating the Egyptian victories in the 1973 Yom Kippur War, Sadat was assassinated by a group of dissident Egyptian soldiers. In uniform, they leaped from a truck that had stopped at the President's reviewing stand, threw hand grenades, and fired automatic rifles point-blank into the stand, killing Sadat and eight others; the wild firing also injured more than twenty people in the reviewing stand. The death of Sadat sent shock waves through the Middle East and the world; the man who had brought some semblance of stability, and the promise of peace, to one of the earth's most volatile trouble spots was dead. His vice-president, Hosni Mubarak, stepped into the presidency and promised that he would continue in the tradition of Sadat (he was eventually elected President), but there were questions in Tel Aviv, Washington, and Moscow as to what his assumption of power would bring to the Middle East.

Sadat was genuinely mourned in many capitals of the world; even his friendly adversary, Menachem Begin, was visibly shaken and sent touching condolences to Sadat's widow and children. Begin sadly stated that he would miss "a friend."

Meanwhile on the troubled, occupied West Bank there was jubilation. A Palestinian writer, Raymonda Tawil, reported a mood of "complete joy . . . It is unbelievable. People are drinking. People are distributing sweets. Children are singing."

There was dancing in the streets in Syria, Iraq, and Libya. In PLO-dominated Beirut, the assassination was celebrated with gunfire and Arafat was heard to say, "We shake the hand that fired the bullets." Virtually all of the government-controlled radios celebrated the death of "the traitor Sadat" and condemned the path upon which he had started at Camp David. Such outpourings were not lost on the stunned but alert Israeli leaders. They were fearful of losing the fragile peace; they had lost their sole powerful friend in the Arab world.

In regard to the question of Palestine, Sadat had maintained and reiterated

October 6, 1981: in the reviewing stand to watch a parade celebrating the initial victories of the Yom Kippur War, Vice-President Hosni Mubarak (left), Anwar el-Sadat, and Defense Minister Abu Ghazala (to Sadat's left) await the opening of festivities.

As recorded by a CBS television camera, several men jumped out of a vehicle in the parade when it stopped before the reviewing stand, while other men, with rifles, began firing.

Chaos in Nasr: Smoke from a hand grenade obscures the scene as one man runs for cover; in the rear, behind him, a gunman fires point-blank into the reviewing stand.

Photos courtesy of Wide World Photos

A gunman with a Kalashnikov assault rifle fires into the presidential stand, killing Sadat and eight others. An abandoned television camera is in the foreground.

An Egyptian security man attempts to bring order so that the stretcher-bearers can evacuate the dead and wounded.

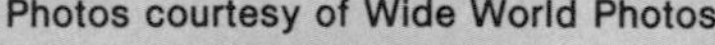

Photos courtesy of Wide World Photos

An unidentified Egyptian officer and Coptic Bishop Samuel lie critically injured in the presidential stand. The Bishop, like Sadat, died later in the hospital.

that a comprehensive peace—not merely one between Egypt and Israel—depended on a "just solution to the Palestinian problem." Speaking before the Knesset, he had bluntly stated: "Nobody in the world today can accept those slogans propagated in Israel ignoring the existence of the Palestinian people and questioning even their whereabouts." Sadat's persistent linkage of the Egyptian-Israeli peace process to the fate of the Palestinians and the future of the Gaza Strip and the West Bank often antagonized the Israelis, but by March 1979 an understanding was reached between the two nations that faced the problem and even provided for the establishment of an autonomous Palestinian Authority in those territories during the transitional phase.

Since the murder of Sadat, despite continual Arab fulminations against Camp David, President Mubarak and other Egyptian leaders have remained true to the Sadat approach to peace in the Middle East. The withdrawal of all Israeli troops from the Sinai in April 1982, as per the Camp David Accords, restored to Egypt its full territorial integrity. Aliza and Menachem Begin celebrated what was, in fact, a day of turbulence, with a telegram to the widow of Sadat which said, in part:

> *Anwar Sadat, of blessed memory, should have been with us to see the glory of his efforts to make peace and achieve reconciliation between the good peoples of Egypt and Israel. To prove that he did not die but will live forever in the hearts of women and men of good will, we will have to work for the sacred cause, No more war, no more bloodshed, peace, salam, shalom between our nations. We embrace you, our dear friend.*

These sentiments did not resound through the Arab world, or even in Israel itself. The Syrian ruling party newspaper *Al Ba'ath* issued a warning against reinstating Egypt among the Arab nations as long as it continued the "treasonous Camp David peace process." Dr. George Habash, leader of the Popular Front for the Liberation of Palestine and physician turned revolutionary, predicted "the escalation of the conspiracy against the Palestinian revolution." The PFLP, even more militant than the PLO, was responsible for several airline highjackings and bombings during the 1970s; some historians attribute to the group the triggering of the Jordanian (1970) and the Lebanese (1975) civil wars. Arafat, in Libya on the day that Egyptians reoccupied Sinai, remained silent.

The transfer of Israeli-held Sinai back to Egypt was not carried out without incidents; many Israeli squatters were removed by Israeli Defense Forces troops by force. Defense Minister Sharon rather nostalgically voiced another view when he said, ". . . the battlefields of Sinai have become an inescapable part of the landscape of our lives." He also invoked the names of several battlegrounds and intimated that this would be Israel's final peace concession and that he would encourage expanded Jewish settlements (as he had as Minister of Agriculture) in the occupied West Bank and the Gaza Strip. No mention was made of yet another troubled area: the Golan Heights, of Syria. Although Israel had demilitarized it in December 1981, the area was immediately annexed for good strategic reasons, placing it under Israeli administration and law.

Although there was no general holiday to commemorate the return of the Sinai—as originally planned by Sadat—there were ceremonies in which large Egyptian flags were raised in the north at Rafah and in the south at Sharm el-Sheikh, symbolizing the restoration of the Sinai to Egyptian control. A more ominous banner appeared above Beirut's once-chic Hamra Street. Its brilliant red Arab message warned that there was "no place for traitors and weaklings in the ranks of the Palestinian revolution."

This appeared to be a warning to the absent Arafat from one of the more aggressive factions of the Palestinian guerrillas. He had agreed to a cease-fire with Israel, negotiated by the American Undersecretary of State, Philip C. Habib, after severe clashes in southern Lebanon in June and July 1981. During this period, Israeli settlements in northern Israel were hit by PLO shellfire, and Israeli jets struck back, with devastating results, against PLO camps in southern Lebanon and as far north as Beirut. The Sinai transfer infuriated the Arabs who opposed the Camp David Accords, and they made a point of reminding Arafat that he was a warrior, not a diplomat.

Arafat was under pressure to reopen the war with Israel; however, hoping to gain worldwide recognition for his organization and to balance his backing from the various fractious Arab states, he preferred diplomacy. With Egypt again intact, and with a new Egyptian President, it would be possible that other Arab nations, fearing that Iran's revolution might engulf the more benign oil-producing nations, would begin to swing back to normal relations with Cairo.

1982 Operation "Peace for Galilee"

Despite the cease-fire and Arafat's nonrevolutionary demeanor, the Palestinian presence in Lebanon, as well as the presence of the twenty-five thousand "peace-keeping" Syrian troops, ushered in a time of strife. Within a month after the cease-fire, Israelis reported that the Palestinians were spotted moving artillery and ammunition south of the Litani River into what was supposed to be the UN buffer zone. In April 1982, Israeli diplomat Yacov Barsimantov was assassinated in Paris and Prime Minister Begin warned of the increasing dangers of PLO guerrilla activities in northern Israel and the arms buildup in Lebanon.

On April 21, 1982, after an Israeli soldier was killed while on patrol inside Lebanon, the Israeli Defense Forces struck at PLO strongholds, killing twenty-three Palestinians. The Israelis announced at the time that, since the cease-fire, there had been one hundred thirty guerrilla attacks inside Israel. On May

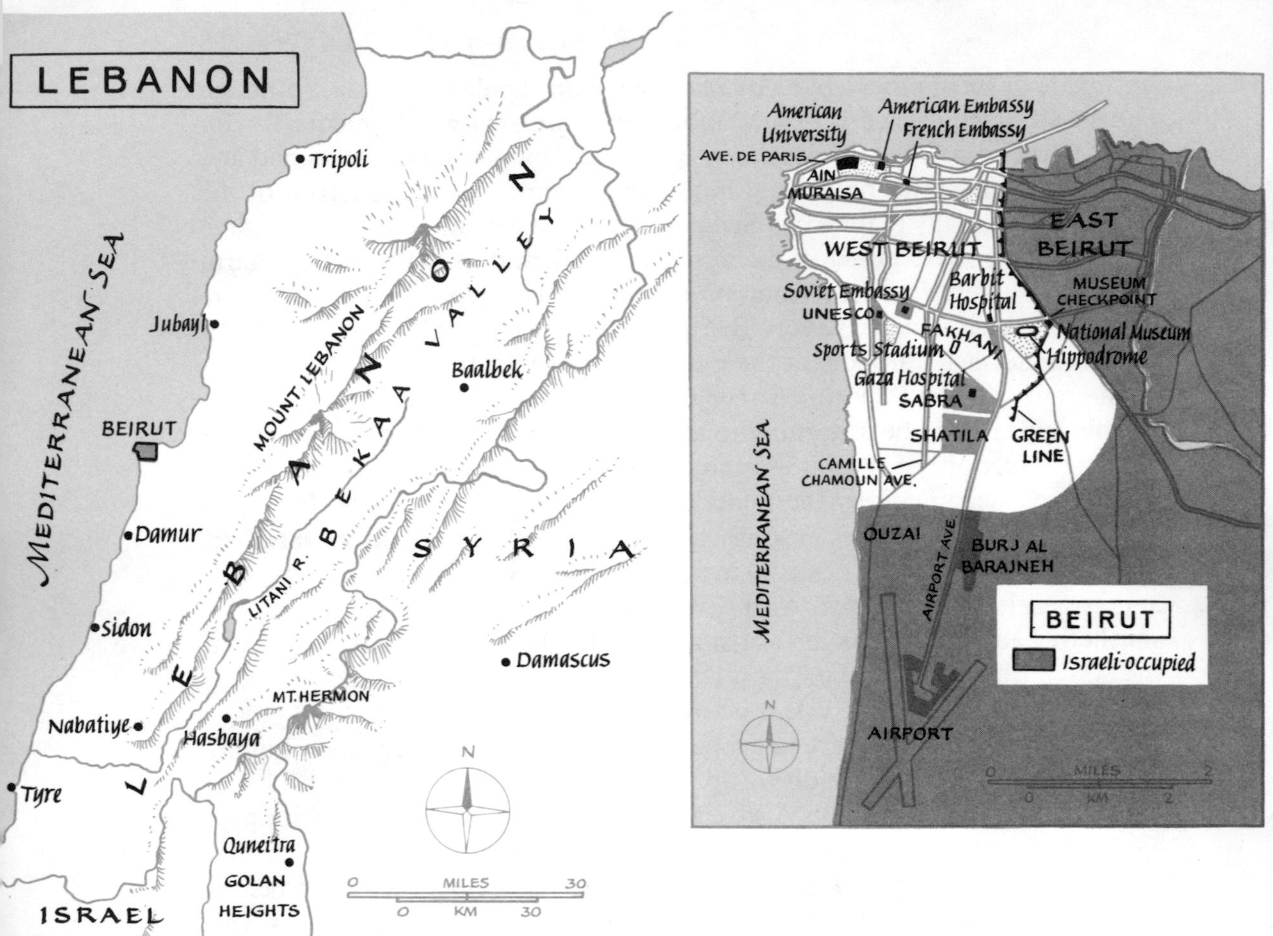

9, the Israeli Air Force attacked PLO bases south of Beirut, killing six and wounding twenty; the PLO reacted with artillery fire on settlements in the Galilee. Rumors that Israel was planning to invade Lebanon began to spread. They were generally discounted.

The shelling in northern Israel disrupted farm life, closed factories and schools, and destroyed property. Casualties were light, but life in northern Israel was described by a government official as "intolerable." The heavy shelling, persistent and damaging, also indicated a heavy cache of arms and ammunition. Israeli intelligence suspected that the PLO was not a scattered band of guerrilla fighters in Lebanon, but a small army (estimated at around six thousand), well equipped with heavy artillery, Soviet-made tanks, and mobile rocket launchers.

And so the duel went on: in time it was difficult to determine if the Israeli strikes initiated the PLO shellings, or vice versa. Then, in a surprise attack on June 3, the Israeli ambassador to Britain, Shlomo Argov, was shot in the head, suffered severe brain damage, and went into a coma. The PLO disclaimed responsibility, and British authorities, who had detained five suspects (with assorted Arab passports) found no PLO connection. One of the suspects was found to be carrying a list of other intended victims; on the list was the London

Photos courtesy of United Press International

Leftist Muslim guerrillas shooting into Christian positions in Beirut. The man on the right has just fired a rocket-propelled grenade.

Covering the withdrawal of the grenade launcher, gunmen fire into Christian-held East Beirut.

Lebanese against Lebanese: the body of a Christian Phalangist is dragged by a car driven by a Muslim through the streets of Beirut.

In December 1981, an explosion inside the Iraqi Embassy in Beirut collapsed the building and killed most of the people caught inside.

Photos courtesy of United Press International

Chairman of the PLO Yasir Arafat in Beirut, September 1981. PLO raids and shellings across the northern border of Israel led to great tensions and provided a reason for Prime Minister Begin to unleash the Israeli Defense Forces into Lebanon in June 1982.

U.S. Navy / Department of Defense

In June 1982, American foreign office advisers predicted trouble in Lebanon. American wives, children, and others—embassy employees—were evacuated from Beirut by the U.S. Navy.

representative of the PLO. The assassination attempt was considered to be a move to discredit Arafat and Al-Fatah, rather than to enhance Arafat's position as an accused "moderate" in the Arab world. Guesswork ascribed the shooting to a maverick Palestinian organization operating out of Damascus that had Arafat on its "hit list."

Before these facts and theories could be fully investigated after the June 3 shooting, Prime Minister Begin and his Defense Minister took action. Alluding to the London assassination attempt and to the shelling of northern Israel (in fact, a retaliation to Israeli air attacks in southern Lebanon), Begin announced operation "Peace for Galilee," which was planned to push the Palestinians in southern Lebanon twenty-five miles away from Israel's northern border, and its settlements there out of artillery range. The invasion was not in any way an assault on Lebanon, Begin maintained, nor was it Israel's intent to acquire Lebanese territory.

In the morning of June 6, 1982 (the fifteenth anniversary of the Six Day War), the Israeli Defense Forces swept into Lebanon with tanks and infantry, even as other strikes were being made on Palestinian positions on the western coast within a few miles of Beirut by the Israeli Air Force and Navy.

Within a week, the Israelis destroyed Palestinian strongholds in southern Lebanon (Beaufort Castle, Nabatiye), while Tyre, Sidon, and Damur, on the coast, were heavily pounded. By the second day, the Israelis were within fifteen miles of Beirut (well beyond the originally announced twenty-five-mile limit).

Consulate General of Israel

Lieutenant General Rafael Eytan (center), chief of staff, during the "Peace for Galilee" incursion into Lebanon, June 6, 1982.

Flying the Israeli and Lebanese flags, an Israeli armored personnel carrier moves through a village in southern Lebanon during the third day of the "Galilee" operation. The Lebanese, many of whom suffered under PLO occupation, welcome the Israelis.

Inside Sidon, Israeli troops search for a sniper who had been firing from the apartment building across the street. (The sniper escaped.) In· civilian clothes, it was easy for a guerrilla to blend in with the Lebanese.

United Press International

United Press International

Inevitably, the clash involved the hapless Lebanese, Palestinians not involved with the PLO, and the Syrians.

Israeli and Syrian jets met in the greatest air battles since World War II; in the first week, Israel claimed more than seventy Syrian MiGs. Even more significant was the destruction of 19 SAM batteries (which had scourged the Israelis during the opening phase of the Yom Kippur War) in the Bekaa Valley, the Syrian stronghold in eastern Lebanon. Having learned a costly lesson from the 1973–74 war, the Israeli Air Force's McDonnell-Douglas F-15s were equipped with radar-jamming devices, and their fighters and bombers were guided by command aircraft circling out of danger over the Mediterranean and directing the battles with electronic computers.

The intensity and extent of the Israeli incursion soon made their objective obvious: the destruction of the PLO in Lebanon. Beaufort Castle, which dated from the Crusades, was situated on top of a cliff with a view of northern Israel, it fell in vicious hand-to-hand fighting on the second day. The market town of Nabatiye, a major guerrilla command post, also fell, as did Hasbaya, in the southern Bekaa Valley. To the west, on the coast, Tyre, another major Palestinian center (one in which guerrilla and refugee lived side by side), went up in flames; Sidon, to the north, also fell. Israeli forces headed northward, toward Beirut.

Damur, less than ten miles south of the capital, was held by a rebel wing of the PLO. When the town fell, after heavy pounding from sea and air, and invasion by the Army, it was found to harbor large caches of arms and ammunition. The Israeli Army arranged for tours of Damur for newsmen, not only to display the piles of war materials, but also to reveal the Palestinians' desecration of the Christian buildings in the town. One church had been converted into a garage; its grease-stained floors were cluttered with engine casings and spare parts. The pews of St. Elias Church had been removed and its nave converted into a volleyball court. Washington *Post* correspondent William Branigin reported that Damur, which had once been populated by some thirty thousand Lebanese (predominantly Maronite Christians), had been overrun by Palestinian guerrillas during the 1975–76 Lebanese civil war between the dominant Christian rulers and the depressed Muslims. In retaliation for the destruction of a Palestinian refugee camp at Karantina by Christian soldiers, the Palestinians took over Damur, drove out the inhabitants, and established a stronghold that dominated the road from southern Lebanon to Beirut.

Branigin also noted the "awesome destruction" dealt by the "fierce Israeli shelling and air strikes. Where facades of deserted buildings have not been blasted away entirely, they are scored with more holes than Swiss cheese. In a few places, all that is left of a building is a set of pillars, giving the appearance of modern-day ruins—the effect of centuries of wear instantly achieved." He, and others, also found evidence of the use of American-made cluster bombs, which had been sold to Israel strictly for defensive purposes.

The destroyed Palestinian refugee camp in Rashidieh, near Tyre, southern Lebanon.

United Nations Relief and Works Agency, G. Nehmeh

United Nations Relief and Works Agency, G. Nehmeh

Operation Peace for Galilee, as it proceeded northward into Lebanon, encountered resistance in numerous Palestinian settlements. This is the damaged United Nations school in the Ein el-Hilweh camp, near Sidon.

United Press International

The body of an Israeli pilot is exhibited in the streets of Sidon on the opening day of the Lebanon war, June 6, 1982.

By the end of the first week, the military outcome was obvious; only the political future was murky. Begin and Sharon were criticized for the extent and savagery of the invasion, likened by some critics to a Nazi blitzkrieg. After some half-hearted fighting, the Syrians agreed to a cease-fire, on June 11. It was a flimsy one, but it freed Israeli Defense Forces to abandon the attempt to cut the Beirut–Damascus highway and to concentrate on the Palestinians as well as Syrians fleeing north and westward into West (Muslim) Beirut. Lebanon's largest city, by the time the vanguard reached its outskirts, harbored some six thousand Palestinian and Syrian troops and housed around a half million civilians. The dash to Beirut left a trail of civilian and military casualties and the destruction of dwellings and other buildings.

What appeared to be a ruthless aggression, rather than a defensive action, brought severe, even unexpected criticism upon Begin, Sharon, and even Israel; it came from the West, including Israel sympathizers and even inside Israel itself. In the United States, regarded as Israel's major ally and supplier of weaponry, advertisements soon appeared protesting the fate of the Lebanese and Palestinian civilians caught in the shattering onslaught.

Before the Israeli Defense Forces entrapped the PLO in West Beirut, some awesome casualty figures were circulated. The International Red Cross estimated that 10,000 Lebanese and Palestinians were killed or wounded and, initially, some 600,000 refugees fled from southern Lebanon. (Israeli sources maintained that the figure exceeded the number of inhabitants of the area.) According to Israeli sources, 400 civilians were killed in Sidon, 50 in Tyre, and 10 in Nabatiye; the dead from refugee camps had not been counted, but the Israelis placed the figure at no more than the 460 in the heavily besieged towns.

The Arab Womens' Council claimed that there were 10,000 killed (the same figure used by the International Red Cross) and 30,000 wounded. The homeless number also coincided with that of the IRC. Since the Red Cross was stationed in Beirut, with all communications with the South cut and travel there impossible, the accuracy of the figures is questionable. In countering these high numbers, the Israeli Defense Forces issued their strikingly small toll figures—which did not account for the dead buried in mass graves or buried in rubble; and Beirut was totally ignored. The IDF also steered correspondents and other observers away from refugee camps in the battle zones.

The suspiciously large Beirut Red Cross figures appeared in several advertisements placed by such groups in the United States as the Ad Hoc Committee in Defense of the Palestinian and Lebanese People, Concerned Americans for Peace, as well as the Arab Women's Council. In a full-page ad in the New York *Times* and other newspapers, the Concerned Americans bitterly chastised Israel for making the Lebanese the "innocent victims of a senseless war." It was made to appear that such relief agencies as the American Red Cross, CARE, UNICEF, the National Council of Churches, Save the Children Federation, and the American Friends Service Committee endorsed the censure. Within days, all had communicated with the newspapers explain-

United Nations, photo by G. Nehmeh

A woman stands in the doorway of what had been her home in the Palestinian refugee camp Burj el-Barajneh, on the approach to Beirut.

ing that none had been approached by the Concerned Americans for the use of their names and that, since neutrality was one of the factors that made it posssible for them to function in troubled areas, any criticism of either belligerent was not in their interests. Also, when an investigation was made, the Los Angeles box number listed for Concerned Americans for Peace did not exist.

It will be a long time, if ever, before the true toll of the war in Lebanon will be known.

In about five weeks of fighting, the Israeli military dead numbered 282—not an imposing number if compared with the casualties of a day on the Western Front in 1916, or the beaches of Saipan in 1944. But to Israel and its tiny population it is a gross figure.

Even as the Israelis closed in on Beirut, scattering leaflets through its streets urging the Syrians trapped there to flee, demonstrations for peace took place in Israel itself. In Tel Aviv a great rally was held, demanding "Stop the madness in Lebanon." Two organizations, Peace Now and the Committee Against War in Lebanon, assembled some 20,000 protestors carrying posters reading "Another Victory Like This and We Are Lost!" and "We Have No Future on the Graves of Palestinians." A hundred troops from an armored brigade, recently returned from southern Lebanon, signed a petition demanding a political solution to the Palestinian problem. Political leaders were also damned for remaining silent about Defense Minister Sharon's conduct of the war, stating that he had "gone too far."

On July 3, Sharon was photographed talking with Israeli soldiers in East Beirut. Three weeks of negotiations with the PLO by the Lebanese Government and U.S. envoy and Middle East troubleshooter Philip C. Habib broke down. Cease-fires were declared and almost immediately violated. Christians living in West Beirut were asked to move into the eastern (i.e., Christian) quarter of the city. Speaking for his splinter group of the PLO, Dr. George Habash, in rejecting the terms of the peace offer, said that his men were ready for a battle in Beirut; "our Stalingrad," he called it, and felt confident that the PLO could hold off the Israelis long enough to be in a better bargaining position than they were on July 2.

On July 3, Israeli armored troops sealed off the western, Muslim section of Beirut, isolating the PLO; after an eight-day cease-fire, the exchange of artillery, machine gun, and rocket fire erupted again. The setting was no longer villages and refugee camps, but one of the most modern—and once beautiful—cities in the Mideast.

By July 4, with Israeli armored troops from the eastern section of Beirut cordoning off the western city, the PLO units, Syrians who had chosen to remain, and thousands of civilians who had not left—or could not—were isolated in the shell-pocked city. Except for some none-too-avid Syrians there was little from the other Arab nations to help the Palestinians. They were virtually written off as an effective fighting unit. Still, inside West Beirut, the Palestinian guerrillas blended in with the civilian population and were using nonmilitary buildings for storage of ammunition and guns. They were, as the New York *Times* put it, "armed to the teeth."

Wide World Photos

Defense Minister Sharon visits Israeli troops near Beirut. His objective: wipe out the PLO.

As the Israelis stopped shipments of food and other supplies into West Beirut and cut off water and electricity, the fate of the PLO was all but determined (or so it appeared). A fellow Arab, Libyan leader Muammar Qaddafi offered Arafat his solution to the hopeless situation: "It would be shameful to give the enemy the right to negotiate on *our* [emphasis added] existence in Beirut," he asserted. "If we allow that, the enemy will have the right to pursue you to the ends of the earth.

"I advise you to commit suicide and not to accept dishonor. Your suicide would immortalize the Palestinian cause for future generations." Arafat may have been willing to fight to the death, but he is not suicidal; also, his death would remove one of Qaddafi's arch rivals in the Middle East.

The destruction, between cease-fires, of West Beirut, its mounting death toll, and the fate of the Palestinian guerrillas trapped there had become the major political issues by the middle of July. Deadlocked talks led to more shelling as attempts by assorted negotiators—some of whom would not speak to one another except through intermediaries—to get the PLO out of Beirut as gracefully as possible, broke down. When asked, during a mid-July cease-fire, if the cease-fire was a hopeful sign, Arafat replied that it was a stall for time and that the Israelis were "preparing for a big operation." When questioned on the chances of the PLO holding out for as long as six months in West Beirut, he replied, "Why not? I have nothing to lose."

The destruction of Beirut, and the saving of thousands of lives, depended on the evacuation of the Palestinian guerrillas. President Ronald Reagan's request that the survivors be escorted out of the city by a contingent of U.S. marines (France also volunteered troops for this procedure) into Syria was rejected by President Hafez al-Assad.

The talks foundered again when Arafat would not agree to leave Beirut—now a hostage city—unless the PLO was recognized by the United States. The United States remained firm in its avowal not to recognize the PLO until it, in turn, recognized Israel and its right to exist—which Arafat refused to do. (There were hints of that possibility, but not enough to resolve the issue.) Meanwhile, Sharon held his forces in check in East Beirut.

Egypt's President Hosni Mubarak, gradually bringing his country back into the good graces of fellow Arabs, also strove toward a resolution by calling for an Arab summit meeting and for direct U.S. negotiations with the PLO.

During the heaviest fighting in June there were two events not directly linked to the war but which, in time, would have some effect on it. On June 13, 1982, King Khalid of Saudi Arabia died of a heart attack and was succeeded by his half brother, Crown Prince Fahd, who came forward with his plan for peace. Fahd's peace plan, in effect, would return to the Arabs all territories taken from them during the Arab-Israeli conflicts. It also provided for Arab recognition of Israel, which earned him criticism from the other Arab nations. More worldly than the reclusive, deeply religious King Khalid, Fahd was experienced in the administration of government, education, economics, and diplomacy.

An Israeli soldier studies a group of luxury apartments in West Beirut; the once-glittering city has become a battleground. The PLO was well entrenched in this section of the city.

PLO artillery position, Beirut. The bag in the foreground once contained food; filled with sand, it serves as a weight for the gun.

Photos courtesy of United Press International

Lebanese militiaman at a checkpoint between East and West Beirut. A Muslim, he carries a copy of the Koran tucked in his ammunition belt.

His accession to the throne of Saudi Arabia would have its impress on the future of the Middle East.

Twelve days later, Alexander Haig resigned as the U.S. Secretary of State. Whether the resignation was voluntary or forced, and whether it involved differences of opinion with the White House over handling of foreign affairs, are unclear.

Haig's successor, George P. Shultz, was unanimously confirmed by the Senate Foreign Relations Committee and by the full Senate in mid-July. A long-time friend of the President, Shultz, a labor economist, had served in the Nixon administration. As president of the Bechtel Group, Inc., an international construction and engineering firm based in California, Shultz had a good deal of experience in the Middle East. His business dealings with the Arab world led to some consternation in the Senate; where Haig had appeared to be conciliatory toward the Israelis, would Shultz be amicable toward the Arabs?

During the hearings before the Foreign Relations Committee, Shultz deported himself with skill and intelligence. He placed the "Palestinian problem" high on the list of American concerns in foreign policy, saying that there would be no peace until there was a solution to the "legitimate needs and problems" of the Palestinians. Shultz also stated that there was a continuing American commitment to the security of Israel. There would be no "comprehensive peace" in the Middle East, no sure guarantee of "true and durable security," until these two problems were resolved.

Meanwhile, Lebanese civilians streamed on foot and jam-packed cars into Israeli-held East Beirut. (By July 16, it was estimated, of the 600,000 who had lived in the western portion of the city, about half had left.) That still left from 200,000 to 300,000 inside PLO-occupied Beirut.

In hopes of solving the impasse, Arafat suggested that the PLO be allowed to evacuate West Beirut and, since they were abandoned and rejected by the Islamic Arabs, move "temporarily" into eastern and northern Lebanon. They could move into Baalbek, in the Bekaa Valley, and join their brother Palestinians in the PLO concentrations in and around Tripoli, a major northern port, and Hermil, close to the Syrian border. (All of these positions were under Syrian control, it might be noted.) The fractured Lebanese Government did not smile on the idea. The response to this "solution" from the Israeli Government in Jerusalem was an unequivocal "We want them out of Beirut and out of Lebanon!"

The "solution" was further complicated by the reluctance of the Arab nations to serve as hosts to the trapped guerrillas once negotiations, guided by U.S. special envoy Philip C. Habib, were arduously and intricately hammered out. Habib's only contact with Arafat was through the former Lebanese Prime Minister, Saeb Safem (the United States does not officially recognize the PLO). Habib found the suggestion "cumbersome," but Salem and he eventually agreed that it might prove feasible—except that the Israelis insisted that the PLO must leave Beirut, taking all military and political personnel with it, and go directly to another Arab capital.

Arafat had begun issuing demands that made it appear as if he were the victor and not the vanquished. He insisted that he and Habib consult directly, without an intermediary. Arafat also wanted American troops to serve in a multinational peace-keeping force to stand between the Israeli Army and the PLO guerrillas. In addition, he invoked a United Nations resolution (drafted by France and Egypt) calling for the right of *all* nations in this troubled area to be permitted to live in peace and that the issue of Palestinian self-determination be included in a Security Council resolution.

This was tantamount to an implied U.S. recognition of the PLO, which would violate an agreement with Israel and place Habib in a nearly impossible position. He could not affront Israel, nor could he ignore Arafat.

The impasse was strengthened by violations of the cease-fire that had ended large-scale fighting since June 25. On July 22, 1982, citing the ambush killing of five Israeli soldiers in the Syrian-held sector near the village of Mansura, the Israeli Defense Forces lashed out with artillery and air strikes along two fronts: in the Bekaa Valley, the barracks at Baalbek, to the north; and the Fakhani quarter, specifically the PLO headquarters, in northwestern Beirut. On July 23, there was a ninety-minute aerial bombardment and artillery barrage on Palestinian neighborhoods in West Beirut. The PLO attributed this new fury to the failure of American negotiations to get the PLO out of Beirut. Meanwhile, patient, hard-working Habib had begun shuttle trips to Syria, Saudi Arabia, and Egypt.

United Press International

During Operation Peace for Galilee, the American special envoy Philip Habib shuttled between Lebanon and Israel in attempts to negotiate a permanent cease-fire. These Palestinian refugees from southern Lebanon picket the British Embassy, expressing their sentiments regarding his efforts.

Palestinian gunners return Israeli fire; their target is an Israeli gunboat offshore from Beirut.

Established in East Beirut, an Israeli heavy-gun position returns fire after the PLO began an attack during a cease-fire. At right, a 175-mm. cannon; in the background, a heavy, 320-mm. cannon.

Photos courtesy of United Press International

Although the eighth cease-fire ended the siege, on July 28, it was only temporarily. On August 1, on a day when Habib had scheduled further peace talks, the Israelis launched heavy strikes on Beirut—the most violent shelling on the capital since the start of the war. Israeli tanks and infantry advanced toward Palestinian camps and positions near the Beirut airport. After fourteen hours of heavy fighting, Habib successfully arranged another cease-fire (which turned out to be temporary). The ominous factor was that the Israeli Defense Forces had begun an approach on West Beirut itself. If Arafat and the PLO would not leave, the IDF would drive them out.

Three days later, under cover of heavy artillery fire, Israeli tanks thrust through two points in West Beirut in the port area in the north and at what was called the Museum checkpoint (near the Hippodrome, a deserted racetrack occupied by Syrian and Palestinian troops). Another armored column pushed northward along the coastal highway, from the Ouzai district (north of the airport), leading into the heart of Beirut itself. The official Israeli communiqué claimed that these moves were not to be regarded as a "general offensive" to take Beirut, but as "a tightening of the siege" and "an improving" of Israeli positions in the airport and the Hippodrome areas. The assault was in response to "repeated breaches of the cease-fire by terrorists."

The new attacks had come in the midst of three-way negotiations among the PLO, Lebanese representatives, and Habib. The mood in Washington was not one of joy. Anita Stockman, of the State Department, expressed the general reaction in saying, "Any military movements which hinder Mr. Habib's efforts to bring about a solution to the Beirut crisis are unhelpful." As the fighting continued, the talks were cut short and civilian casualties mounted.

Under criticism, even by his American friends, Prime Minister Begin countered sharply: "Nobody should preach to us," he told two hundred American members of the United Jewish Appeal visiting Israel on the day the assaults

McDonnell-Douglas F-15 "Eagle," which was used by the Israeli Air Force in the fighting over Lebanon; it was one of the most powerful aircraft operating in the Middle East.

McDonnell-Douglas

Photos courtesy of United Press International

While the Israeli Air Force bombed and strafed West Beirut, mobile artillery shelled it from nearby hills. The artillery commander is poised to order his battery to fire.

Captured Soviet rocket launchers are used by the Israelis to fire on PLO positions near Beirut's International Airport.

An Israeli tank stationed near Beirut's Raouche amusement park. The building in the right background appears to have escaped damage, as has the Ferris wheel.

had begun. "Yesterday," he told them, "the terrorists broke the tenth cease-fire, so of course we should hit back. When the Israeli Defense Forces hit back, they hit hard."

An unnamed Israeli official defined what he called the PLO game: "If they can draw us into shooting and hitting civilian targets in the city, they create world opinion against us and it is a political victory. When there is shooting, negotiations tend to stop and they think time is working in their favor. We have to show them that the game is costly."

And cost it did. Even as peace talks continued, on August 11, Israeli tank units plunged beyond Beirut, into northern Lebanon toward Jubayl, the Laqluk ski resort area, and along the Metun River. (This moved them closer to the Syrian and Palestinian-held Bekaa Valley.) Beirut erupted in new fighting as Israeli gunboats shelled the Ain Muraisa district (in which the American Embassy was situated); fighting broke out around the Museum crossing, and Israeli aircraft bombed the Palestinian camps at Shatila-Sabra.

The plans for the evacuation of the PLO from Beirut went awry again on August 12, when an eleven-hour air raid by the Israeli Air Force ravaged West Beirut. Bomb runs were made on residential areas in the northwestern tip of

An Israeli air strike on an eight-story apartment building, presumably sheltering PLO guerrillas, left more than two hundred fifty people dead. This woman, who lost members of her family, is being led from the building.

United Press International

United Press International

Operation Peace for Galilee evolved into an operation to wipe out the PLO in Lebanon. Israeli soldiers, supported by tanks, move into West Beirut.

National Council of Tourism in Lebanon

While fighting raged in eastern Lebanon and in Beirut, the Israeli Defense Forces also attacked Syrian troops and Palestinians entrenched in the Bekaa Valley, in east-central Lebanon. The major agricultural section of Lebanon in peaceful times (as in this photograph), the valley was churned up by shelling and heavy vehicles.

United Press International

PLO leader Yasir Arafat and an aide, with their Soviet AK-47 assault rifles, walk the streets of Beirut. Arafat, one of the last of the PLO to leave Lebanon, moved on to Greece on August 30.

the city as well as the known Palestinian strongholds at Burj el-Barajneh Camp, Sabra-Shatila, and Fakhani. In central Beirut, the operating room of the Berbir Hospital was hit by an Israeli bomb. White House Deputy Press Secretary Larry Speakes, shaken and pessimistic, relayed word that President Reagan was "outraged" by the new round of intensive attacks and that such bombings resulted in "needless destruction and bloodshed."

Lebanese Prime Minister Shafik al-Wazzan, after a brief meeting with the American negotiator, informed newsmen: "I have told Philip Habib that I cannot carry on in these talks while these thousands of tons of explosives are wreaking mass destruction in my city, my capital." Although he did not cancel the talks, Wazzan emphasized that he held Habib and the United States responsible "for the consequences."

He also noted that, indeed, the talks had been progressing, that the Lebanese Government and the PLO had given "all the concessions requested from us and we had reached the stage of defining the PLO's departure routes." He raised his voice in an eloquent question: "What is the meaning of all these thousands of destructive devices, especially at a time everyone knows everywhere we are very close to a peaceful solution. Enough!" he exclaimed; "stop this wholesale devastation."

In Jerusalem the Knesset angrily confronted Defense Minister Sharon, who had ordered the air raid—and demanded that it be stopped. Around the same time, Prime Minister Begin received heated calls from Washington insisting on an end to the bombings; President Reagan went so far as to threaten the recall of Habib and his staff. But the Israeli Cabinet had already curbed the controversial Sharon. Thus, in a flurry of charges and raised voices, the twelfth cease-fire was initiated and talks resumed.

The negotiations continued to be as labyrinthine as before, but Habib persevered: the PLO agreed to provide him with a list of the guerrillas to be evacuated to several Arab countries and the list of those nations finally willing to accept them (Jordan, Iraq, Tunisia, Yemen, People's Yemen, Syria, Algeria, and Sudan). Then the Israeli Cabinet accepted the plan for the deployment of a Multinational Force, of French, Italian, and American troops, to cover the evacuation; the Cabinet dropped its demand for the names of the guerrillas shipping out. On August 19, all details were ironed out regarding the disposition of Palestinian and Syrian troops trapped in West Beirut. The ten-week siege of the city was over.

Peace, of a sort, had come to Beirut, if not to Lebanon. It was still a nation infested with warriors and their weapons. The "peace" came with much bitterness. Arafat, smiling, confident, maintained his stance as the victor, not the vanquished, as his men started on what the Lebanese newspaper *As Safir* described as a "new diaspora." The PLO leader, as he saw them off and prepared for his own departure, hinted at his opinion of some of his Arab brothers. "Some regimes," he said, "were even in collusion with the Israeli invaders." *Al Liwa*, in an editorial, claimed that "Arafat has emerged a big-Palestinian hero that ever."

A Multinational Force for maintaining peace in Lebanon was sent by France, Italy, and the United States. Marines of the 32nd Marine Amphibious Unit stand guard in Beirut.

Photos courtesy of Department of Defense

An air of celebration—more like a festive Dunkirk than a Waterloo—marked the Palestinian departures from Lebanon as the guerrillas waved flags, held aloft Arafat's photograph, and fired weapons into the air. (Some wild shots resulted in the death of civilians, among them children.) In the first group were some 265 Palestinians, who were flown to Jordan, where they were greeted with kisses by King Hussein, who had driven them out of his country in Black September 1970. "You have held the flag high and fought well for your rights," he told them. "It's still a long struggle, but we are sure of victory." One of the evacuees, Lieutenant Nasser Shawar, did not quite agree. Instead, he had arrived with "a feeling of victory." "Our fight in Beirut was confronting the United States military machine and all its sophisticated weapons," he said. When, in mid-October, the Israelis began displaying captured arms at the Khordani army base, near Haifa, the cache was impressively formidable; the PLO had not lacked weapons and ammunition. One officer, obviously surprised by the variety and quantity, said, "We took out 200 truckfuls of arms from one depot alone in the Fakhani section of West Beirut." During the fighting it sometimes required a hundred trucks a day to haul the captured equipment.

"The biggest surprise," he said, "was the incredible amounts. If I had 35,000 men I could line them up and give each one a rifle or automatic weapon. It was a huge army, armed to the teeth. I don't know how they got that stuff.

"What I'd like to know is how the P.L.O. had crates of G-3's, the current NATO rifle, if nobody is selling arms?"

The captured matériel had originated in Hungary, Romania, Czechoslovakia, East Germany, North Korea, Soviet Russia, China, Japan, Belgium, France, Britain, West Germany, and the United States.

On August 30, as a demonstration of his disdain for certain "regimes" that had not come to his aid in Lebanon, Arafat sailed off on a Greek cruise ship, *Atlantis*, and instead of landing in an Arab country, stopped over in Athens, where he was warmly greeted by Prime Minister Andreas Papandreou. A spokesman for Arafat explained in Beirut that this was done "as a deliberate gesture to criticize all Arab leaders for their stand during the siege of Beirut . . . He wants to show that all Arab leaders are not worthy of respect . . ." No names were mentioned.

From his position of isolation, Libyan dictator Colonel Qaddafi was not so circumspect. On the anniversary of the ousting of King Idris, which put him in power thirteen years before, Qaddafi asked, "What was the stand of Saudi Arabia, Jordan, Morocco, Sudan, or any other Arab country? They did not attend a summit meeting for fear of being embarrassed and asked to enter the battle." Qaddafi described King Hassan of Morocco as "cowardly" and Jordan as "worthless." He promised to send revolutionary committees to every Arab country to mobilize the masses "to take over the authority and to destroy the governments." This canceled out any invitation he may have had to attend high-level conferences to be held in Fez, Morocco, on September 6 to discuss the Palestinian question, since he had publically scourged most of the participants.

By this time, Arafat had flown to Tunisia, as various peace plans were discussed, disagreed over, and set aside. Skirmishing did not actually stop, for there were still PLO guerrillas and Syrian troops in central and eastern Lebanon. However, with most of the PLO out of Beirut (it was believed that perhaps three thousand had remained), the Lebanese Assembly elected a new President. He was thirty-four-year-old Bashir Gemayel, a tough commander of the Christian Phalangist militias. Lebanese tradition calls for a Christian President (a Maronite Catholic), balanced by a Sunni Muslim Prime Minister and a Shi'ite Muslim Speaker of Parliament. Because of his reputation for toughness and the presence of Israeli troops, Gemayel appeared to be the most logical strong man to establish a new Lebanese Government, which had hardly existed since the 1975–76 civil war and the occupation by the PLO and the Syrian Army.

His "election"—there was no other candidate—was greeted in the Christian quarter of Beirut with jubilation, and with dread in the Muslim section of the city. Washington, D.C., and Jerusalem were pleased, especially when a less belligerent than usual Gemayel said, "It's time to unite the country, return people to their proper homes, and restore the pride and sovereignty of the Lebanese nation." At least half of his nation did not believe him: the Muslims.

On September 14, nine days before his scheduled inauguration, Gemayel was crushed to death in his military headquarters in the heart of East Beirut. Just minutes after 4 P.M., as the President-elect was about to address about one hundred members of his Christian Phalangist Party, some seventy-five-pounds—early reports gave the number as four hundred—of high explosive was detonated on the third floor of the building. The blast shattered the structure, causing the upper floors to smash down onto the first floor, where the meeting was being held. East Beirut shook as the air filled with debris and smoke; fragments of the building spewed into the street, along with parts of human bodies. Automobiles parked nearby were crushed by the force of the explosion.

It was hours before the mutilated body of Gemayel was found. Early reports had him walking to the hospital to have superficial wounds treated. At midnight, the official radio announced the assassination of the President, along with twenty-one other people, with dozens more injured.

No one group claimed responsibility for the assassination, although Yasir Arafat, in an unusual audience with Pope John Paul II in Rome, attributed it to "the Americans and Israel so that the Israelis could enter Beirut." Early in October the Phalangist Party paper, *Al Amal*, announced that the party's security agents had seized a suspect who had confessed to the assassination. The TNT had been placed on the building's second floor and was detonated by a Japanese electronic device about a mile away from Phalangist Party headquarters.

On the same day as Arafat's meeting with the Pope, Sharon ordered Israeli troops into West Beirut, a move that Prime Minister Begin rationalized as necessary to "stem chaos" in the wake of the assassination. Pushing upward from the south, the Israelis isolated the Palestinian strongholds—now theoretically cleared of guerrillas, although suspect—at Burj el-Barajneh and Sabra/Shatila. Two forces pushed into the heart of West Beirut from the east. Although the positions were secured by evening, it was reported that the Israeli advances had encountered some resistance from PLO troops still hiding in Beirut. On hearing this, Sharon made the "immediate decision" to send in either Lebanese or Christian troops to attend to the remaining guerrillas and to disarm them.

On Thursday, September 16, the day after Gemayel's assassination, the Multinational Force returned to their respective countries. Unsuccessful in persuading the Lebanese Army to enter the suspected camps (house-to-house fighting is invariably costly), chief of staff Lieutenant General Rafael Eytan and commander-in-chief of the northern units of the Israeli Defense Forces Major General Amir Drori decided to turn the job over to the Phalangists.

In Jerusalem, Begin and the Israeli Cabinet were informed of the decision; no vote was taken, nor did it seem necessary. Permission was given to clear the camps of Sabra and Shatila. Foreign Minister Yitzhak Shamir later indicated that before the action was taken, the Israelis "emphasized" that it was "against terrorists and that the civilian population should not be harmed, especially women, children, and old people."

On Thursday morning, the Israeli Army had surrounded the Sabra/Shatila area and had sealed off the camps. By 3 P.M., Phalangists from East Beirut, under the direction of Gemayel's intelligence chief, Elias Hobeika, joined up

United Press International

Major Saad Haddad (right, with cap), commander of the Phalangist Christian militia in southern Lebanon. During the tragedy that occurred after the Multinational Force withdrew from Lebanon and the assassination of President Gemayel, Haddad testified, he had been inside the city of Beirut offering his condolences to Gemayel's family and then visited friends north of the city. The youthfulness of his militiamen is obvious in the photograph.

near the airport with some units of the Haddad militia from the South. (Major Saad Haddad has denied that any of his men participated in the events that followed.) Although the numbers are disputed, about five hundred to six hundred troops, probably more, moved out of the staging area through the Israeli lines. They had given their word not to harm civilians. Hobeika was known as a murderous leader who carried a knife, a pistol, and a hand grenade in his belt. He was also no friend of Amin Gemayel, who would succeed to the presidency; he hated the Palestinians—men, women, and children.

Moving through the Israeli positions, the Phalangists established a command post across the street from an Israeli Army observation post on Camille Chamoun Avenue, overlooking the two camps. The entrances had been sealed off by Israeli tanks; the soldiers were there, Sharon explained, "to coordinate the entry of the Phalangists into Shatila camp." The entry was made at about 4 P.M.; forty hours of carnage followed.

Hobeika asked for, and received, Israeli flares to light up the area to make the *kasach* (Arabic for a chopping operation) easier for his men. The sound of gunfire and cries came from Shatila. It was 11 P.M. when it was obvious that a massacre, not a clearing-up operation, was underway in the camps. Women had run from Shatila and told Israeli soldiers stationed there that their children were being butchered, but nothing was done. A Phalangist commander informed an Israeli officer during the night that, up to then, "300 civilians and terrorists have been killed." This was also contained in a cable sent by the commander to Israeli headquarters in East Beirut, as reported by Jerusalem *Post* correspondent Hirsch Goodman and forwarded to Sharon in Tel Aviv.

On Friday, when General Drori was informed of the massacre via the Jerusalem *Post* and ordered a stop to the killings, the Phalangists moved northward through Shatila into Sabra. By this time, too, the hospitals in the vicinity—Akka Hospital, to the south of Shatila, and Gaza Hospital, at the northwestern corner of Sabra—overflowed with fleeing refugees, many wounded.

At around 11 A.M. a division commander, Amos Yaron, met with General Drori and "raised suspicions concerning the method of operation of the Phalangists." Later that afternoon, Sharon and General Eytan met with Phalangist leaders and agreed to their remaining in the camps until Saturday morning, the next day. About an hour later, at 5 P.M., a doctor serving on the staff of Akka Hospital left for safety in an International Red Cross convoy. As they moved out, he saw, at the southern end of Shatila, bulldozers scooping some ninety corpses, mixed with sand, into a mass grave.

Although the firing had slackened after Drori's stop order, it did not end. Hysterical, protesting, and terrified residents of the camps attempting to flee were tragically and unaccountably turned back by Israeli soldiers. It was Friday afternoon before American journalists dropped by the American Embassy to report that they had heard rumors of Phalangists who had entered Shatila camp and had begun an indiscriminate bloodbath. Chargé d'affaires Robert Barret immediately phoned Amin Gemayel, who apparently had not been informed that some of his troops had gone into the camps.

During Friday night and early Saturday morning, bulldozers were kept busy covering up the handiwork of the Phalangists. Buildings were knocked down over bodies, corpses were collected into piles of sand with portions of bodies, arms, and legs protruding; others were simply covered with rubble and iron sheets. The buildings that would not serve as concrete shrouds were wrecked to make them uninhabitable.

Around 6 A.M. on Saturday, bullhorns boomed through the Sabra camp, ordering the several hundred remaining residents to gather in the street for evacuation to Shatila. The soldiers identified themselves as Israeli and assured the people they had nothing to fear. The soldiers, it was soon learned, were not Israelis, but Phalangists. An hour later, a half dozen militiamen entered Gaza Hospital and ordered everyone to march down to Shatila, except for two nurses, who were permitted to remain with the patients.

Meanwhile the Phalangists in Shatila camp had begun to separate the Lebanese from the Palestinians. The latter were marched off behind a sand pile and killed. When the women began screaming, some of them were returned to the group to quiet their screams. Later, however, the men were ordered out of the camp and passed by a parked Land-Rover in single file to be identified. Those who were pulled out of the line and forced to sit in a ditch were never seen again. Eventually the surviving men were turned over to the Israelis and marched to the nearby sports stadium, where the wounded were treated and given food and water. The women were told to return to their homes, if they still existed.

Around 9 A.M., Saturday, September 18, 1982, the first outsiders entered Shatila/Sabra, to be sickened by the inhuman carnage wrought by Hobeika's

Shatila camp, Beirut, Saturday, September 18, 1982. The killings are over, as are the attempts to cover the bodies with building rubble. A distraught woman passes by the bodies of two children.

Ninety-year-old Adnan Nouri, shot through the head, sprawls in the street, his cane nearby.

Photos courtesy of United Nations Relief and Works Agency

militiamen. Because of the many bodies covered over by rubble, the number of dead will probably never be known—certainly more than three hundred and probably closer to a thousand. (In 1976, Hobeika led a slaughter of "thousands" of Palestinians in Tel Zaatar while the world's attention was focused on the drama of Entebbe.)

The number of victims is not as crucial as the victims themselves: a three-year-old girl, aged Adnan Nouri, a white horse—and hundreds of others, not all of whom could possibly have been "terrorists."

In Israel, articles critical of Begin and Sharon appeared in newspapers—even *Yediot Ahronot*, the conservative and consistent supporter of the Begin government; and the horrors of Shatila and Sabra were seen on television. With the end of the Sabbath, on Saturday night, nearly four hundred thousand Israelis swarmed into Tel Aviv's Square of the Kings of Israel to protest the massacre in Lebanon and to mourn the deaths. Their chant was a call for the resignation of the Prime Minister. The demonstration in Tel Aviv was subdued, orderly, and large in number (bringing together in one place 10 percent of the total population of Israel). Signs depicted Sharon as Israel's Idi Amin; others branded him a "monster." Many signs said, "Children's Blood Is Not Water."

The mood of the people was clear. Even so, Begin and Sharon stood together. In the Knesset, both Begin and Sharon were challenged and reprimanded, but held their ground. Sharon insisted that he had not known about the massacres until Friday, although word had begun to seep through by Thursday evening. Begin, insisting that it would be an admission of complicity, denied a request for a full-scale probe of the killings. This was followed by the sobering resignations of Energy Minister Yitzhak Berman and Israeli Minister of the West Bank Menachem Milson. These were a decided setback for the Begin-Sharon alliance; eventually a promise of an investigation of the Beirut murders was made.

Opposition leader Shimon Peres, of the Labor Party, himself a former Minister of Defense, addressed the two men: ". . . Mr. Prime Minister, Mr. Defense Minister, I want to ask you, whose stupid idea was it to send the Phalangists to the refugee camps in order to locate the terrorists. After all, you don't have to be a political genius or a famed commander. It is enough to be a country cop in order to understand from the outset that those militias, which were more emotional than ever, following the murder of their leader, were likely to commit atrocities also among innocent people."

Peres concluded with "What have you wrought, Mr. Prime Minister and Mr. Defense Minister?"

Long after the impassioned meeting of the Knesset, the questioning continued. Israel's status in the world community was undermined, although no complicity in the murders in Beirut has been uncovered. Nor had the investigation of the incident gotten underway when, on October 11, the casualty figures of the Israeli Defense Forces were released: 368 dead and 2,383 wounded. The Lebanese-Palestinian (estimated) toll was 17,825 dead and 30,103 wounded; the figures do not include the Shatila/Sabra *kasach* victims.

Elusive peace, so intrinsic to the future lives of millions in a sorely troubled

Photos courtesy of United Nations Relief and Works Agency

Palestinian women search for members of their families in the Shatila camp, Monday, September 20.

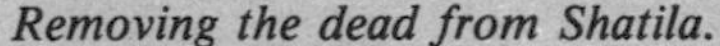

Removing the dead from Shatila.

region, lies buried under the shattered bricks, mortar, and dust that have been bulldozed over some thousand butchered innocents. It will haunt the course of events in the Middle East for years, even generations, to come.

❦

The Begin-Sharon incursion into Lebanon succeeded in one of its major objectives: the elimination of the Palestinian threat to the Galilee. The subsequent diaspora of the Palestinian guerrillas has not answered the Palestinian question, nor, in fact, has it eliminated the threat of future terrorist activities. Although the PLO concedes to having lost its "74-Day War" in Lebanon, the general mood would seem to indicate that it has won the political war. Scattered throughout nine nations in the Middle East, demoralized but not defeated, the PLO is bitter, especially in the wake of the Beirut massacre.

In his new headquarters in Bourj Cedria, Tunisia (some fifteen hundred miles from the homeland for which he has been fighting for decades), Yasir Arafat, his stature enhanced, rather than weakened, by the destruction of his army, waits. He firmly believes that peace in the Middle East cannot come without the participation of the PLO. "Palestinians," he has said, "are the odd number in the Middle East equation." Omitting the odd number will only produce the wrong answer. He also knows that his objectives have not been achieved via "military options"; there are intimations of a "negotiated settlement," once the question of a Palestinian homeland is resolved.

United Nations Relief and Works Agency

Shatila camp, Beirut. The Christians have long gone, and the dead are being counted (if found) and buried. An abandoned, twisted bicycle lies in the blood-splotched street.

This introduces many questions. Will Israel, the most powerful military force in the Middle East, vacate Gaza, and especially the West Bank, now dotted with Jewish settlements that threaten the Palestinian presence in the area Arafat calls Palestine? Will the other Palestinian factions—there are at least a half dozen—agree with Arafat's negotiated settlement? Will Habash's Popular Front for the Liberation of Palestine accept any kind of peace with Israel? Will Hawatmeh's Democratic Front for the Liberation of Palestine, violently anti-Jordanian, recognize King Hussein as a peacemaker? Also to be reckoned with is Abu Nidal's Black June, a terrorist group that broke away from Arafat's Fatah because Arafat was considered too "accommodating." There are other independent, rejectionist Palestinian groups, marshaled under the heading of PLO, but who simply and unequivocally refuse to recognize Israel's right to exist. Any Arab leader who does becomes the assassin's target. This was the fate of Anwar el-Sadat and illuminates Jordan's Hussein's cautious approach to the role of negotiator between Israel and the Arab world. His contribution to the "peace process" will depend on Israel's agreements on the fate of the Palestinians, stopping the mushrooming of settlements in the West Bank; also, he awaits a public signal from the PLO, and such states as rich, influential, and moderate Saudi Arabia, to proceed in pursuit of Reagan's peace initiative.

The plan places pressure on the current Israeli government, which resists some of its features, especially the curtailment of Jewish settlements in Israeli-held territories and the withdrawal of troops from Lebanon and the Golan Heights. The Israeli arguments for holding onto these territories is that they are necessary to the defense of Israel. With Judaea and Samaria (the West Bank) in Israeli control, population centers and airfields inside Israel would be safe from ground attack by invading troops. Or, at least, if troops invaded from Jordan, there would be sufficient warning time during which to mobilize the Israeli Defense Forces reservists. As stated by the deputy chief of mission at the Israeli Embassy Ben Netanyahu, "No amount of electronic gadgetry can substitute for the control of artillery positions and armor routes that lead from Jordan to the Mediterranean. Given modern technology and advances in warfare, he who controls the heights of Judaea and Samaria controls Israel." It can be assumed that this is the official Israeli view on the West Bank (certainly the Begin-Sharon position) and does not bode well for peace or the fate of the Palestinians.

Meanwhile, as the year 1982 closed, negotiations between Lebanon and Israel began in Khaldah, a southern suburb of Beirut. Head of the Lebanese delegation Antoine Fattal opened the talks with a statement that made it clear that he viewed the negotiations as a means to achieve the withdrawal of Israeli troops in Lebanon, after which the Syrian and Palestinian forces would follow. (Israel has maintained that the remaining Palestinian guerrillas would have to go first, then Israel and Syria would follow.)

Israel's chief negotiator, David Kimche, presented a more elaborate concept, aiming at a formal peace treaty with Lebanon, which has proved so elusive since 1949. Such a treaty would provide for the establishment of a "security zone" in southern Lebanon of about thirty miles in width. Fattal was discussing sovereignty, and Kimche, strategy; while this was a beginning, it was clear that there were complex negotiations ahead.

Israel's military victory in Lebanon, the dispersal of the Palestinian Liberation Organization, the aloof indecisiveness of the moderate Arab states (Saudi Arabia, Egypt, and Jordan), as well as the internal wars between states (Iraq and Iran) or within states (the clashes between Lebanese Christian and Druse militias as well as Muslim Sunnis and Shi'ites, after the large-scale fighting ceased) have contributed little to peace in the Middle East.

Peace in Lebanon? Since the end of fighting in 1982, neither the Syrians nor the Israelis have withdrawn from the ravaged country, although the Israeli Defense Forces moved out of Beirut; and despite internal wrangling that has weakened Arafat seriously, the scattered Palestinian fighters have returned. Lebanon has become a political military quagmire, defying rational solutions.

In late August 1983, Begin, tired and distraught, offered his resignation as Prime Minister and was succeeded by another strongman, Yitzhak Shamir. Almost concurrently, U.S. Marines stationed around Beirut Airport, as members of the international "peacekeeping" force, died and were wounded in clashes between the Lebanese Army and Shi'ite and Druze dissidents; the day after, French troops died. These casualties were added to the toll of 63 who perished when a bomb exploded in the American Embassy in April. This was a prelude to the carnage that resulted when a TNT-laden truck, driven by a suicidal zealot, rammed into Marine Headquarters on October 23, 1983, killing more than 200 marines. Simultaneously, another truck attacked the French barracks, killing more than 20 troops.

Shocked, aroused, even angered, Americans began to question the role of their peacekeepers (which had metamorphosed in a few months from keeping the peace to protecting President Gemayel's unpopular militia) in a land where those who most needed peace stubbornly and bloodily rejected it.

Peace is heavily dependent upon security, and security, tragically, is dependent upon weapons. What is lost in high-level negotiations is humanity. For two generations, children have been born and have survived in refugee camps, nurtured on fear, hatred, and a hunger for vengeance. A tiny sliver of a nation has existed as an armed camp since 1948, its sons and daughters trained to use weapons in the defense of their right to exist. Both camps will have to recognize each other's existence, or there will never be peace in the Middle East; this may be simple, or even obviously simplistic, but the solution must begin there or end with Armageddon.

There are no simple solutions, and for too long in this anguished area, no happy endings. There has been, in truth, one continuous Arab-Israeli war since the founding of Israel. "If," as a very wise man once said, "we merely celebrate their war, we've missed the essence of our heritage."

Bibliography

DOBSON, CHRISTOPHER; and PAYNE, RONALD. *The Terrorists.* New York: Facts on File, 1979.
DONOVAN, ROBERT J., et al. *Six Days in June.* New York: New American Library (Signet Books), 1967.
ELON, AMOS. *Understanding Israel.* New York: Behrman House, 1976.
HERZOG, CHAIM. *The Arab-Israeli Wars.* New York: Random House, 1982.
LAFFIN, JOHN. *The Dagger of Islam.* New York: Bantam Books, 1981.
______. *Fedayeen.* New York: The Free Press, 1973.
LEWIS, BERNARD. *The Middle East and the West.* New York: Harper Torchbooks, 1964.
Life, the editors of. *Israel's Swift Victory.* New York: Time, Inc., Book Div., 1967.
MARSHALL, S. L. A., *Sinai Victory.* New York: William Morrow Company, 1967.
O'CONNOR, PATRICIA ANNE, ed. *The Middle East.* Washington, D.C.: Congressional Quarterly, Inc., 1979.
PATAI, RAPHAEL. *The Arab Mind.* New York: Charles Scribner's Sons, 1976.
______. *The Jewish Mind.* New York: Charles Scribner's Sons, 1977.
PIVKA, OTTO VON. *Armies of the Middle East.* Cambridge, England: Patrick Stephens, Ltd., 1979.
POLK, WILLIAM R. *The Arab World.* Cambridge, Mass.: Harvard University Press, 1980.
RUBENSTEIN, MURRAY; and GOLDMAN, RICHARD. *Shield of David.* Englewood Cliffs, N.J.: Prentice-Hall, 1978.
SAADAWI, NAWAL EL-. *The Hidden Face of Eve* (Women in the Arab World). Boston: Beacon Press, 1982.
SAID, EDWARD W. *Orientalism.* New York: Pantheon Books, 1978.
______. *The Question of Palestine.* New York: Times Books, 1979.
SCHMIDT, DANA ADAMS. *Armageddon in the Middle East.* New York: The John Day Co., 1974.
SHAPIRA, AVRAHAM. *The Seventh Day.* New York: Charles Scribner's Sons, 1970.
STERLING, CLAIRE. *The Terrorist Network.* New York: Holt, Rinehart & Winston, 1981.
STEVENSON, WILLIAM. *90 Minutes at Entebbe.* New York: Bantam Books, 1976.

Other sources: Recent and current events in the Middle East are comprehensively recorded in the New York *Times,* the Washington *Post,* and the Jerusalem *Post,* all of which have served as sources for eyewitness accounts and views—pro, con, and objective. An invaluable source, both for views and an expanding bibliography, is *Foreign Affairs,* published by the Council on Foreign Relations. Especially important is the annual, truly book-sized edition devoted to the topic "America and the World." I have also regularly read *The Middle East,* published in London, and *MERIP Reports* (Middle East Research and Information Project), published in Washington, D.C. These publications, presenting the Arab position on the controversies in the Middle East, contributed a great deal to whatever objectivity or, indeed, fairness this work may evince. But as a writer who has had a long experience with war and with writing about war, it is difficult to be objective or fair about man's most wasteful activity. It is more difficult when both groups of belligerents strongly believe that it is their cause only which is just; war will not solve this dilemma; only understanding, trust, and love.

Index

Page numbers in italics indicate pictures or maps.

INDEX

INDEX

INDEX